DATE			

SERVICING THE PROFESSIONAL CORPORATION

A Complete Manual and Guide

SERVICING THE PROFESSIONAL CORPORATION

A Complete Manual and Guide

Steven K. Riemer

PRENTICE-HALL, INC. Englewood Cliffs, N.J.

Prentice-Hall International, Inc., *London*
Prentice-Hall of Australia, Pty. Ltd., *Sydney*
Prentice-Hall of Canada, Ltd., *Toronto*
Prentice-Hall of India Private Ltd., *New Delhi*
Prentice-Hall of Japan, Inc., *Tokyo*

Second Printing . . . . . August, 1977

This publication is designed to provide accurate and authoritative information with regard to the subject matter covered. It is sold with the understanding that the publisher is not engaged in rendering legal, accounting, or other professional advice. If legal advice or other expert assistance is required, the services of a competent professional person should be sought.

. . . From a Declaration of Principles jointly adopted by a Committee of the American Bar Association and a Committee of Publishers and Associations

Library of Congress Cataloging in Publication Data
Riemer, Steven K
Servicing the professional corporation.

Includes bibliographical references and index.
1. Professional corporations--United States. I. Title.
KF2901.R5 346'.73'066 75-28127
ISBN 0-13-806968-9

Printed in the United States of America

To my wife, Dale,

whose patience and understanding
made this book possible

ABOUT THE AUTHOR

Steven K. Riemer, practicing attorney with his own firm in Boston, counsels almost exclusively in the areas of professional corporations, pension and profit sharing plans, and estate planning. He has personally incorporated more than 140 professional corporations and acted as a consultant on many others.

The author was one of the first attorneys in Massachusetts to incorporate his own practice. He has spoken extensively on the subjects of professional corporations, pension and profit sharing plans, and estate planning procedures before medical, dental, accounting and other societies, insurance companies and varied financial groups. In addition, the writer is a director of the Greater Boston Association of Financial Planners, a member of the Tax Section Committee and Professional Corporation Committee of the American Bar Association. Mr. Riemer is also a member of the Massachusetts Bar Association, the National Health Lawyers Association and the Boston Estate and Business Planning Council.

WHAT THIS BOOK WILL DO FOR YOU

This book offers the professional adviser a detailed, step-by-step guide to organizing and operating a professional corporation. It provides a practical how-to-do-it approach to obtain maximum tax savings for the professional who incorporates, while minimizing or avoiding the pitfalls that can occur. The Pension Reform Act is discussed in clear and understandable language, and procedures and guidelines are provided in order to meet compliance requirements. The author offers a practical analysis of specific cases and suggested solutions to everyday problems — sharing his extensive experience in organizing and representing professional corporations. He addresses the professional adviser representing either the one-man professional corporation or the multi-shareholder corporation. Countless examples, illustrations, charts, forms, and successful estate planning techniques — all part of the latest and most comprehensive information on the subject — make this the most complete handbook available for insuring the success of a professional corporation.

HERE ARE SOME SPECIFIC WAYS THAT THIS BOOK CAN WORK FOR YOU

Chapter One shows the benefits and advantages of the professional corporation and answers the question "Why should a professional incorporate?"

- Gives eleven key tax and non-tax reasons why a professional should incorporate.
- Provides a simple five-step procedure on how to determine whether a professional should incorporate — sample case provided illustrates that a professional with taxable income of $65,000 will save $9,400 in federal taxes alone each year after incorporating.
- Demonstrates how a professional can reduce his taxable income without appreciably affecting his spendable income after incorporating — sample case indicates how a professional can reduce his taxable income by over $18,000 while hardly affecting his spendable income.
- Provides a complete twenty-two point comparison between a qualified corporate retirement plan and the Keogh plan — sample case illustrates that a professional at age 50 may accumulate more than $132,000 in a corporate plan vs. a Keogh plan.

Chapter Two provides step-by-step procedures on how to organize a professional corporation to achieve maximum tax savings and avoid potential tax pitfalls.

- A twenty-eight point checklist of matters to be discussed and decided upon at the organizational meeting of the corporation.
- A twenty-point checklist of the basic corporate documents — from the Articles of Organization to the Stock Redemption Agreement.

— An eight-point checklist of procedural steps to be completed after incorporating to insure the integrity of the corporation.
— Three solutions which may avoid or minimize the "bunching of income" problem.
— Eight steps to follow to qualify under Section 1244 of the Internal Revenue Code.
— How to set up a tax-free incorporation.
— How to handle the fixed assets, accounts receivable, accounts payable, real estate and good will upon incorporating; different fact situations and guidelines for handling each are provided.
— How to choose the tax year of the corporation.
— How to determine whether or not to elect Subchapter S status.
— How to handle the recapture of depreciation and investment credit provisions of the Internal Revenue Code.

Chapter Three presents in detail the tax traps to avoid — disregard of corporate entity, reallocation of income, personal holding company, unreasonable accumulations — and shows how to head off these potential pitfalls.

— A nineteen-point checklist on how to "Look Like, Sound Like and Act Like a Professional Corporation."
— Three preventive steps to avoid Internal Revenue Code Section 269.
— Five steps to take to avoid the personal holding company.
— Six preventive steps to avoid the accumulated earnings tax.

Chapter Four examines the unreasonable compensation problem in detail and provides nineteen preventive steps to take to avoid or minimize a successful Internal Revenue Service attack upon the reasonableness of a professional's corporate salary.

— How to establish a "reasonable salary."
— How to handle bonuses and Contingent Compensation Agreements.
— How to avoid or minimize the "imputed dividend" problem.

Chapter Five presents in detail eighteen steps to take in drafting the employment contract to achieve maximum efficiency and to avoid misunderstanding and friction among professional employees.

— How to handle salary continuation agreements in the event of employee disability.
— How to handle restrictive covenants.
— How to handle business expenses.
— How to establish and handle severance pay.

Chapter Six describes in detail procedures to follow to maximize tax savings and to avoid expensive tax traps in expanding, contracting and liquidating the professional corporation.

— Four different procedures the corporation may take in admitting a non-shareholder professional employee as a shareholder in the corporation — each explained and guidelines given for selecting the most advantageous.
— Three methods of how to merge two unincorporated practices into a professional corporation — each explained and guidelines provided for choosing best route to follow.
— How to merge two incorporated professional practices.

— How to redeem the stock of a withdrawing stockholder — eleven-point comparison checklist between stock redemption and cross purchase agreements is provided, with guidelines to use in selecting the appropriate method.

— Four methods of determining the value of the corporate stock — each explained and guidelines provided for selecting appropriate value.

— Steps to take in liquidating a professional corporation — an eighteen-point checklist comparing Section 331, Section 333, and Section 337 liquidations is provided, together with guidelines to use to secure maximum tax savings in a particular case.

Chapter Seven explains in detail how a professional corporation can save the professional thousands of dollars each year by providing him with non-retirement fringe benefits.

— Seven-step checklist on how to draft a medical reimbursement plan which will qualify under Sections 105 and 106 of the Internal Revenue Code, with sample plan language.

— How to draft a tax-qualified wage continuation plan, with sample plan language.

— How to draft a $5,000 tax-free death benefit, with sample plan language.

— How to draft a qualified group term insurance plan, with sample plan language.

Chapter Eight examines the qualified retirement plans available to a professional corporation — fixed benefit, money purchase, target benefit, and profit sharing plans — and how to determine which plan or combination of plans will provide the greatest benefits to a particular corporation.

— Explains in detail the effect of the new rules established by the Pension Reform Act.

— Gives a summary checklist of the basic characteristics of each plan.

— Provides a ten-point comparison checklist of all retirement plans, which simplifies selection dilemna.

— How to reduce contributions to non-professional employees, with illustrated example.

— How to provide maximum retirement benefits to older professionals, with example.

Chapter Nine tells point by point, in clear and understandable language, how to qualify a corporate retirement plan under the Pension Reform Act.

— How to determine who is an employee for coverage requirements.

— How to handle past service with a proprietorship or partnership.

— How to avoid "discrimination in operation" rules.

— How to meet minimum vesting requirements.

— How to avoid plan terminations and partial terminations.

Chapter Ten reveals retirement plan drafting techniques — cash option profit sharing plans ... loans and withdrawals ... voluntary contributions ... integration with Social Security ... segregated accounts — which will provide maximum flexibility and security for the participants.

— Provides a four-point checklist on how to provide for withdrawals from a profit sharing plan which will avoid the constructive receipt problem, with sample language.

— Gives a five-point checklist on how to provide loans to participants from retirement plan.

— How to handle professional employees who do not wish to participate in retirement plan.

— How to receive retirement benefits while still working.

Chapter Eleven details the various methods of funding a qualified retirement plan — fully insured, split funded, and all equity — and provides guidelines for determining the best method to use in a particular corporation.

- Clear-cut procedures to follow in order to comply with the Pension Reform Act.
- Guidelines to follow in order to comply with the "diversity of investment" requirement.
- A four-point checklist of steps to take to meet "exclusive benefit of employees" rule.
- A fourteen-point checklist of the advantages and disadvantages of life insurance in a retirement plan.
- How to purchase life insurance in a retirement plan to reduce P.S. 58 cost. Example provided shows how one professional reduced his taxable income in one year from $620 to $51.
- A nine-point checklist on how to transfer personally owned life insurance to a qualified retirement plan.
- A four-point checklist on how to transfer Keogh assets to a qualified retirement plan.
- How to save thousands of dollars in estate taxes by excluding death benefits from professional's and spouse's estates.

Chapter Twelve provides a unique step-by-step approach on how to allocate the value of retirement plan assets among plan participants.

- Guidelines will save countless hours of time and will enable quick compliance with the Pension Reform Act.
- Formulas are given and all you do is fill in the blanks.
- Tests are provided to check results.
- Six problem examples are provided in clear and understandable language.

The author, in preparing this book, hopes to have provided, in one source, the helpful answers and guidelines that will enable the reader to serve clients in an effective and professional manner.

Steven K. Riemer

CONTENTS

2. How to Organize a Professional Corporation Tax Wisely (cont.)

SERVICING THE PROFESSIONAL CORPORATION

A Complete Manual and Guide

1

WHY A PROFESSIONAL SHOULD INCORPORATE

"Why should I incorporate?" This question is constantly being raised by almost all professionals throughout the country. If the answer can be stated in one sentence, in the author's opinion, it would be as follows: *"A professional who incorporates is able to do with his pre-tax dollars what he is now doing with his after-tax dollars, without, in many cases, affecting his spendable income."* That is, the corporation is able to provide the professional certain fringe benefits which are available only to corporate employees. The cost of these programs which were once paid by the professional personally with after-tax dollars, will now be considered "business expenses" by the corporation, and thus, deductible. As a result of this shifting from after-tax dollars to pre-tax dollars, the professional is able to save thousands of dollars of taxes each year.

Although the advantages of incorporating are substantial, it will not fit the needs of all professionals, and, as a result, there are many considerations which must be examined and evaluated by the professional and his advisor before a decision to incorporate can be made. The purpose of this chapter is to discuss these various factors. The topics to be discussed are:

1. What are the advantages of incorporating
2. What are the disadvantages of incorporating
3. How to determine whether a professional should incorporate
4. What effect does the increase in Keogh contributions have upon the decision to incorporate
5. What effect will incorporating have upon the professional's spendable income
6. The future of professional corporations after pension reform

WHAT ARE THE ADVANTAGES OF INCORPORATING

Tax-Advantages

The fringe benefit programs which the professional is able to adopt through the corporation are as follows:

1. *Pension and profit sharing plans*[1]

a. Contributions to a qualified corporate retirement plan are deductible by the corporation;

b. The contributions are not included in the professional's taxable income;

c. The earnings generated by these contributions are not taxable to either the trust or to the professional; and

d. In the event of the professional's death prior to retirement, his retirement account will be distributed to his named beneficiary without being included in his gross estate for federal estate tax purposes.[2]

e. In many states, the death benefit will not be subject to inheritance taxes.

f. The contributions made to this plan may be used to purchase a wide variety of investments, including life insurance.[3]

2. *Medical reimbursement plans*[4]

a. The corporation may purchase health insurance for the professional and his dependents.

b. The corporation may reimburse the professional for all medical expenses incurred by him and his dependents which are not covered by his health insurance policy.

c. All employees do not have to be covered by the medical reimbursement plan, and those covered do not have to receive the same benefits.

3. *Wage continuation plans*[5]

a. The corporation may provide disability income protection insurance for the professional. The payments made for such insurance will be deductible by the corporation.

b. The payments made for disability income protection insurance by the corporation will not be taxable to the professional.

c. The corporation does not have to purchase this insurance protection for all employees.

4. *Group term insurance*[6]
The corporation may purchase up to $50,000 of group term insurance for its employees, the premiums for which will not be taxable to the employees.

5. *Tax-free death benefits*[7]
The corporation may pay a $5,000 tax-free death benefit to the professional's beneficiary.

Non-Tax Advantages

In addition to the tax advantages of incorporation, there are certain non-tax advantages of incorporating, which are:

1. Centralized management

The corporation permits a greater centralization of management than a partnership by having the business aspects of the practice conducted by its corporate officers.

2. Limited liability

A professional corporation will not limit a professional's liability for his own acts, but the professional will be protected from personal liability of the acts committed by the other professionals in the corporation. In a partnership, any partner is personally liable for the acts commited by the other partners.

3. Continuity of life

A corporation, unlike a partnership, will not terminate upon the withdrawal, for whatever reason, from the corporation, by a shareholder. This will result in greater stability than available in a partnership.

4. Transfer of shares

It is generally much easier for a professional to transfer his shares in a professional corporation to another professional than for a partner to transfer his partnership interest.

5. No estimated taxes to pay

The salary a professional receives as a corporate employee is subject to withholding taxes, and thus, the check he receives represents his net salary after taxes. Therefore, for many professionals, the need to file estimated tax returns is eliminated.

6. Professional becomes more aware of business aspects of practice.

WHAT ARE THE DISADVANTAGES OF INCORPORATING

The following are some of the disadvantages of operating as a corporation:

1. The professional becomes subject to unemployment taxes and workmen's compensation insurance coverage after incorporating. The amounts required to be paid for these items are very small and therefore, are not really significant.

2. Additional annual filing fees may be imposed upon the corporation by the state in which it was incorporated. For instance, Massachusetts requires that the corporation file an annual certificate which certifies that each shareholder of the corporation is licensed to practice medicine ($75), an annual financial statement of the corporation must be filed ($35), and a minimum corporate income tax is imposed irrespective of the fact that the corporation may have no profits for that particular year ($114.00).

3. An additional premium is usually charged by the malpractice insurance companies for issuing a policy covering the corporation. This additional coverage may be equal to 20% or more of the professional's present insurance premium.

4. The professional's Social Security tax is higher as a corporate employee than what he was required to pay as a self-employed individual. In 1975, the self-employment tax on the wage base of *$14,100* is *$1,113.90*. On the other hand, the Social Security tax after incorporation will be $1,649.70, half of which is paid by the corporation and the other half is paid by the professional. However, the tax which is paid by the corporation is deductible by the corporation, whereas no portion of the self-employment tax is deductible. Therefore, although the professional will now pay an additional *$535.80* in Social Security taxes, he will be deducting $824.85 ($1,649.70 ÷ 2) and thus, there is no additional out-of-pocket cost to the professional.

5. The corporation will be subject to federal income taxes. The amount paid will, in almost all cases, not be significant since the corporation's taxable income will be very small after the professional's salary, fringe benefits and retirement plan contributions have been made.

6. The professional will incur additional annual legal and accounting fees in order to maintain the corporation on an annual basis and for filing any state and federal forms for the corporation and retirement program.

7. After incorporating, the professional subjects the corporation to Internal Revenue Service scrutiny upon additional grounds which he did not have to be concerned as a sole practitioner, i.e., the reasonable compensation problem, personal holding company attack, disregard of corporation as a taxable entity, the tax on unreasonable accumulation, and the reallocation of income problem. As will be subsequently discussed, with proper planning and draftsmanship, these problems are more academic than real.[8]

8. The professional, after incorporating, must comply with corporate formalities. For instance, corporate records must be kept and indiscriminate withdrawals of corporate funds by the professional for personal use are not permitted. In other words, the professional must treat his corporation as a separate entity.

9. The corporation may be required to make larger contributions to the corporate retirement plan that what would be contributed to the same employees in a Keogh plan. However, this may result in an advantage to the corporation, since full vesting may be postponed over a stated number of years, whereas contributions made in a Keogh plan are 100% vested.

OBSERVATION

Although there are certain negative factors which arise when a professional incorporates, these disadvantages, in almost all cases, become insignificant in comparison to the advantages the professional gains after incorporating. For instance, the costs of maintaining the corporation will often appear negligible in relation to the tax savings resulting from the adoption of the fringe benefit programs enumerated previously. In addition, when the chances of a successful Internal Revenue Service attack upon the corporation are weighed against the benefits to be gained, incorporation would be advisable in almost all cases, since, with proper planning, these attacks are more academic than real.

This author does not wish to infer that the disadvantages of incorporating are unimportant. They certainly must be considered, and the practitioner must fully discuss the pros and cons in order that the professional will know exactly what obligations and responsibilities he will assume if he incorporates. What this author is stressing is that many professionals for the first time will be able to take advantage of certain benefits which were never previously available to them, and that these benefits in many cases will far exceed the disadvantages listed above. Thus, the issue really becomes an economic one; that is, are the benefits of incorporating worth incurring the disadvantages of doing so, or, stated in other words, does the tax savings generated by incorporating make incorporating advisable. If the tax savings are significant, then the disadvantages should, in almost all cases, not be reason enough to decide against incorporating. The next section discusses how to determine whether a professional should incorporate.

HOW TO DETERMINE WHETHER A PROFESSIONAL SHOULD INCORPORATE

When a professional asks "Should I incorporate?" the practitioner should not be concerned with whether the Internal Revenue Service recognizes professional corporations as corporations for tax purposes, but instead should determine whether incorporating makes sense based upon the professional's particular economic circumstances. Thus, the decision to incorporate or not to incorporate will, in almost all cases, be made by determining the professional's tax savings if he incorporates and whether the tax savings warrants the annual additional expense of maintaining the corporation. This section will show the practitioner how to make such a determination.

Example

Dr. Smith, age 50, is married and has two children, nets $70,150 on his Schedule C and has $6,500 of outside income. He has one full-time employee who earns $7,500 per year. In addition, he pays $1,000 for health insurance, $750 for disability income protection insurance, and $400 for other medical and dental expenses not covered by insurance. His total itemized deductions are $8,500 and he has not participated in a Keogh plan. He is interested in incorporating his practice and would like to contribute 25% of his income to a pension and profit sharing plan.

Step 1 — *Compute tax before incorporating*[9]

Net income Schedule C	70,150	
Other income	6,500	
Gross income	76,650	76,650
minus		
Itemized Deductions	8,500	
Exemptions (4 x 750)	3,000	
	11,500	11,500
Taxable income		65,150
Tax		24,995

Step 2 — *Establish corporate structure*[10]

Corporate net income		70,150
Salary	52,000	
Pension and profit sharing contributions (52,000 x .25)[11]	12,995	
Health insurance	1,000	
Disability	750	
Medical reimbursement	400	
	67,145	67,145
Surplus		3,005
Corporation maintenance expense (approximate)	1,000	
Contribution for nurse[12]	1,425	2,425.00
Corporate surplus subject to tax		580.00
Corporation's tax 580.00 x .22		127.60

Step 3 — *Compute personal tax after incorporating*

Personal Tax		
Corporate salary	52,000	
Other income	6,500	
	58,500	58,500
minus		
Itemized deductions and exemptions		11,500
Taxable income		47,000
Tax		15,560
Tax savings after incorporating		9,435

Step 4 — *Determine net tax savings*

Subtract annual costs of maintaining corporation and contribution to non-professional employee from total tax saving to arrive at net tax saving.

Gross tax savings		9,435
1. Annual corporate expense	1,000	
2. Employee's contribution	1,425	
	2,425	
Total		2,425
Net tax savings		7,010
Total net tax savings until retirement (age 65) (7010 x 15)		105,150.00

Step 5 — *Compare corporate plan to Keogh plan*

This is determined by multiplying the annual contribution to the corporate plan and Keogh plan by a compound interest factor assuming a certain investment return over the period remaining until Dr. Smith's normal retirement date (65). This example assumes an interest rate of 6½.

Corporate
12,995 (contribution) x 24.1821 = 314,246.39

Keogh
7,500 x 24.1821 = 181,365.75

Additional accumulation in corporate plan — 132,880.64

OBSERVATION

The above example, which is not unusual, demonstrates quite dramatically the significant tax savings which can be generated by Dr. Smith incorporating his practice, and a recommendation to incorporate would certainly appear to be warranted.[13] Although there is an annual additional expense which is incurred by incorporating, this expense is minimal in comparison to the tax savings which results. Furthermore, the contribution to the doctor's employee will be forfeited in its entirety or in part if she should terminate her employment prior to her becoming fully vested in her benefits, which will further reduce the expense to the corporation.

HOW A PROFESSIONAL CAN REDUCE HIS TAXABLE INCOME WITHOUT AFFECTING HIS SPENDABLE INCOME

"I can't afford to live on less than what I am now earning." This is a statement which is often heard by practitioners when discussing the advisability of incorporating a particular professional's practice. However, most professionals don't realize that in many cases they can reduce their taxable income without really affecting their spendable income. Referring back to our previous example, let's add one more fact; Dr. Smith has continually invested $6500.00 a year out of earnings as a hedge against inflation and for retirement. Now, let's compare Dr. Smith's spendable income before incorporating and after incorporating.

WATCH THIS

In order to arrive at true spendable income, the professional's fixed expenses or commitments should be subtracted from his net income after taxes. Money spent for health and disability income protection insurance, and other such items are not really spendable dollars.

Spendable Income

before incorporating			*after incorporating*	
taxable income	65,150		taxable income	47,000
tax	- 24,995		tax	- 15,560
spendable income after taxes	40,155			31,440
minus	-6,500	investments		
	- 1,000	health ins.		
	- 750	disability ins.		
	- 400	medical, dental expenses		
actual spendable income	31,505			31,440

result: Dr. Smith has given up $65.00 of additional spendable income.

WATCH THIS

This example does not intend to imply that a professional's spendable income will never be affected. Whether or not spendable income will be reduced will depend upon the amount the professional's taxable income is reduced and the professional's insurance (including life insurance) and investment program, which will be shifted to the corporation. The more the professional's taxable income is reduced the greater the reduction in his spendable income. Similarly, if the professional has a small personal insurance and investment program, the greater the effect will be upon his spendable income, since the professional is shifting less after-tax items to the corporation. However, in many cases, a professional, through tax savings and by shifting certain after-tax expenses to the corporation, will not experience any loss of spendable income. Therefore, a practitioner must examine his professional client's particular circumstances to determine what effect incorporating will have upon his spendable income. Many professionals have been pleasantly surprised to learn that they are able to incorporate without affecting their standard of living.

OBSERVATION

Incorporating will provide many professionals an opportunity to accumulate significantly greater retirement funds than would be possible by investing after-tax dollars. For example, assume a professional in the 50% tax bracket decides that he will use the last $10,000 of his income for retirement accumulation purposes. Unfortunately, taxes do not permit the maximum use of this money for such purposes. In such a case, $5,000 of the $10,000 must be used to pay federal income taxes. If the remaining $5,000 is then invested at 6%, federal taxes will eat up another $150 of the $300 which was generated. Thus, out of a total of $10,000, the professional is left with $5,150 after one year. However, if this $10,000 was contributed to a corporate retirement plan, then the professional will have $10,000 to invest and assuming the same annual interest rate of 6%, he will keep the entire $600 earnings on his investment. Thus, by incorporating, after the first year the professional will have $10,600.00 compared to $5,150. When this is continued over a period of years, the results are magnified beyond belief.

WHAT EFFECT DOES THE INCREASE IN KEOGH CONTRIBUTIONS HAVE UPON THE DECISION TO INCORPORATE

The Pension Reform Act has increased the maximum deduction under H.R. 10 plans from $2,500 or 10% of earned income, whichever is less to $7,500, or 15% of earned income, whichever is less. As a result, many professionals who do not wish to contribute more than $7500 to a retirement plan are beginning to seriously question whether incorporating is advisable or even necessary in view of this increase. However, there are substantial differences between a Keogh plan and a corporate retirement plan, and before an intelligent decision can be made whether or not to incorporate these differences must be examined and carefully considered. The following is a comparison between the Koegh Plan and the Corporate Retirement Plan.

WATCH THIS

There are two types of Keogh Plans:[14] 1, Plans which cover one or more owner employees (Regular Keogh)[15] and 2, plans which cover self-employed individuals, none of whom are owner employees (Super Keogh).

Generally, Super Keogh plans are similar in most respects to the corporate retirement plans.[16] However, there are substantial differences between the regular Keogh plan and the corporate plan. Since there must be at least ten partners to have a super plan, most professionals will have to evaluate the differences between a regular Keogh plan and a corporate retirement plan. For this reason, Figure 1 compares a Keogh plan which contains one or more owner employees to the corporate plan.

OBSERVATION

If a professional desires to contribute more to a retirement plan than what is permitted to be contributed to a Keogh plan, the decision to incorporate is easy. The decision becomes more difficult, however, when the professional only desires to contribute the Keogh limitation to a retirement plan. In such a case, the professional may feel that the expense of incorporating is not warranted, since the contributions which will be made to the corporate plan will be the same as what would have been made to a Keogh plan.

As one can readily observe, there are more important considerations in determining whether or not incorporating is advisable than the amount of the desired contribution. A corporate plan provides substantially greater flexibility than a Keogh plan, and the importance of this flexibility should not be underestimated. Although flexibility may not seem very important when the plan is adopted, it may prove to be indispensable some time in the future. Although a Keogh plan will cost nothing to establish and substantially less to maintain than a corporate plan, the restrictions and limitations of a Keogh plan may prove to be more costly to the professional than the initial

Figure 1

KEOGH PLAN vs. CORPORATE PLAN

A COMPARISON

Characteristics	*Keogh*	*Corporate*	*Observations*
1. *Eligibility*	All full-time employees with more than three years of service must be covered.[17]	70%/80% test must be met; however, the plan cannot require as a condition of participation a minimum age over 25 and a minimum service requirement greater than one year.[18]	The three-year service requirement will probably result in fewer nonprofessional employees being covered by the Keogh plan than would be covered in the corporate plan. However, if there is a rapid turnover of nonprofessional employees within a three-year employment period, the contribution which is made by the corporation on behalf of these employees will be forfeited entirely or in part, when they terminate their employment. Thus, in such cases, it will make little difference if the nonprofessional employees are covered or not. (See comment for vesting.)
2. *Vesting*	All covered employees must be 100% vested in the contributions allocated to their account.[19]	Vesting in benefits is usually gradual, and is based upon the number of years the employee has been participating in the plan. Generally, vesting may be postponed over an 11-year period of time.[20]	This is a serious disadvangate of the Keogh plan. If the common law employees tend to continue their employment for three or more years, then it will probably be more expensive to contribute to a Keogh plan than to a corporate plan, since the employee is fully vested in his Keogh contributions whereas, he will probably only receive a portion or none of the contribution allocated to his account in the corporate plan.

Characteristics	*Keogh*	*Corporate*	*Observations*
3. *Contributions*			
a. deductible limits	Deductible contribution limited to $7,500 or 15% of earned income, whichever is less. If a defined benefit plan is adopted, the retirement benefit is limited to the corporate limits i.e., $75,000 or 100% of compensation, whichever is less. Thus, in some situations the maximum deductible contribution may be greater or lesser than $7500 or 15% of compensation, whichever is less.[21]	Deductible contributions substantially in excess of $7,500 are generally permitted; in defined benefit plans, corporation may deduct that amount necessary to provide retirement benefits equal to 100% of compensation not in excess of $75,000 per year.[22] In a money - purchase and target benefit plan, the corporation may deduct an amount equal to 25% of employee's compensation or $25,000, whichever is less.[23]	Corporate plans permit a professional to contribute substantially greater amounts than are permitted under a Keogh plan. If a professional wishes to maximize his contribution, he will probably have to incorporate.
b. increase in contribution deduction based upon cost of living adjustments	Maximum deductible contribution may not be adjusted as a result of cost of living increase.	$75,000 and $25,000 limits will be increased based upon cost of living index.[24]	This is a very attractive advantage of corporate plans, since the present maximum limits of $75,000 and 25,000 will be adjusted for cost of living increases. Thus, the deductible limits in the corporate plan will continue to increase, whereas, the Keogh limits will remain frozen.
c. excess contribution	A 6% tax is imposed upon excess contributions.[25]	No tax is imposed if a contribution is made in excess of what is properly deductible.	This is another disadvantage of the Keogh plan. Excess contributions may be made inadvertently, and the tax imposed will place an unexpected cost upon the professional.

Characteristics	*Keogh*	*Corporate*	*Observations*
d. carryover of excess contribution to subsequent years.	Excess contribution may be carried over and deducted in succeeding taxable years.	Excess contribution may be carried over and deducted in succeeding taxable years.	
e. Credit carryover of permitted contributions which were not made in taxable year to succeeding taxable years.	Credit carryovers in profit sharing plans are not permitted.[26]	Credit carryovers in profit sharing plans are permitted. However, deductible contributions in succeeding taxable years may not exceed 25% of compensation.[27]	This is a very attractive feature of a corporate profit sharing plan, since a professional who does not contribute the full deductible limit in one year can carry it forward and deduct it, within limits, in succeeding years. This will result in an increased deductible limit in these succeeding years (i.e., 15% annually to 25% annually which includes credit carryovers), whereas, the Keogh contribution will always remain the same
4. *Integration*	Integration is permitted in a limited manner, but is very complex and not very practical.[28]	Integration is not as difficult or complex as in Keogh plan.[29]	
5. *Distribution*			
a. Minimum age before distribution can be made without penalty	Distribution, other than for disability or death, may not be made prior to age 59½ without penalty.[30]	Distribution may be made prior to age 59½ without penalty for various stated reasons, such as loans, hardship withdrawals in profit sharing plans, early retirement, and distribution of a terminated employee's vested interest.	Some of the most serious disadvantages of a Keogh plan are its inflexibility in regard to when benefits can be distributed. Professionals who contribute the maximum amount to a Keogh plan are, for practical purposes, freezing large sums of money which cannot be withdrawn prior to age 59½.

Characteristics	*Keogh*	*Corporate*	*Observations*
b. Maximum age when benefits must commence	Distribution of benefits must begin by age 70½.[31]	There is no stated age when benefits must commence.	Thus, if a financial emergency should arise, there is no way to reach their Keogh funds without incurring a penalty. Alternatively, if the professional desires to work beyond age 70½, he will be forced to begin withdrawals from his Keogh plan while he is still earning a high income. None of these problems are found in corporate plans.
c. Penalty on premature distribution.	An owner employee will be subject to a penalty equal to 10% of the premature distribution. This is an increase from the penatly imposed under prior law.[32]	There is no similar penalty.	
d. Lump sum distribution.	Accumulation attributable to contributions made before 1974 will be taxed as capital gain; accumulation attributable to contributions after 1973 will be treated as ordinary income which will be taxed under a 10-year forward averaging rule.[33]	Rules which apply to Keogh plans are equally applicable to corporate plans.	
6. Death benefits			
a. estate tax exclusion.	Death benefit is included in gross estate of self-employed employee.[34]	Death benefits are not included in gross estate of employee.[35]	This is a significant advantage of corporate plans. The ability to transfer corporate retirement plan death benefits to a named beneficiary free of federal estate taxes may result in a savings of $10,000, $20,000 or more in taxes. This advantage alone may be reason enough to incorporate.

Characteristics	*Keogh*	*Corporate*	*Observations*
b. $5,000 death benefit exclusion	The beneficiary of a self-employed individual's death benefit is not entitled to the $5,000 death benefit exclusion.[36]	The $5,000 exclusion from income is available to the beneficiary of an employee's death benefit from a qualified corporate plan.[37]	
7. Disability benefits	Very rigid definition of disability — disability must be of such a nature that death can be expected or disability will continue for an indefinite period of time.[38]	Definition is more flexible. May be defined as inability to perform the services for which the employee was employed.	The extreme definition of disability in a Keogh plan will prevent most professionals from ever receiving benefits under the plan since most disabilities are not of such a severe nature. Therefore, if a surgeon loses the use of a hand, he will become totally disabled as far as practicing his profession is concerned, but will not be entitled to receive a distribution of his Keogh account for "disability." Thus, when the professional needs money the most, he cannot receive it without penalty. This is not a problem in corporate plans.
8. Voluntary contributions			
a. When permitted	Only permitted if plan covers one or more common law employees.[39]	Voluntary contribution may be made by a professional even though there are no non-professional employees participating in the plan.	
b. Penalties for withdrawal of voluntary contributions	An owner employee may now withdraw any voluntary contribution he made to the plan without penalty. Prior law did impose a penalty if voluntary contributions were withdrawn.[40]	Employee's voluntary contribution may be withdrawn without penalty.[41]	

Characteristics	Keogh	Corporate	Observation
c. Maximum voluntary contribution	Limited to $2500 or 10% of compensation, whichever is less.	Limited to 10% of the employee's aggregate compensation.	Larger voluntary contributions are available in corporate plans, but voluntary contributions may result in reduced corporate contributions. Thus, whether or not maximum voluntary contributions are advisable will depend upon the factors in the particular case.[42]
9. *Trustees*	An owner employee may be the trustee of the plan provided he can satisfy the Secretary of the Treasury that he will administer the trust consistently with the requirements of the Internal Revenue Code.[43] Prior law required a bank to be trustee.	The professional may be trustee of the retirement plan.[44]	
10. *Profit sharing plans*	Plan must contain a definite formula for determining the contribution that must be made by the employer on behalf of employees other than owner employees. That is, the plan must specify the portion of profits to be contributed.[45]	No requirement for definite formula.[46]	One of the advantages of a corporate profit sharing plan is that there is no requirement as to what amount of profits must be contributed to the plan. This provides the professional with maximum flexibility in determining what he will contribute annually to the plan. This flexibility is lost in a Keogh profit sharing plan.
11. *Prohibited transaction*	Plan cannot permit loans to be made to an owner employee.[47]	A qualified corporate plan is permitted to make loans to a plan participant.[48]	This is another example of the rigidness of Keogh and the advantages of a corporate plan. Professionals in a corporate plan may borrow funds in the event of a financial emergency without penalty.

cost of incorporating and the annual cost of maintaining the corporation. Furthermore, the professional will be able to save substantial tax dollars by shifting the cost of his medical and disability income protection insurance premiums, as well as medical and dental expenses not reimbursed by insurance, to the corporation. These items are not deductible to the professional personally.[49]

Therefore, it is most important that the practitioner be sure that his professional clients fully understand the differences between a Keogh plan and a corporate plan, their advantages and disadvantages, and the other fringe benefits which are available to them under a corporation which are not available to them as sole practitioners or as partners in a partnership, before the decision to incorporate or not to incorporate is made.

THE FUTURE OF PROFESSIONAL CORPORATIONS AFTER PENSION REFORM

Professional corporations are alive and well, and the increase in Keogh contributions will not deter their growth in the years ahead. Although the Pension Reform Act has decreased the amounts which can be contributed to a corporate money purchase and target benefit pension plan, these plans still enable the professional to contribute more than three times the amount which can be contributed to a Keogh plan ($25,000 maximum limit in corporate plan vs. $7500 in Keogh). In addition, the limitations to a corporate defined benefit plan have not been significantly affected by the Pension Reform Act, and, in many cases, older professionals will be able to contribute amounts in excess of $25,000. Therefore, incorporating still provides a professional vehicle through which he may accumulate funds for retirement purposes and to meet current income needs, in amounts and in a manner just not available to self-employed individuals. In addition, the Pension Reform Act has not affected the fringe benefits that may be provided a corporate employee. Thus, for those professionals who wish to maximize the amount they can accumulate for retirement, maintain the maximum flexibility in plan provisions, and to take advantage of certain fringe benefits only available to corporate employees, then they must incorporate.

FOOTNOTES

[1]See chapter 8 "Selecting the Retirement Plan," p. 125.

[2]See chapter 11 "Handling Investments and Life Insurance in the Qualified Plan," section entitled "Estate Tax," p. 200.

[3]Ibid., section entitled "Funding the Retirement Plan ... The Trusteed and Insured Plan," p. 189.

[4]See chapter 7 "How to Take Advantage of Non-Retirement Fringe Benefits," section entitled "Medical Reimbursement Plans," p.102.

[5]Ibid., section entitled "Wage Continuation Plan and Disability Income Protection Insurance," p. 115.

[6]Ibid., section entitled "Group Term Insurance," p. 119.

[7]Ibid., section entitled "Tax Free Death Benefit," p. 118.

[8]See chapter 3 "Operating the Corporation to Avoid Internal Revenue Service Problems," p. 40.

[9]This computation is generally not necessary if the practitioner has the professional's tax return. But for purposes of illustration, the computation is made.

[10]Salary and fringe benefits plus other costs should be very close to the expected net income of the corporation. This will reduce the corporate tax.

[11]Integrated money-purchase plan with contribution formula of 4% of first $7500 of compensation and 11% of excess plus 15% profit sharing plan.

[12]Ibid.

[13]The tax savings will be even greater since state income taxes are also reduced.

[14]Regs. §1.401-10(a).

[15]An owner employee is defined as an individual who owns either more than 10% of the capital interest or more than 10% of the profits interest of a proprietorship or partnership. Regs. §1.401-10(d).

[16]The only significant differences between a Keogh plan covering no owner employees and a corporate retirement plan are that the maximum deduction permitted under the Keogh plan is $7500 or 15% of earned income, whichever is less, and there is no estate tax exclusion for death benefits payable under the Keogh plan.

[17]IRC§401(d) (3).

[18]See chapter 9 "Qualifying the Retirement Plan," section entitled "Coverage Tests-After Pension Reform," p.151.

[19]IRC§401(d)(2)(A).

[20]See chapter 9 "Qualifying the Retirement Plan," section entitled "Vesting," p. 155.

[21]IRC §404(e)(1).

[22]IRC §415(b)(1).

[23]IRC §415(c).

[24]IRC §415(d).

[25]IRC §4972(a).

[26]Regs. §1.401(a)-8(a)(2).

[27]IRC §404(a)(3)(A).

[28]Regs. §1.401-12(h).

[29]See chapter 10 "Retirement Plan Drafting Techniques," section entitled "Integrating the Retirement Plan with Social Security," p. 181.

[30]IRC §401(d)(4)(c).

[31]IRC §401(a)(9).

[32]IRC §72(m)(5)(b).

[33]IRC §402(e).

[34]IRC §2039(c).

[35]Ibid.

[36]IRC§101(b)(3): Regs.§ 1.101-2(f).

[37]IRC §101(b)(2).

[38]Regs. §1.401-12(m)(l)(i).

[39]IRC §401(d)(5)(B).

[40]IRC §72(m)(5)(A).

[41]See chapter 10 "Retirement Plan Drafting Techniques," section entitled "Withdrawing Voluntary Contributions," p. 180.

[42]See chapter 8 "Selecting the Retirement Plan," section entitled "Corporate Contributions to Money-Purchase Pension Plan." p. 132.

[43]IRC § 401(d)(1).

[44]See chapter 11 "Handling Investments and Life Insurance in the Qualified Plan," Section entitled "Trustees," p. 194.

[45]Regs. § 1.401-12(d).

[46]See chapter 8 "Selecting the Retirement Plan," section entitled "Contribution formula not required," p. 127.

[47]IRC § 503(j); Regs. § 1.503-(j)-1(a).

[48]See note 29. Section entitled "Loans," p. 176.

[49]An individual taxpayer is only able to deduct those medical expenses which exceed a certain specified percentage of his gross income. See chapter 7 "How to Take Advantage of Non-Retirement Fringe Benefits," section entitled "Medical Reimbursement Plans," p. 102.

2

HOW TO ORGANIZE A PROFESSIONAL CORPORATION TAX WISELY

Once the decision has been made by the sole practitioner or partnership to incorporate, the immediate question raised is how the new corporation should be organized. In this context, the practitioner must carefully study the assets and structure of the incorporating professional or partnership and find answers to the following questions.

1. Should the professionals elect a tax-free incorporation or a taxable one?
2. Should the furniture, fixtures and equipment of the prior entity be transferred to the new corporation?
3. Should real estate be transferred to the corporation?
4. Should the accounts receivable be transferred to the corporation?
5. Should accounts payable and liabilities be transferred and assumed by the new corporation?
6. What effect will the recapture of depreciation provision and recapture of investment credit have on the decision of whether or not to transfer property to the corporation?
7. How should the bunching of income problem be handled for fiscal year partnerships?
8. What accounting method should be adopted?
9. Should the corporation adopt a fiscal or calendar year?
10. Should the corporation elect to be taxed under Subchapter S of the Internal Revenue Code?

The purpose of this chapter is to discuss these questions in detail and to provide guidelines which will enable the practitioner to organize the professional corporation in a tax-wise manner.

TAX-FREE VS. TAXABLE INCORPORATION

Tax-Free Incorporation

The Internal Revenue Code provides that no gain or loss will be recognized if property is exchanged solely for the stock or securities of a controlled corporation.[1] Thus, a professional who has property, i.e. furniture, fixtures and equipment, whose fair market value exceeds its basis may transfer this property to his corporation in exchange for its stock without a taxable transaction. The basic premise for this nonrecognition is that there has only been a change in the form of doing business and the transferor has not really recognized a gain in the economic sense from the transaction.[2]

In a tax-free exchange, the corporation's basis for the property transferred is the same as it was in the hands of the professional,[3] and the basis of the stock and securities acquired by the professional is the same as the property transferred.[4]

How to set up a tax-free incorporation

In order to have a tax-free incorporation, the following requirements must be met.[5]

1. One or more persons must transfer property to the corporation
2. The transfer must be solely in exchange for the stock or securities of the corporation, and
3. The person or persons are in control of the corporation immediately after the exchange.

What constitutes property?

Property includes all real and personal property, such as professional buildings and all furniture, fixtures and equipment. In addition, money,[6] accounts receivable[7] and good will[8] are considered property for purposes of Section 351.

However, §351(a) specifically states that services are not considered property, and a person who secures stock for services will not be considered a transferor in determining whether the requisite control is present. Thus, if the person receiving stock for service has more than a 20% interest in the corporation, the corporation will not be a tax-free incorporation, since the other transferors, who are considered part of the control group, have not acquired 80% of the stock of the corporation.

However, if a person has received stock for services and property, he will be considered part of the control group unless the transfer of property was solely for the purpose of obtaining a tax free incorporation and served no other purpose.[9] A person who receives stock for services will report as ordinary income the value of the stock received.

What constitutes "stock and securities"

This requirement is quite important since the receipt of anything other than stock or securities (referred to as "boot") by the transferor will result in taxable gains to him.[10] Normally, this requirement will present no problem to almost all professionals. However, if debt financing is desired, the question arises whether the debt instrument is in fact a security of the corporation or a short-term note. If the latter, a taxable gain occurs.

Generally, if the corporate obligation is of a long-term duration, it will be considered a security. However, the courts have varied widely on what constitutes a long-term obligation, which makes the job of the practitioner quite precarious when issuing bonds in exchange for property. It appears that notes with a five-year term or less will not qualify as securities, whereas notes with a term of ten years or more will qualify.[11]

WATCH THIS

If the corporation is undercapitalized, then it is quite likely that the Internal Revenue Service will treat debt instruments as a substitute for stock. Thus, professionals who felt they were loaning money to the corporation will find this loan is considered part of their capital investment which can only be returned in the form of dividends.

In addition, stock rights and stock warrants are not considered "stock or securities."[12]

What constitutes control

The transferors must control at least 80% of the total combined voting power of all classes of stock entitled to vote and at least 80% of the total number of shares of each non-voting class of stock.[13]

Taxable Incorporation

Since the basis of the transferred property is carried over to the corporation, many incorporators have chosen to have a taxable incorporation. In a taxable incorporation, the property transferred receives a stepped-up basis equal to the value of the property, thus creating larger depreciation deductions for the corporation against its ordinary income. Alternatively, if the fair market value of the property has fallen below its basis, the professional will recognize loss in a taxable incorporation.[14]

There are three methods available by which the professional may realize a taxable exchange, which are as follows:

Partial taxable exchange - receipt of "boot"

If the professional receives property ("boot") other than stock or securities from the new corporation in exchange for his assets arising from his practice prior to incorporation, he will be taxed on the gain to the extent of the fair market value of the "boot."[15] Normally, the other property will be short-term notes. If the adjusted basis for the property transferred exceeds its fair market value, a realized loss would not be recognized under Internal Revenue Code §351(b), even though "boot" is received. Whether the gain will be treated as capital gain or as ordinary income and whether short-term or as a long-term gain will depend upon the type of asset that was transferred, the length of time it was held by the professional and by other Internal Revenue Code sections.[16]

The corporation obtains a stepped-up basis for the transferred assets to the extent of the gain which is taxed.[17] When several assets are transferred to the corporation, each is treated separately, and the boot is allocated among the assets in proportion to their value. A loss on one of the transfers, if any (in addition to not being recognized under S351(b)), may not be used to offset the gain of any other transfer.

WATCH THIS

If the professional transfers accounts receivable in an exchange when stock is received, a portion of the boot will be allocated to the accounts receivable. This will result in the recognition of ordinary income to the extent of the boot which is allocated to the accounts receivable and a reduced basis on the other depreciable property. Thus, in a taxable incorporation, the accounts receivable should not be transferred.

Sale of assets by corporation

By this method, the professional incorporates tax free under §351(a) and then, in a separate transaction, sells his high valued, low basis equipment and other such property to the corporation. The corporation's basis is the purchase price of said property, and the gain to the professional is based upon the difference between the purchase price and his basis in the property.

However, the Internal Revenue Service may successfully argue that the sale is really part of the entire transaction, and treat the property sold as part of the non-taxable exchange under §351(a) or as a contribution to capital.[18] This would be especially true if the corporation was thinly capitalized.

> ...whenever property is 'sold' to a controlled corporation, the taxpayer must be prepared to establish that appearances correspond with reality. The Internal Revenue Service has more than once argued, sometimes with success, that a corporation's promise to pay for property should be disregarded, either because the corporation's capitalization was tax 'thin' or for some other reason, and that the 'sale' should be treated either as a §351 transfer or as a contribution to capital.[19]

Avoiding section 351

The professional can achieve a taxable incorporation by avoiding the provisions of §351. However, this is not as easy as it may seem. Once the requirements of §351 are met, then a tax-free exchange has occurred even though the parties have intended to have a taxable incorporation.[20] For corporations consisting of two or more professionals, the easiest way to avoid §351 is to issue more than 20% of the stock to a professional solely in exchange for his services. However, for most professionals, it will be almost impossible to sidestep §351 by trying to avoid its provisions. The Internal Revenue Service will look at the reality of the transaction and treat it accordingly, despite the label placed upon it by the incorporators.

Thus, of the three alternatives available to a professional for obtaining a taxable incorporation, the "boot" transaction will probably achieve the best results.

Limited Usefulness of Taxable Incorporation

Existing Internal Revenue Code provisions effectively eliminate taxable incorporation as a tax-savings device. The following are some of the undesirable consequences which might result under a taxable incorporation.

1. *Possible recapture of depreciation under §1245 and §1250* - If depreciable property, whether real or personal, is sold to the corporation, some or all of the gain on the sale may be taxed to the transferor as ordinary income under the recapture provisions of §1245 and §1250 of the Internal Revenue Code.
2. *Loss of accelerated depreciation* - The transferee corporation may not continue the accelerated depreciation method which has been adopted by the transferor, since the corporation is not the original user of the property.[21]
3. *Recapture of investment credit* - The sale of property upon which the investment credit was taken by the transferor may result in the recapture of some or all of the credit taken by the transferor.[22] The transferor will treat the amount recaptured as ordinary income.
4. *Internal Revenue Code §1239* - In addition to the recapture provisions of sections 1245 and 1250, section 1239 provides that any gain recognized on the sale of depreciable property to a controlled corporation will be treated as ordinary income if the transferor owns more than 80% of the stock of the corporation.

   Although this section may not be applicable to many corporations consisting of two or more shareholders, it will always apply to the one-man professional corporation.
5. *Internal Revenue Code §267* - This section will disallow a loss on the sale of property by a transferor to a corporation in which he owns more than 50% of the outstanding stock of the corporation.

An individual is deemed to own the stock of his partners and, thus, the transferor will only be able to avoid this section by dissolving the partnership before incorporating. However, *§267 can never be avoided by the one-man professional corporation.*

6. *Good will* - If good will is deemed transferred to the new corporation,[23] the professional may be confronted with a large tax based on the value of the good will, since there is no basis for the good will. This tax may affect any potential benefit sought by the taxable incorporation.

OBSERVATION

Thus, it appears that the tax-free incorporation under §351 will be used in almost all cases, since the "cost" of obtaining the stepped-up basis for the new corporation may offset some or eliminate all of the benefits sought by the taxable incorporation.

WHAT ASSETS SHOULD BE TRANSFERRED TO THE NEW CORPORATION

The above section was concerned with whether a tax-free or taxable incorporation should be utilized. Once the decision has been reached, the next question confronting the practitioner is whether or not the assets used by the professional or partnership prior to incorporating should be transferred to the professional corporation, and if so, what assets. Since almost all corporations will elect to incorporate tax free under §351 of the Internal Revenue Code, it will be assumed for purposes of this section that §351 route was adopted.

Accounts Receivable

One of the most discussed topics in regard to the formation of a new professional corporation is whether the outstanding accounts receivable of the professional or partnership should be transferred to the corporation. The problem raised is that a cash basis taxpayer does not report income until its receipt, and by transferring accounts receivable, the taxpayer is in effect transferring income earned by him to another entity. Thus, a distortion of income may arise.[24] This is not a problem for accrual basis professionals or partnerships since the accounts receivable have already been reported as income when earned.

The Internal Revenue Service's initial position on this matter was that accounts receivable were not property within the scope of §351 and that the accounts receivable should be taxable to the transferors either at the time the exchange was made or alternatively, when the corporation collected the receivables.[25] The Internal Revenue Service, in most cases,has been unsuccessful in persuading the courts to this position, and it now appears that the Service will permit a cash basis taxpayer to transfer the accounts receivable tax free to the new corporation under §351. This new position is evidenced by the following Service actions or statements:

1. The Service acquiesced to the L. Kniffen Case,[26] in which the court held that accounts receivable should be considered property for §351 purposes.
2. In Rev. Rul. 69-442 1969-2 CB 53, the Service implied that accounts receivable could be transferred to the new corporation under §351 by stating that the basis for the accounts receivable of the corporation would be zero.
3. Rev. Proc. 73-10 IRB 1973-17, 37 set forth procedures to follow for securing an advance ruling in regard to the tax-free transfer of property, including accounts receivable, to a new corporation under §351.
4. A statement by K. Martin Worthy, when he was Chief Counsel of the Internal Revenue Service that "It would seem that the basic policy of Section 351 is to recognize that the new corporation represents a substantial continuation of the business formerly conducted by the transferor. This policy would suggest that the transferor should not be taxed on the accounts receivable and the new corporation should be taxed when it collects them."[27]
5. In a recent case, the taxpayer partnership argued that the accounts receivable which were transferred to the new successor corporation should not be the income of the corporation, but the income of the partnership since it was the partnership who earned the income. The court

disagreed stating that when there is a bona fide transfer of a total business from a non-corporate to the corporate form with no tax avoidance purposes, it was congressional intent that there be no taxable event to the transferors.[28]

Thus, it seems quite certain that a professional or partnership may safely transfer his accounts receivable to the new corporation without fear that they will be taxed to the professional or partnership.

Should accounts receivable be transferred to the corporation

Notwithstanding the strong evidence indicating that accounts receivable can be transferred under §351, the issue has not been finally settled and several commentaries feel that accounts receivable should not be transferred to the professional corporation. The basic premise for this position is that section 482 of the Internal Revenue Code providing for the reallocation of income between related taxpayers supersedes the provisions of §351,[29] and if §482 is applied, then it is possible that a double taxation situation may arise. That is, the transferors will be taxed upon the accounts receivable transferred either at the time they are transferred or when they are collected by the corporation and taxed a second time, when the corporation pays its salaries from the income generated by the accounts receivable which have already been taxed to them. As a practical matter, this should not pose a real threat to most professionals who incorporate their practices. If there is a bona fide transfer of the professional's practice to the new corporation, §482 or the assignment of income doctrine will almost never be raised by the Internal Revenue Service.

If accounts receivable are not transferred, then the professional or partnership must establish two sets of books; one for the new corporation and another for the outstanding accounts receivable. This can become cumbersome and confusing. In fact, it might necessitate keeping the partnership alive until the accounts receivable are collected. In addition, two sets of bills would have to be sent out. Furthermore, if accounts receivable are not transferred, then the corporation may be cash poor for several months or more until the corporation's bills are collected. From the author's personal observation, the greatest disillusionment with professional corporations has come from professionals whose accounts receivable were kept outside the corporation. For these individuals, there never seemed to be money to meet current corporate expenses, money was required to be loaned to the corporation from their personal funds, and there were no funds available to meet their required contributions to the corporate retirement plans.

Thus, it is the author's opinion that, in view of current Internal Revenue Service positions and court cases, the benefits to be gained versus the negligible chances for adverse tax consequences warrant the transfer of accounts receivable to the corporation.

Organizational problems in handling accounts receivables

When a professional corporation adds a new shareholder or when two or more practices are combined to form a new corporation, a problem arises as to how the accounts receivable should be handled. Since the new shareholder or combining professionals will not have an equal amount of accounts receivable, the person with the greater amount of outstanding accounts receivable will be sharing income which he generated with his new colleagues. Therefore, this problem must be considered in such situations.

Some possible solutions to this problem are as follows:

Formation of Corporation Consisting of Two or More Shareholders

A. *Retain accounts receivable* - Under this method, each professional would retain his own accounts receivable and collect them personally. When this is done, it makes little difference that each professional has a different amount of outstanding accounts receivable. However, all of the problems created with the retention of receivables as discussed above will be present.

B. *Purchase of receivables* - In this case, the professional with the smaller amount of outstanding accounts receivable will purchase a sufficient amount of receivables from the other professionals so that each professional now owns an equal amount. The difficulty here is that some of the professionals are going to have to come up with the money to purchase these receivables and it is difficult to determine whether all of the receivables purchased will ever be collected. In addition, the professionals selling their receivables recognize an immediate tax on their sale. For these reasons, the purchase and sale of receivables is not the best vehicle to solve this problem.

C. *Corporation collects accounts receivable for professionals* - Under this method, the new corporation will act as the collection agent for each professional for his receivables. The corporation normally receives a small percentage of the amount collected as an agency fee. The receivables collected will then be disbursed to the individual professionals. This will eliminate the need for double billings or the need to keep the prior entity alive until the receivables are collected. But, the corporation is cash poor until its new bills are collected, which presents a host of problems as discussed above.

OBSERVATION

The author has found a satisfactory solution by having each professional transfer a minimum amount of their accounts receivable to the corporation. Any excess above this amount will then be collected by the corporation as agent for each professional. By this method, the corporation receives the needed cash in order to conduct its ordinary business affairs without having to borrow money, and no professional is benefiting from the income generated by his colleagues prior to incorporating.

Addition of New Shareholder to an Existing Corporation

Where an existing corporation brings in a colleague as a new shareholder, it is often felt that the new shareholder will be receiving an interest in the accounts receivable of the corporation which he did not help generate. Thus, the issue arises as to how the accounts receivable should be handled. One solution is to have the new shareholder purchase his share of the accounts receivable when he enters the corporation. In many cases, the new man may not be able to afford this initial expenditure, in which case, it is often suggested that the new man should draw a smaller salary for several years until his share of the accounts receivable is paid off. If the new man withdraws from the corporation for whatever reason, he is usually paid his share of the accounts receivable then outstanding.

OBSERVATION

This author does not feel that is is necessary for the new professional to be required to purchase his "share" of the accounts receivable when being admitted as a new shareholder in the corporation. In most cases, the new man will not be admitted as a shareholder until he has been with the corporation for a certain period of time and has proven his ability to generate and attract new patients or clients. Thus, in many cases, the new man, when he becomes a shareholder, is already directly responsible for a portion of the accounts receivable that he is being required to buy. Therefore, the author feels that in such cases, accounts receivable should not be reflected in the price of the stock, since the new man is not receiving a benefit to which he is not entitled.

If a new man has not been with the corporation for a sufficient period of time to generate his share of the accounts receivable at the time of his admission as a shareholder, the author still feels that it is still not necessary for him to purchase his interest in the receivables. In such a case, the parties can always agree that if the employee terminates his employment he will not be entitled to any portion of the outstanding receivables of the corporation at that time.[30]

Furniture, Fixtures and Equipment

Whether or not furniture, fixtures and equipment should be transferred to the corporation will depend upon the facts in each case. Generally, if the value of such assets is considerable, many practitioners have taken the position that they should not be transferred but retained personally and leased to the corporation, for the following reasons:

1. *Minimizing unreasonable compensation problems* - Some courts have adopted the "fair return of invested capital" theory whereby a dividend is imputed based upon the capital of the corporation. If these assets are retained by the professional or partnership, then the capitalization of the corporation is smaller and the ability to impute a dividend based on the corporation's invested capital is reduced.[31]

2. *Loss of accelerated depreciation* - If the professional or partnership has been using an accelerated method of depreciation, it cannot be utilized by the corporation.[32] In many cases, a greater tax saving can be generated if the professional continues to utilize this method of depreciation to offset his personal income than would be generated if the corporation were to use the straight line method of depreciation.

3. *Facilitate admission of new shareholders* - If the furniture, fixtures and equipment have a substantial value, and they are retained personally by the incorporating professional, it will be easier for a new man to purchase shares in the corporation, since the value of the stock will not be increased by the value of these assets.

WATCH THIS

In professional practices, it is not uncommon to permit a potential shareholder to purchase shares of stock at a nominal value. This will result in unexpected tax consequences if the stock is sold for less than adequate consideration. If the new man receives the stock at a price which is less than its true value, then the differences between the value of the stock and the consideration paid may be considered a gift of the difference to the new man or given in exchange for services, and the new shareholder will be taxed at ordinary income rates.[33] This problem is eliminated if assets of substantial value are not transferred to the new corporation.

4. *Easier to withdraw money from corporation* - Normally, assets which are retained will be leased to the corporation by the professional. These will provide another vehicle by which corporate funds can be withdrawn other than through compensation, thus providing another method of minimizing the unreasonable compensation problem.[34]

WATCH THIS

Retention of these assets will trigger the recapture of investment credit provision of the Internal Revenue Code,[35] since substantially all of the assets are not being transferred to the corporation. Thus, the cost must be considered in determining whether the furniture, fixtures and equipment should be transferred or retained. In many cases, the "recapture" will be the cost of retaining these assets.

OBSERVATION

The author agrees that the advantages of retaining the furniture, fixtures and equipment outside the corporation will provide substantial tax advantages to the professionals for the reasons stated above. However, completely stripping the corporation of all assets may create a "shell," thus giving an appearance of lack of corporateness. This will obviously make the corporation more vulnerable to Internal Revenue Service attack that the corporation is not really operating as a corporation, especially in one- or two-man professional corporations.[36] Therefore, the author is of the opinion that a minimum amount of assets should be transferred to the corporation in order to give more substance to the corporation. Although it is impossible to give a definite dollar amount as a cut-off point, the author has selected the book values of $10,000 to $15,000 before additional assets will be retained by the professional and leased to the corporation.

Organization Problems in Handling Furniture, Fixtures and Equipment

When two or more professionals with independent practices decide to incorporate, there is a problem of how to handle the furniture, fixtures and equipment since the value of such assets which each professional will transfer to the corporation will differ. If the total contribution to the capital of the corporation by each professional consists of just these assets, then the professional whose equipment has the highest value will either be deemed to have made a gift equal to the difference in value of his property and the value of the other professional's assets, or the professional with the lowest value will be deemed to have been compensated for personal services.[37] Thus, some adjustments must be made to avoid this problem. The following are some solutions.

1. *Purchase and sale of assets between professionals* - The professional whose assets have the highest value sells some of his equipment to the other professionals to equalize the value of their property, and they then transfer their assets to the corporation. The problem with this solution is that it may result in adverse tax consequences to the selling professional. If the sales price exceeds the seller's basis, then the seller will be faced with a tax on the gain, which may be treated as ordinary income if the recapture of depreciation provisions of the Internal Revenue Code are applicable. In additon, the recapture of investment credit provisions may also be applicable, resulting in further income taxed at ordinary income rates.
2. *Additional cash contribution by professionals whose assest have a smaller value* - Under this method, the professionals whose assets have the lowest value will contribute a sufficient amount of cash to the corporation to equalize their contribution to the contribution of the professional with the high-valued furniture, fixtures and equipment. Thus, if in a three-man professional corporation, "A" is going to transfer assets with a value of $15,000 and "B" and "C"'s assets are worth $5,000 and $10,000 respectively, then "B" will contribute an additional $10,000 and "C" will contribute an additional $5,000, in order that the contribution of each professional will be $15,000. The only difficulty with this solution is that the professionals who are required to contribute cash to the corporation may not be able to afford to do so.
3. *Issuance of corporate securities* - In this instance, the professional whose assets exceed the value of the assets of the other contributing professionals will receive a corporate security for the difference in this value. Thus, in the preceding example, "A" will receive a corporate security equal to $10,000 and "C" will receive a corporate security equal to $5,000. The net effect is that the contributions of "A", "B", and "C" will now be $5,000. The disadvantages to the use of securities in this manner are that while the corporation is in effect paying for a portion of the equipment, it will not be entitled to a depreciation deduction for such, and to the extent of the securities-holding shareholder's interest in the corporation, he is making repayments to himself.[38]
4. *Lease of equipment to the corporation* - In this case, the professionals will retain their respective furniture, fixtures and equipment and lease them to the corporation. Alternatively, each professional could transfer equipment having the same value and retain the excess, which would then be leased to the corporation.

OBSERVATION

In trying to equalize the contributions to the corporation, the practitioner must consider the effect of the accelerated depreciation provision and recapture of investment credit provision of the Internal Revenue Code. If the professional was using the accelerated method of depreciation and transfers equipment to the corporation, the corporation will not be able to continue this method. However, if the professional retains his equipment, he may be subject to the recapture of investment credit provisions. If the equipment is sold, then he may be subject to the recapture of depreciation rules. Thus, it will not always be possible to provide each professional with the best possible tax advantages, and the practitioner should be primarily concerned with the solution which is as fair as possible to all parties and which will insure the overall success of the corporate venture.

Real Estate

If the professional or a partnership owns the real estate in which its office is situated, then a decision must be made whether to transfer the medical building to the new corporation or whether it should be retained. Generally, the considerations and principles set forth for furniture, fixtures and equipment are equally applicable to real estate. In fact, there are even stronger reasons for retaining the real estate than personal property assets. Real estate will almost always have a high value which will increase the value of the stock much more than transferring personal assets. Thus, it becomes even more difficult for a new man to purchase stock in the corporation and makes an attack upon the reasonableness of the professional's compensation even easier under the "return of invested capital" theory since the capitalization has been increased by the value of the real estate. In addition, the rental income that would be generated by the real estate which was transferred to the corporation would be difficult to distribute to the professional employee shareholders as compensation since it was not generated by personal services.[39] Therefore, the rental income would be distributed as dividends and subject to tax at the corporate level and then at the personal level. Furthermore, the losses generated by the real estate, i.e., depreciation, interest and taxes, are better utilized against the professional's high tax rate than against the corporation's ordinary income, the tax upon which will probably be at the 22% rate.

Transfer of Accounts Payable and Liabilities

The practitioner should be aware that a distinction is often made between accounts payable which are incurred for currently deductible expenses, such as supplies, salaries, utilities and other operating expenses, and liabilities which are incurred for capital expenditures, such as a mortgage on equipment. The transfer of both will be treated separately.

Accounts payable

One of the most discussed issues in regard to the incorporation of a professional's practice is whether a professional who is on the case basis of accounting should transfer his accounts payable to the new corporation. The problem raised is that the professional, when he transfers his accounts payable to the corporation, will not receive a deduction when they are paid since he did not pay them.[40] At the same time, the corporation may not be able to deduct the payments since they were not expenses of the corporation.[41] In such a case, the cost of paying the accounts payable will be considered part of the cost of incorporating the professional's practice, i.e., it will be treated as a capital item.

On the other hand, there is ample authority indicating that the payment of the accounts payable by the new corporation can be deducted by the corporation.[42]

Although it appears that congressional intent under §351 should permit the transfer corporation to deduct the payment of the accounts payable transferred to it, the issue is still unclear. Therefore, in the absence of obtaining an advance revenue ruling from the Internal Revenue Service,[43] it will be advisable to have the professional retain his accounts payable arising from his practice and to retain a sufficient amount of accounts receivable that can be used to pay the accounts payable. Most commentaries agree with this position.[44]

Liabilities

The assumption of the liabilities of the predecessor organization by the new corporation does not generally create as much concern among commentators as does the transfer of accounts payable. It is generally felt that liabilities can safely be transferred to the corporation and the corporation will be able to deduct the payments made.

> In situations where money has been borrowed to finance the purchase of equipment and the equipment is transferred to the corporation, no problem exists with respect to transferring the liability. To a certain extent, assumption of the liability by the corporation might be advantageous because to the extent the liability must be repaid at a faster rate than depreciation deductions provide case flow for such payments, the excess will be coming from income taxed at corporate rates which in all probability will be lower than individual rates.[45]

Assumption of accounts payable and liabilities in excess of basis

As a general rule, the assumption by the new corporation of the liabilities of the incorporating professionals will not be treated as money or other property (boot) for purposes of §351(b) nor will it prevent the exchange from qualifying under §351.[46] Instead, the assumed or acquired liabilities will reduce the basis of the stock received by the professionals in the exchange.[47]

However, there are two exceptions to the general rule. First, if the principal purpose of the professional in making the exchange was for the purpose of avoiding federal income taxes or the exchange does not serve a bona fide business purpose, then the assumption of the liability will be treated as boot and taxable to the transferor.[48] An example of this would be if the professionals prior to incorporating mortgaged their equipment and other assets and then transferred them subject to the liability tax to the new corporation. If this was not prevented, the incorporators could receive money tax free. However, the incorporators will now be taxed to the extent of the liabilities assumed. As a general rule, the exception should not prove to be a problem to almost all professional corporations.

The second exception presents a more serious and real problem to the incorporating professional. If the corporation assumes liabilities in excess of the basis of the property transferred, the excess is taxable to the professional and will be treated as a gain from the sale or exchange of the property transferred under Section 357(c) of the Internal Revenue Code.

Example

> Professional transfers property with an adjusted basis of $5,000 and a fair market value of $35,000, subject to a $15,000 mortgage in exchange for stock in his corporation for $20,000 plus the assumption of the mortgage.
>
> Professional's realized gain is $30,000 (value of the stock received plus the mortgage assumed minus the professional's basis in the property).
>
> Professional's recognized gain is $10,000 and his basis for the stock will be zero since his basis has been reduced by the liability assumed.[49]

The practitioner is then faced with the difficult problem of allocating the gain among the different assets transferred to the corporation for the purpose of computing the character of the gain. The gain will be allocated among the assets transferred in proportion to their relative fair market values.[50] The nature and the holding period of the property transferred will determine whether the gain recognized should be treated as long-term or short-term capital gain or as ordinary income.

At first blush, it may appear that most professionals will not be troubled by this problem. However, if accounts payable are transferred to the corporation, the professional may very well be confronted with the provisions of Section 357(c).

For most professional corporations, the principal asset that will be transferred to it will be the accounts receivable of the incorporating professional. If the professional has been on the cash basis of accounting, then these receivables will have a zero basis since they have not been taken into income by the professional.[51] Assuming the extreme, and the only assets of the incorporating professional which are transferred to the corporation are his accounts receivable and accounts payable, then the professional will be taxed on the amount of the accounts payable transferred to the corporation, since the accounts payable exceed the basis of the accounts receivable.[52]

The court in the Bongiovanni case[53] reached a different conclusion. The court held that the word "liabilities" as used by §357(c) was meant to apply to "tax liabilities," i.e., liens in excess of tax costs, particularly mortgages encumbering the property transferred in a Section 351 transaction; and that accounts payable are liabilities only for accounting purposes and not "liabilities" for tax purposes. Therefore, the court concluded that the taxpayer should not be taxed on the difference between the accounts payable and the basis of the property transferred.

However, in a more recent case, the court did not agree with the Bongiovanni conclusion and held that accounts payable are liabilities for purposes of §357(c).[54]

Thus, the trap of §357(c) provides another reason why the practitioners must proceed with great care when handling accounts payable of a cash basis professional, and another reason why they should, in most cases not be transferred to the new corporation.

INCORPORATING THE PARTNERSHIP

In almost all cases, the working relationship and understanding between the partners prior to incorporating will be continued in the corporation. Thus, the practitioner, after studying the partnership agreement and familiarizing himself with the unwritten obligations of the partners to each other, will incorporate these terms into the minutes of the first meeting of the Board of Directors, in which corporate policy and procedure is discussed and decided, and in the employment agreements.

Nevertheless, there are two aspects of incorporating a partnership which require careful planning in order to achieve the maximum tax advantage to the incorporating professionals. These areas are as follows:

1. Determining the best method of incorporating the partnership
2. How to minimize the bunching of income problem

The Mechanics of Incorporating a Partnership

There are three ways to incorporate a partnership tax free under §351:

1. The partnership can transfer all of its assets to a corporation in return for all of its stock, which will then be distributed to the partners in relation to their respective shares upon the liquidation of the partnership.
2. The partnership can liquidate and distribute assets to the partners who will then exchange these assets to the corporation in exchange for its stock.
3. The partners can transfer their interest in the partnership to the corporation in exchange for its stock.

The Internal Revenue Service has taken the position that any of the above methods will qualify as a tax-free exchange under §351.[55] The Service considers that in each case, the partnership is transferring its assets to the corporation in exchange for its stock and then distributes the stock to the partners upon its liquidation. As a result,

> The basis of the property acquired by each corporation will be the same as its basis in the hands of the transferor partnership. Section 362(a) of the Code. The basis of the stock

received by a partner will be an amount equal to the adjusted basis of his partnership interest. Section 732(b) of the Code.[56]

Notwithstanding the Internal Revenue Service's position, it appears that it does make a difference which method is adopted when determining the corporation's basis for the property transferred.[57] If the partnership incorporates under Method 1, the corporation will assume the partnership's basis for the assets transferred.[58] However, if the partners incorporate under Method 2 or 3, the corporation will assume the partners' basis for their interests in the partnership as its basis for the assets transferred.[59] In all cases, the partners' basis in the stock will be equal to the basis they had in their partnership interests.

Therefore, if the partnership's basis for its assets is greater than the partners' basis for their partnership interest, Method 1 should be used. If the reverse is true, then Method 2 or 3 should be used. In most cases, however, the partner's interest in his partnership will be equal to the basis of his share of the partnership assets unless he has acquired his interest by purchase. In that case, it is quite possible that the partner's basis in the partnership will exceed the basis of his share of the partnership assets.

However, if the partnership is incorporated under Method 1, then section 1244 cannot be used, since the stock was not issued directly to the partners.[60] Thus, if the 1244 election is important, then Method 2 or 3 should be used. Furthermore, if state law prohibits the issuance of stock in a professional corporation to anyone other than a licensed professional, the Method 1 would not be available.

If it is desirable to retain some of the partnership assets outside the corporation, the Method 2 would have to be used.

Thus, no method is correct in all cases, and the practitioner will be required to examine his particular set of facts in order to determine the most advantageous method of incorporating his client's partnership.

The Bunching of Income Problem

One of the biggest problems faced by the practitioner in incorporating a partnership is to minimize the bunching of income problem which may arise in fiscal year partnerships. A partner must include in his income for his taxable year his distributive share of partnership income for any taxable year of the partnership ending within or with his taxable year.[61] This will not create a problem when the partners are on the same fiscal year as the partnership. But this is rarely the case, since most partners will be on the calendar year. Thus, if a partnership whose year ends on June 30, 1974 incorporates on July 1, 1974, a calendar year partner will include in income for his 1974 tax returns his share of the partnership income for the year ending June 30, 1974 plus all compensation he receives from the corporation from July 1, 1974 to December 31, 1974. In effect, the partner will be reporting 18 months' income in his 1974 tax returns. An extreme example of this problem is presented when a partnership whose fiscal year ends January 31, 1975 incorporates on February 1, 1975. In this instance, the partner will report 23 months of income on his 1975 tax returns.[62]

Generally, this problem will arise only with partnerships formed prior to 1954, since the Internal Revenue Code has provided since that year that, without the consent of the Internal Revenue Service, a partnership must adopt the taxable year of its partners.[63] Neverless, some partnerships have attained such Internal Revenue Service permission or have adopted a fiscal year for their partnership without realizing that they couldn't, which was never noticed by the Service.[64]

Unfortunately, although the bunching of income problem may be minimized, as will be observed, it can rarely be entirely avoided. The following are some possible solutions to this problem.

Pay Reduced Salaries

Under this method, the corporation will pay a minimum or no salary to the former partners for the balance of the calendar year in which incorporation took place. The deferred income would then be spread out over the subsequent years.

However the Internal Revenue Service has recently taken the position that a controlling shareholder will be taxed on his salary which was due him by the corporation in his calendar year under the theory of constructive receipt if the shareholder could have had the corporation pay his salary.[65] Thus, the payment of minimum salaries may not find Internal Revenue Service approval if there were funds available in the corporation to pay the full salaries of the shareholder employees.

It has been suggested that the threat of constructive receipt could be minimized by having the corporation pre-pay as many expenses as possible, including the pre-funding of the pension profit sharing plan during the remainder of the calendar year, thus reducing the amount of money which would otherwise be available for salaries.[66]

However, even if the threat of constructive receipt can be avoided, the bunching dilemna is not solved by paying reduced salaries; it is merely postponed to subsequent years. It is even possible that the postponement of income may create a larger income for the former partner in later years than if he received his regular salary during the remainder of his calendar year in the year in which the corporation was formed.

Keep the Partnership in Existence

In this case, the partnership would not be terminated upon incorporation but would be maintained for the purpose of collecting its outstanding accounts receivable. Thus, if a partnership whose fiscal year ends on June 30 incorporates on July 1, 1974 and retains the accounts receivable, the partners (calendar year) will not report the income from the receipt of their share of the accounts receivable until they file their income tax return for 1975. Since the new corporation will not be generating income during the initial months of operation since there is always a significant time span between when services are rendered and paid for, the corporation will not be able to pay full salaries to the former partners.

Although this will reduce the bunching problem, it also defeats the purpose of incorporating. Not only will there not be sufficient funds available to pay salaries, but there will not be sufficient funds to provide for pension and profit sharing contributions.[67]

Elect Subchapter S

The bunching problem can be eliminated if the corporation elects to be treated as a subchapter S corporation and adopts the same fiscal year as the partnership being terminated. However, the contribution limitations placed upon subchapter S corporations to the Keogh limit effectively eliminate the method as a realistic solution, unless the professional does not wish to contribute more than $7500 to a retirement plan.

Use of Tax Shelter Investments

The former partner can always reduce the tax impact caused by the bunching problem by investing in various tax shelter investments which will reduce his taxable income. Of course, such an approach has its risks, but tax shelter investments vary in the degree of risk an *investor* may assume, and the partner may find a relatively conservative investment which will reduce his tax liability.

OBSERVATION

The impact of the bunched income may be reduced by the income averaging provisions of the Internal Revenue Code[68] and also by the 50% maximum tax on earned income. If incorporation makes sense when viewed in a long-term perspective, then the additional tax which each partner will pay as a result of the bunching of income problem will be an additional cost of incorporating which will be more than offset by the long-term benefits.

1244 Stock

When an investor sells stock in a corporation at a loss or if his investment becomes worthless, his loss is usually treated as a capital loss rather than as an ordinary loss. However, if a corporation issues stock pursuant to the provisions of section 1244 of the Internal Revenue Code, any loss incurred on its sale, or if the stock becomes worthless, will be treated as an ordinary loss, up to $25,000 per year or $50,000 if a joint return is filed.[69] Section 1244 was enacted by Congress as a tax incentive to encourage the flow of new funds into small businesses. It was felt that section 1244 would place shareholders in small corporations on the same basis as proprietors and partners, who were always able to deduct business losses against their ordinary income.[70] Thus, section 1244 provides an effective vehicle by which an investor may recover a portion of his investment if he sells his stock at a loss or if it becomes worthless. On the other hand, if the stock is sold at a gain, it will be treated as a capital gain. Thus, the best of both worlds is obtained.

As a practical matter, the usefulness of the provisions of Section 1244 to a professional who incorporates will be remote, since the chance of his stock becoming worthless or being sold at a loss is negligible. Nevertheless, there is always that possibility, and since it doesn't cost anything to elect 1244 stock, and the professionals have everything to gain and nothing to lose, the 1244 stock should be issued as a matter of course.

How to qualify under 1244

In order to qualify for the benefits provided under S1244, the stock must be issued pursuant to a valid Section 1244 plan. Recent court decisions have construed this section very narrowly and the practitioner must be careful to follow the requirements of Section 1244 or the desired potential benefits will be lost. The requirements for a valid 1244 plan are as follows:

1. Plan must be in writing.[71]
2. At the time the plan is adopted, no other offering of stock can be outstanding.[72] If there is an outstanding stock offering before the plan is adopted, that offering must be withdrawn.
3. A plan to offer stock under a 1244 plan may extend no longer than two years from its adoption.[73]
4. When the plan is adopted, the corporation must be a small business corporation. A corporation will qualify as such if:
   a. The total amount of common stock that is offered under the plan, plus other stock offered by the corporation before the plan was adopted, does not exceed $500,000, and
   b. The equity capital of the corporation does not succeed $1,000,000.[74]
5. The stock issued by the corporation must be common stock, which may be either voting or non-voting. Preferred stock will not qualify, nor will securities which are convertible into common stock or common stock which is convertible to securities qualify.
6. The stock issued under the plan must be for money or other property other than for stock or securities. In addition, stock issued for services will not qualify for 1244 stock.[75]
7. The plan must specifically state, in terms of dollars, the maximum amount to be received by the corporation in consideration for the stock issued pursuant thereto.[76]
8. For the five most recent years prior to the time the loss occurs, the corporation must derive more than one-half its gross receipts from sources other than royalties, rents or dividends.[77]

WATCH THIS

The stock issued must be held by the individual or partnership to whom it was issued in order to derive the benefits of §1244. Therefore, if a partnership is being incorporated and the §1244 election is important, then the partnership should either liquidate and distribute its assets to its partners, who will then transfer them to the corporation in exchange for its stock, or the partners should transfer their partnership interests in exchange for the stock of the corporation. However, if the partnership transfers its assets to the corporation in exchange for its stock and then liquidates, distributing the stock to its partners, the plan will not qualify.[78]

If the assets which are being transferred to the corporation in exchange for stock are actually transferred before the plan is adopted, it is possible that the stock issued will not be considered issued under a section 1244 plan. Therefore, the practitioner should make sure that a plan is formally adopted before the assets are transferred in exchange for stock.[79]

ACCOUNTING METHODS

Cash Basis vs. Accrual Basis

Since the principal asset of a professional corporation will be its accounts receivable and there will be only a small amount of outstanding accounts payable at any period of time, the corporation will almost always adopt the cash basis of accounting.

If the accrual method is elected it is important that the incorporating professional or partnership retains the accounts receivable; otherwise, the corporation will have a bunching of income problem, since the transferred accounts receivable will be treated as income in the corporation's first year.

Fiscal Year vs. Calendar Year

The ability to adopt a corporate taxable year different from the professional's calendar year provides a unique opportunity for maximum tax planning. One of the most common methods of tax savings available was for the corporation to postpone the payment of compensation to the professional employee during the last months of his calendar year. Then, if the professional had exceptionally high earnings, the tax could be minimized by postponing the payment of additional salary to the professional's next calendar year. Thus, shareholder employees of small corporations had the ability to pay or defer income, depending upon which decision would produce the greatest tax advantage. However, as previously discussed, this has been effectively eliminated as a tax-saving device by Rev. Rul. 72-317.[80]

Nevertheless, there is still a substantial advantage of having the corporation adopt a fiscal year as opposed to a calendar year. For example, if the corporation is going to pay substantial bonuses to its employees and the corporation is on the calendar year, then the professional employees will receive additional compensation at the end of their tax year, leaving no opportunity for tax planning. If the corporation was on a fiscal year, then the bonuses could be paid and the employees would have ample time to take effective steps to reduce their tax liability.

For this reason alone, the author favors the adoption of a fiscal year by the corporation.

TAX-OPTION CORPORATIONS (SUB-CHAPTER S)

In 1958, Congress enacted Sub-chapter S of the Internal Revenue Code, which permits certain businesses the right to utilize the corporate form without having to be taxed as a corporation.[81] Generally, it is thought that a sub-chapter S corporation is taxed as a partnership. This is not entirely accurate. A sub-chapter S corporation is taxed as a corporation except as to those rules which are specifically modified by sub-chapter S of the Internal Revenue Code. Thus, in effect, a sub-chapter S corporation is a hybrid, having both corporate and partnership tax attributes.

Tax Effects of Electing Sub-chapter S

The following are some of the tax results which a corporation realizes when electing sub-chapter S status.

1. The corporation pays no corporate tax on its income.[82]
2. The corporate income is taxed to the shareholders, whether distributed or not. To the extent the income is paid out, it is taxed to the shareholders who receive it. Undistributed taxable income is taxed ratably to those who are shareholders at the end of the corporation's taxable year.[83]

3. Except for the pass through of net long-term capital gains, income which is received by the shareholder is generally treated as ordinary income, regardless of its character at the corporate level. Corporate income consisting of long-term capital gains will be taxed as such by the shareholders.[84]
4. The corporation may pass through any net operating losses to its shareholders which may be used to offset their income from other sources.[85]
5. Undistributed taxable income previously taxed to the shareholders may be distributed to them without additional tax.[86]

Advantages of Sub-chapter S

As can readily be observed, the principal tax advantage derived from electing under Sub-chapter S is the ability to pass through all corporate earnings to the shareholders, thus avoiding the "double-taxation" problem often faced by non-electing corporations. As a consequence, the unreasonable compensation problem is effectively reduced, as well as avoiding the application of the unreasonable accumulation tax under §531 or the personal holding company tax under §541.

It should be noted, however, that although the unreasonable compensation problem is effectively minimized, it is not entirely eliminated. The problem will certainly be present once the election is revoked or terminated.[87] In addition, it would appear that contributions to the corporate retirement plan would be based only upon the shareholder's stated salary and not his taxable income. Furthermore, the Internal Revenue Service may examine the entire compensation of the shareholder, which includes fringe benefits, and determine that the contribution to the plan is unreasonable. To the extent the Internal Revenue Service finds the contribution to be unreasonable, it will be disallowed as a deduction.[88]

Nevertheless, notwithstanding the possible problems remaining in the unreasonable compensation area, these problems would be present if the election was not made, and Sub-chapter S, without question, certainly minimizes the problem of determining whether the shareholder's salary is reasonable, as well as eliminating the unreasonable accumulation and personal holding company problem. Moreover, the reallocation of corporate income to the shareholders under §482 would also be avoided. For these reasons, many practitioners have advocated adopting sub-chapter S status. As will subsequently be discussed, the Tax Reform Act of 1969 and other inherent problems connected with sub-chapter S have effectively reduced its usefulness to professional corporations.

Who Can Elect

A corporation, to be able to elect sub-chapter S status must qualify as a small business corporation. A corporation will be eligible as such if it meets all of the following requirements:[89]

1. It is a domestic corporation
2. It is not a member of an affiliated group as defined by Internal Revenue Code §1504
3. It does not have more than ten shareholders
4. Each shareholder must be an individual or a decedent's estate. No stockholder may be a non-resident alien.
5. It may have only one class of stock.

How to Elect

Any small business corporation may elect to be taxed under sub-chapter S of the Internal Revenue Code if all shareholders consent to such election and such election is filed with the Internal Revenue Service within one month before or after the start of its taxable year.[90] The election will be effective for the year the election was made and for all subsequent years until it is terminated.[91]

Disadvantages

The most serious disadvantage of the sub-chapter S election was created by the Tax Reform Act of 1969. This legislation restricted deductible contributions to the H.R. 10 (Keogh) limits.[92] Since most professionals who incorporate do so for the primary purpose of increasing their retirement plan contributions, the limitation upon sub-chapter S corporations reduces the attractiveness of this election.

In addition, sub-chapter S contains numerous technical rules and regulations which reduce its attractiveness. These problems were fully expressed by Berrien C. Eaton, Jr. as follows:[93]

> There are so many things to watch — such as how to handle distributions if a change of ownership is anticipated within the first two and one-half months of a corporation's year — how to avoid "trapped" income — how to arrange sales and redemtptions — and generally how to handle distributions of either cash or property ... a constant danger is unintentional disqualification by reason of such events as having more than ten shareholders — or having stock transferred to a trust or other holder which is not an individual or estate — or failing to make a timely election because of confusion as to when the first taxable year commences — or failing to obtain a timely consent from a new shareholder — or having a consent treated as invalid because not given by the beneficial owner — or having passive investment income exceeding 20 percent of gross receipts — or being charged with having two classes of stock because of disproportionate debt or an agreement affecting voting rights — or becoming part of an affiliated group by forming a subsidiary. Although an inadvertent termination of Subchapter S status applies to the entire year in which the transgression occurs, it may not be discovered for several additional years. Its belated discovery by the Service may then lead to substantial corporate tax deficiencies and interest for the intervening years, distributions to shareholders being taxed as dividends, and other unthinkable disasters.

OBSERVATION

In spite of the pitfalls, with the increase of H.R. 10 contributions to $7500, together with the elimination of other tax problems, as discussed, Sub-chapter S will again become a more attractive vehicle which should be examined carefully by the practitioner.

THE MECHANICS OF INCORPORATING

The following four checklists will serve as a guide to the practitioner of the various matters which should be discussed and decided upon by the incorporators and initial Board of Directors and the steps which must be taken in organizing the corporation.

Basic Corporate Documents

1. Articles of Organization
2. Meeting of the Incorporators
3. First Meeting of the Board of Directors
4. Employment Contracts
5. Pension and/or Profit Sharing Plans
6. Stock Certificates
7. Federal Identification Number for Corporation
8. Federal Identification Number for Retirement Plans
9. Federal Identification Number for Trustees of Retirement Plans
10. Bank Resolution
11. Medical Reimbursement Plan

12. Group Term Insurance Plan
13. By-Laws
14. Bill of Sale
15. Documents changing leases from sole practitioner or partnership to corporation.
16. Forms 5301,5301 Schedule A and 5302 for Pension Plan and Profit Sharing Plan
17. Power of Attorney

If corporation consists of more than one shareholder employee, then the following documents should also be drafted.

1. Agreement to form Corporation
2. Dissolution of Partnership
3. Stock Redemption Agreement

Meeting of Incorporators - Items to be Decided Upon

1. Name of Corporation
2. Principal place of business of the Corporation
3. Officers and Directors
4. Target date of Corporation.
5. The amount of stock to be authorized
6. The classes of stock to be authorized
7. Whether or not Section 1244 stock should be created
8. Whether or not Subchapter S election should be taken
9. The fiscal year of the corporation
10. Whether accrual or cash basis of accounting should be elected
11. Date to be selected for annual meeting of Board of Directors and shareholders

Initial Meeting of Board of Directors - Matters to be Discussed and Decided Upon

1. The adoption of the Stock Certificate which will be used by the Corporation.
2. The adoption of the Corporate Seal
3. The stock subscription offers by the shareholders
4. The acceptance of the stock subscription offers
5. The appointment of a bank who will act as a depositary for corporate funds.
6. The consideration of the various professional shareholders for employment by the corporation.
7. The establishment of the salaries to be paid each professional employee of the corporation.
8. The basis upon which increases in said salary will be made
9. The authorization of the President to conduct the ordinary business affairs of the corporation.
10. The authorization of the corporation to pay organizational expenses.
11. The authorization of the corporation to purchase malpractice insurance for the corporation.
12. The adoption of a wage continuation plan for professional employees.

13. The adoption of a medical reimbursement plan.
14. The adoption of group term insurance.
15. The authorization of the corporation to assume the lease presently in the name of the sole practitioner or partnership prior to incorporation.
16. The consideration of what business expenses will be reimbursed to the professional employees in the course of their business for the corporation.
17. The adoption of the Pension of Profit Sharing Plans for the corporation.

Other Procedural Steps

1. Order Corporate Seal
2. Notify Blue Cross to obtain new number for corporation for billing purposes.
3. Change letter heads, billboards, bills, business cards to corporate name.
4. Notify telephone company to bill corporation.
5. Change malpractice coverage
6. Change casualty insurance coverage to cover corporation.
7. Complete all forms required by the state in which the corporation is located; such as unemployment compensation insurance forms and workman's compensation insurance forms.
8. Be sure all documents are signed

FOOTNOTES

[1]IRC §351; §351 provides in part, "No gain or loss shall be recognized if property is transferred to a corporation ... by one or more persons solely in exchange for stock or securities in such corporation and immediately after the exchange such person or persons are in control ... of the corporation."

[2]Portland Oil Co. v. Commissioner 109 *F2d* 479 (1st Circuit) 1940.

[3]IRC §362(a).

[4]IRC §358(a)(1): The rules just stated are general and the basis of the property received and the stock and securities acquired will be adjusted if the professional has received property other than stock or securities ("boot") or if gain is recognized by the transferor.

[5]IRC §351(A).

[6]Rev. Rul. 69-357 CB1969-1, p. 101.

[7]See section entitled "Accounts Receivable" in this chapter, page 21.

[8]S. Levine 24 T.C. 147 (1955); See discussion on whether good will is in fact transferred by the professional to the corporation upon incorporating - Chapter 4 Planning For and Avoiding the Unreasonable Compensation Dilemma, Section entitled "Goodwill as an Income Producing Factor," p. 64.

[9]Regs. s1.351-1(a) *(1)*(ii).

[10]IRC §351(b).

[11]Bittker and Eustice *Federal Income Taxation of Corporations and Shareholders* Section Edition, 1966, *Section 3.03* P. 73; However, in one case the court held that a one-year note was a security. U.S. v. Mills, Jr. 399 F2d 944 (Fifth Circuit) 1968.

[12]*See Note 9.*

[13]IRC §368(c).

[14]IRC §1001 and §1002.

[15]IRC §351(b).

[16]IRC §1245, §1250, § 47, § 1239, and § 267.

[17]IRC §362(c); Regs. §1.362-1.

[18]Camp Wolters Enterprises, Inc. 230 F2d 555 (1956); Aqualane Shores, Inc. 269 F2d 116 (1959).

[19]Bittker and Eustice, *See Note 11, Section 3.12, p. 104.*

[20]Gus Russell, Inc. 36 TC 965 *(1961)*.

[21]IRC §167(c)(2).

[22]*IRC* §47.

[23]See Footnote No. 8.

[24] See chapter 3 "Operating the Corporation to Avoid Internal Revenue Service Problems" — section entitled "Assignment of Income and Section 482," p.43.

[25]Thomas W. Briggs 15 T.C.M. 440 (1956); L. Kniffen 39 T.C. 553 (1962).

[26]Ibid.

[27]"Internal Revenue Service Chief Counsel outlines what lies ahead for professional corporations" 32 J Tax 88, 90 February, (1970).

[28]Hempt Bros., Inc. v. U.S. 354 F. Supp. 1172 (1973) Third Circuit.

[29]Rooney v. U.S. 305 F2d 681 (Ninth Circuit) 1962; National Securities Corporation 137 F2d 600 (Third Circuit) 1943.

[30]For further discussion see chapter 6 "How to Expand, Contract and Liquidate the Professional Corporation" section entitled "How to Value the Stock," p.92.

[31]See chapter 4 "Planning for and Avoiding the Unreasonable Compensation Dilemma" section entitled "Reasonable But Nondeductible Compensation," p. 62.

[32]*See Footnote No. 21.*

[33]Regs. §351-1(b)(1).

[34]See chapter 5 "Drafting the Employment Contract" section entitled "Automobile" subsection 6. Reasonable Compensation Problem, p. 80.

[35]*IRC* §47.

[36]"Strip Away Practice Assets after you Incorporate" Medical Economics, September 25, 1972, p. 129.

[37]*See Footnote No. 33;* See section entitled "Facilitate Admission of New Shareholders," this chapter, p. 24.

[38]Dunn "Income Tax Considerations In The Transition To A Professional Corporation" 6 Akron Law Review, Winter, 1973, pps. 23, 32.

[39]See chapter 4 "Planning For and Avoiding the Unreasonable Compensation Dilemma" section entitled "Relationship of Compensation to Billings", p. 58.

[40]Kniffen v. Commisioner, *See Footnote No. 25.*

[41]Holdcroft Transportation Co. v. Commissioner 153 F2d 323 (Eighth Circuit 1946).

[42]K. Martin Worthy "International Revenue Service Chief Counsel outlines what lies ahead for professional corporations" *32 J Tax,* February 1970, p. 91; "It could be agreed that to the extent the payments are attributable to services performed prior to incorporation, they are capital items and non-deductible. Again, however, it may be that such a result would be inappropriate in view of the basic policy of Section 351 of treating the new corporation as a continuation of the previous business. This policy would seem to suggest that the new corporation should be regarded as standing in the shoes of the transferor for purposes of taking tax deductions so that it could deduct payments which the transferor could have deducted if he had continued to operate the business." Arnold C. Goldstein "Tax-free Incorporation: Are Courts Today Taking Too Restrictive Views of Section 351?" J

Tax, September, 1973, pps. 165, 167, "Without attempting to reconcile these conflicting cases, it seems fairly well-established that payables are only deductible by the transferee corporation ... it has also been reported that the Service has granted private rulings approving deductibility by the transferee."

[43]Rev. Proc. 73-10, IRB 1973-17, 37.

[44]Eaton, *Professional Corporations and Association,* Matthew Bender Volume 17, Section 12.06, p. 12-37, "Whatever disagreements there may be about handling receivables, very little dispute exists about payables, at least those which represent unpaid deductible expenses. Nearly everyone concurs that these should not be assumed or paid by the corporation."; Dunn "Income Tax Considerations in the Transition To A Professional Corporation" Volume 6; Akron Law Review, pps. 23, 35, "... it is suggested that accounts receivable may be transferred without the concurrent transfer of accounts payable to professional corporation under Section 351 without adverse income tax consequences and that payables incurred prior to incorporation representing deductible expenses should not be transferred."; Crapo and Farnam "Professional Corporations and Tax Benefit Retirement Plans - A Review of Emerging Pitfalls for the Professional Incorporation" 7 Idaho Law Review, pps. 25, 31 (1970) "It should therefore be recommended that the partners or proprietor retain the payables and pay them as they become due, thus preserving the deduction."

[45]Dunn, ibid., p. 34.

[46]IRC §357(a).

[47]IRC §358(d).

[48]IRC §357(b).

[49]IRC §358(d).

[50]Bittker and Eustace, *See Footnote No. 11,* Section 3.06, p. 84.

[51]Rev. Rul. 69-442, 1969-2 CB 53.

[52]Peter Raich v. Commissioner 46 T.C. 604 (1966).

[53]470 F2d 921 (1972).

[54]Thatcher v. Commissioner 61 T.C. No. 4 filed Oct. 4, 1973. It is interesting to note that the court pointed out that a different result would have occurred if the accounts payable were retained and an equivalent amount of accounts receivable was retained to pay the accounts payable.

[55]Rev. Rul. 70-239, *1970-1 CB, 74.*

[56]Ibid.

[57]"Incorporating a Partnership: New Problems on IRS' Ruling" J Tax, December, 1970, p. 382.

[58]*IRC* §362(c).

[59]*IRC* §732(b).

[60]Regs. §1.1244(a)-1(c) Example 2; See section entitled "1244 Stock" this chapter, p. 30.

[61]IRC §706(a).

[62]The reason why a partnership often adopted a fiscal year accounting period was the ability of the partners to postpone the payment of taxes on the income earned during his calendar year. Thus, if a partnership is organized on July 1, 1953 and its fiscal year ends June 30, the partner would only have reported as income on his 1953 tax return six months' income. If the partnership was formed on February 1, 1953 with the fiscal year ending January 31, then the partner would have only reported one month's income on his 1953 tax returns. However, as can be readily observed, the *day* of reckoning arrives when the partnership incorporates.

[63]IRC §706(b)(1).

[64]Prentice-Hall Professional Corporation Guide,¶3002.

[65]Rev. Rul 72-317 *1972-1 CB 128;* See "new constructive income threat for close corporations" J Tax, October, 1972, p. 243.

[66]Prentice-Hall Professional Corporation Guide,¶3003.

[67]If the partnership is terminated, then its taxable year is immediately closed and the bunching of income problem arises. (IRC §706(c)(1)) The problem raised when the partnership remains in existence to collect its retained receivables is whether the retention of accounts receivable by the partnership is sufficient to avoid its termination under §708(b)(1) which provides in part that a partnership shall be considered terminated "if no part of any business, financial operation, or venture of the partnership continues to be carried on by any of its partners in a partnership." The case of David A. Foxman (41 T.C. 535 (1964)) held that the retention by a part of its notes was a sufficient activity to prevent its terminations. However, there is always the possibility that when all the partnership assets except its accounts receivables are transferred to the corporation that the Service might argue that the partnership is terminated under §708(b)(1)(B) which provides that a partnership is terminated if within a 12-month period there is a sale of 50% or more of the total interest in the partnership capital and profits. Thus, if the bunching problem is to be minimized by adopting this route, it is suggested that the partnership retain sufficient assets to avoid this section. The retained assets could then be leased to the corporation.

[68]*IRC* §1301-1305.

[69]*IRC* §1244(b).

[70]H.R. Rep. No. 2198, 85th Congress, 1st Session (1959), 1959-2 CB 711.

[71]Regs. §1.1244(c)-1(c).

[72]*IRC* §1244(c)(1)(C).

[73]*IRC* §1244(c)(1)(A).

[74]IRC §1244 *(c)(2).*

[75]*Regs.* §1.1244(c)-1(f).

[76]Regs. §1.1244(c)*(4).*

[77]*IRC* §1244(c)(1)(E).

[78]Regs. §1.1244(a)-1(c) Example 2.

[79]Newland "How Section 1244 benefits can be lost through premature asset transfers" J Tax, October, 1972, p. 238.

[80]See Note 65; See also section entitled "Pay Reduced Salaries" this chapter p. 29.

[81]Internal Revenue Code §1371-1378.

[82]Internal Revenue Code §1372(b)(1).

[83]Internal Revenue Code §1373(b).

[84]Internal Revenue Code §1375(*a*).

[85]Internal Revenue Code §1374 *(c) (1)*.

[86]Internal Revenue Code §1375(d)(1).

[87]Paula Construction Co. v. Commissioner 58 T.C. 1055 (1972). Court held that distribution to shareholders was not compensation and thus, not deductible after Subchapter S status was involuntarily terminated since distributions were not classified as compensation.

[88]See chapter 4 "Planning For and Avoiding the Unreasonable Compensation Dilemma" Section entitled "What is Compensation," p. 57.

[89]IRC § 1371(a).

[90]IRC § 1372(c)(1).

[91]IRC § 1372(d); § 1372(c) states when an election will terminate.

[92] §1379.

[93]Eaton, *Professional Corporations and Associations,* Matthew Bender, Volume 1, §11.08(5), p. 11-80.3.

3

OPERATING THE CORPORATION TO AVOID INTERNAL REVENUE SERVICE PROBLEMS

Prior to August 8, 1969, the Internal Revenue Service attack upon professional corporations was based upon the theory that professional corporations did not have the necessary characteristics of a corporation and therefore should not be taxed as such. After losing every case tried on this issue, the Service conceded this point on the above data, and in T.I.R. 1019 indicated that "... organizations of doctors, lawyers, and other professional people organized under state professional association acts, will generally be treated as corporations for tax purposes." The effect of this ruling is that the Internal Revenue Service has conceded its attack upon professional corporations for lack of "corporateness." This does not mean that there will be no further attacks from the Internal Revenue Service on professional corporations. The Service has clearly indicated it may conclude differently in a particular case if the facts warrant a different conclusion.[1]

The Internal Revenue Service has now changed its approach. Instead of arguing that a professional corporation is not a corporation for tax purposes, it is going to carefully scrutinize professional corporations to determine whether in fact they are conducting themselves as corporations. Merely creating a paper entity will not suffice. The professional corporation is going to have to "look like, act like, and sound like a corporation if it is going to be able to take advantage of the fringe benefit programs "corporations" are entitled to adopt.

Therefore, the issue now confronting the practitioner is not whether his professional client can incorporate his practice, but having done so, to be sure that he OPERATES as a corporation.

The Internal Revenue Service has various grounds — both common law and statutory — for attacking the professional corporation for not operating as a corporation, which are as follows:[2]

1. **Disregard of corporate entity doctrine**

Under this doctrine, the Service may determine that the corporation is not following any of the procedures inherent to a corporation or that the corporation is, in fact, a "sham," in which case it will disregard the corporation as a taxable entity.

2. **Assignment of income doctrine and Internal Revenue Code § 482**

This doctrine and code section may determine that the income reported by the corporation was in fact earned by the shareholder employee, and not the corporation, in which case it will reallocate such income to the true person who earned it.

3. **Internal Revenue Code § 269**

Under this section, the Internal Revenue Service may find that the sole purpose of the corporation was for tax avoidance and disallow all deductions for contributions to retirement plans and other fringe benefit programs adopted by the corporation.

Under this section the IRS may impose a 70% penalty tax on the "undistributed personal holding company income" of the corporation.

4. **Personal Holding Company Penalty - Internal Revenue Code §541.**

Under this Section the IRS may impose a 70% penalty tax on the "Undistributed personal holding company income" of the corporation.

5. **Penalty on Unreasonable Corporate Accumulation - Internal Revenue Code §531**

The above code sections and doctrines present more of a theoretical problem than a real one to the professional corporaton, provided it is operating as a corporation. This chapter will discuss these problem areas, and provide extensive checklists which will demonstrate "how to operate as a professional corporation to avoid an Internal Revenue Service attack."

WHO EARNED THE INCOME

Disregard of Corporate Entity

It is a basic doctrine that the Internal Revenue Service may disregard a corporation as a taxable entity if it determines that the corporation is, in fact, a sham or serves no business purpose whatsoever.[3] The courts have been most reluctant to uphold an attack upon the integrity of a corporation except in extreme circumstances. In almost all cases, if the court can find some business purpose for the corporation, it will be recognized as such for tax purposes.

> Whether the purpose be to gain an advantage under the law of the statutes of incorporation or to avoid or to comply with the demands of creditors or to serve the creator's personal or undisclosed convenience, so long as that purpose is the equivalent of business activity or is followed by the carrying on of business by the corporation, the corporation remains a separate taxable entity.[4]
>
> However, incorporating merely to escape taxation is not a business purpose,[5] and the Internal Revenue Service has been successful in numerous cases in disregarding the corporation as a taxable entity when this appeared to be its sole purpose.

The most significant case in this area is the case of Jerome J. Roubik[6] since it represents the first victory the Service has had in disregarding a professional corporation as a taxable entity. This case should be read carefully by the practitioner and should serve as a guideline for how not to operate a professional corporation.

In this case, four radiologists, all having their offices at different locations, formed a professional corporation but continued to engage in their private practices of medicine substantially as they had prior to incorporating. Each doctor continued to hold himself out to patients and hospitals in his own name, continued the exclusive responsibility for the operation of his separate office and practice, and continued, in fact, to incur individual expenses and to receive the income of his individual practice.

The court found that the corporation consisted of a mere set of bookkeeping entries and a bank account, rather than serving any meaningful business purpose.

> The corporation must be given substance through the manner in which it actually operates. This was not done here ... petitioner herein simply did not put flesh on the bones of the corporate skeleton, irrespective of its existence under local law. Within the context of the federal income tax, the corporation never became operative in any meaningful sense. The individuals, not the corporation, continued to earn the income and separately to enjoy their own earnings.

The following is a 13-point checklist of what the Roubik corporation did wrong and what could have been done to avoid the court's conclusion.

13 POINT ROUBIK CHECKLIST FOR HOW NOT TO OPERATE A CORPORATION

Where the Corporation Went Wrong	*What Should Have Been Done*
1. Hospital checks were made payable to individual physicians after incorporation.	*1.* Checks from hospitals and other payors should be made payable to corporation and not to professional personally.
2. Contracts between hospital and physicians after incorporating continued to be in the name of the individual physicians.	*2.* After incorporating, contracts for services between a hospital and a doctor should be redrafted to be between the hospital and the corporation.
3. Lease for office space continued to be in name of physician personally after incorporating.	*3.* All leases should be assigned to or new leases drafted in the name of the corporation.
4. Doctors continued to own equipment in their own names and were not reimbursed for the use of such equipment or for the use of their automobiles on corporate business.	*4.* Board of Director's minutes should state whether equipment is to be transferred to corporation or continued to be held personally by professionals. If the latter, the professionals should be reimbursed for the use of such equipment and for the use of their automobiles. If reimbursement is not possible, the Board of Directors should so note and provide that employee must incur these expenses personally as a condition of his employment.
5. Stationery and office bills were issued in name of individual doctors.	*5.* Professionals must hold themselves out as corporate employees after incorporating. All bills, stationery, cards should be in the name of the corporation and never in the name of the doctor personally.
6. Telephone was answered in doctor's name.	*6.* After incorporating, the telephone should be answered in the name of the corporation and not in the doctor's name.
7. Doctor submitted bills to Blue Shield in his own name.	*7.* After incorporating, Blue Shield should be notified to make checks payable to corporation.
8. Doctors continued to assume and pay expenses for rent, office and medical supplies, and for salaries of secretaries and nurses; items continued to be billed directly to individual doctors.	*8.* After incorporating, the corporation should pay for all expenses incurred in the operation of the business; all bills should be made out in the name of the corporation.

9. Doctors did not give up the direction and control over their own activities to the corporation. Corporation had authority to assign doctors to different locations, but this right was never exercised.	*9.* If corporation has more than one office, the corporation should actually assign the professional employees to different offices. Rotation will indicate that the doctors are not conducting their practices at their respective offices as they had prior to incorporating.
10. Secretaries and nurses were hired by each doctor individually, who established their salaries and duties without consultation with the others.	*10.* The hiring of personnel should be done in behalf of the corporation. Appropriate authority should be given to president, business manager, or other appropriate individual to hire personnel in specific instances.
11. The doctors arranged coverage for each other as a matter of convenience, without it being continuous, extensive, or regular.	*11.* In multi-employee corporations, there should be a formal arrangement providing for coverage. It should not be based upon an informal basis or as a matter of courtesy, but as a required obligation to be on call at certain stated times.
12. The doctors themselves controlled the manner in which they conducted their practices. They had little or no contact with each other in their respective offices, and spoke only occasionally when they met in the hospital.	*12.* After incorporating, the corporation should actually establish the responsibilities of each employee and the manner in which he is to conduct his practice. Corporate policy is decided upon by the Board of Directors, and should be evidenced in the minutes of the Board of Directors.
13. The cost and type of liability insurance was selected by the individual doctor and not by the corporation.	*13.* The type of coverage that each doctor has should be decided by the Board of Directors, and liability insurance should be later put in name of corporation.

The second victory for the Internal Revenue Service came in the Dean P. Epperson case.[7] There were few facts presented in the case, but it appears that Dr. Epperson observed few if any of the corporate formalities and frequently withdrew corporate funds in the guise of loans, suggesting no intent to repay. One fact that was mentioned was that the doctor did not even conduct his practice in the corporate name. As a result, the Treasury Department was successful in its argument that the professional and not the corporation was the true earner of the income, and that all the income earned by the corporation during the years in issue should be taxed directly to the professional.

The Roubik, Epperson and other cases in this area[8] represent extreme examples of how not to operate a corporation and corporations whose existence served no business purpose whatsoever other than tax avoidance. As a rule, almost all professional corporations will be able to avoid the "Roubik" pitfalls. The key to success is that once a decision has been made to incorporate that the professionals conduct their practices in the name and for the benefit of the corporation, rather than in their own name and in the same manner as before incorporating. The above checklist will provide an excellent guide on how to avoid the problem. Remember, THE CORPORATION MUST ACT LIKE A CORPORATION.

ASSIGNMENT OF INCOME AND SECTION 482

The assignment of income doctrine and Section 482 of the Internal Revenue Code are very closely interrelated and under both, the basic position of the Internal Revenue Service is that the shareholder employee and not the corporation is the true earner of the income and therefore, all or a portion of such income should be taxed to the shareholder. No attack is made upon the validity of the corporation under this approach.

However, there are some differences between them which are listed in the following checklist.

Assignment of Income	*Section 482*
1. Based upon judicial decisions	*1.* Statutory
2. Doctrine is usually raised when Internal Revenue Service determines that taxpayer is assigning income *already earned* to another entity.[9]	*2.* Internal Revenue Service has power to allocate income among two or more businesses if such allocation is necessary to prevent evasion of taxes or to clearly reflect income.[10]
3. Doctrine has all or nothing effect. If Internal Revenue Service is deemed correct in its use of the doctrine, then all of the income allegedly earned by corporation will be allocated to taxpayer.	*3.* Under Section 482, Internal Revenue Service has authority to allocate all or part of corporation income to taxpayer.

As a practical matter, the assignment of income doctrine should not prove to be a problem to the practitioner since its real applicability to professional corporations appears, in the opinion of the author, to be limited. For example, the Internal Revenue Service could argue that the employment contract between the corporation and the shareholder employee is only a device whereby the income actually earned by the employee is being assigned to the corporation. Unless the corporation is a sham and serves no real business purpose, then it would appear that there is an extremely weak argument. In fact, the court in the Rubin case[11] cited the fact that the corporation did not have an employment contract with his corporation which was employing his services as one of several reasons for allocating the corporation income to him. The problem could also arise when the professional transfers his accounts receivable to his corporation as part of the initial capitalization. In such cases, the Internal Revenue Service could argue that the income received by the corporation when the transferred accounts receivable are collected is the income of the professional and therefore, he should be taxed on its receipt. As discussed elsewhere,[12] it appears well settled that accounts receivable may be transferred to a corporation under Section 351 of the Internal Revenue Code.

Furthermore, its applicability appears to have been even further curtailed by the Court of Appeals in the Rubin case. The Tax Court used the assignment of income doctrine to allocate all the corporation income to the taxpayer. On appeal, the Court of Appeals remanded the case back to the Tax Court with instruction that this common law doctrine should not be used when there is adequate statutory provision which could have been utilized, to deal with the problem, to wit, Section 482.[13]

Therefore, it appears that Section 482 will be the appropriate tool in the hands of the Internal Revenue Service. This section gives the Internal Revenue Service broad power to apportion gross income, deductions, credits or allowances between two or more commonly controlled organizations if the commissioner deems that apportionment is necessary to clearly reflect income to the proper earner thereof or to prevent evasion of taxes.

A reallocation of income under Section 482 is preferable to the readjustment of income under the assignment of income doctrine. The latter has an "all or nothing effect." That is, under the assignment of income doctrine, once a determination has been made that the taxpayer is the true earner of the income, all of the income is allocated to him. Although under Section 482, the court may also allocate 100% of income from one entity to another, there is no requirement that this be done, and it may allocate only a portion of the income of one entity to another. Thus, the results may not be as harsh under Section

482 as under the assignment of income doctrine.[14] Moreover, under the assignment of income theory, the corporation would have to pay the taxpayer a dividend to allow him to meet his additional tax liability. Under Section 482, the corporation can pay the taxpayer the reallocated amount up to ninety days after the final determination of the case without further tax liability to the taxpayer.[15]

There are three cases which are often cited as prime examples of the application of Section 482. The facts, their findings and preventive steps to take to avoid the mistakes cited by the court are given in the following chart.[16]

ACH, BORGE AND RUBIN CHART

Case	*Taxpayer's Objective*	*Issues*	*Facts Cited By Court*
Pauline W. Ach 42 TC 114 (1964). Appealed 358 F2d 342	Taxpayer sold the assets at their book value in her profitable dress business to her son's losing corporation, of which she was President, treasurer, chairman of the Board, to take advantage of the net operating loss carryover provisions of the Internal Revenue Code to offset the profits of her business.	Should the income of the corporation derived from taxpayer's dress business be allocated to taxpayer.	*1.* No arm's length transaction - terms of sale were completely unrealistic. *2.* Taxpayer worked for corporation without compensation. Her services were not transferred to corporation — corporation did not receive right to her services. No contract of employment. *3.* No covenant not to compete.
Victor Borge v. Commissioner 26 TCM 816 (1967) (aff'g, mod'g and rem'g TC) 405 F2d 673 (2nd Cir. 1968); cert. denied 395 U.S. 933.	The taxpayer, to offset the losses of his controlled corporation, agreed to perform entertainment and promotional services for the corporation for which the corporation received income in excess of the taxpayer's compensation. The excess earnings were used to offset the corporation's losses.	Whether a portion of the income earned by the corporation from the taxpayer's services was properly reallocated by the corporation to the taxpayer.	*1.* Taxpayer assigned only a portion of his entertainment business to the corporation while continuing to conduct an independent entertainment business. *2.* Corporation did nothing to earn or assist in the earning of the entertainment income. *3.* Taxpayer would not have agreed to perform the same services for the same compensation for an unrelated party. *4.* Corporation business was completely unrelated to taxpayers entertainment business.

		Court Held	*Preventive Steps*
	(Pauline W. Ach, continued)	Sufficient aspects of clothing business remained with taxpayer in order to hold that her activities were a separate trade or business under Section 482 to reallocate a portion of corporation's income to her.	Taxpayer should have employment contract and covenant not to compete. In other words, provide that employee cannot work for other corporation without permission of Board of Directors.
	(Victor Borge v. Commissioner, continued)	That there was a distortion of income by the taxpayer's arrangement with the controlled corporation since the corporation did nothing to earn the money and the sole purpose of the arrangement was to permit the corporation to affect its losses with the income from the entertainment business.	Professional should assign and conduct his entire practice through the corporation and should not conduct an independent practice. If this is not possible, then such outside activities should be permitted by Board of Directors and should not be material in relation to services to be rendered to corporation. Professional should devote substantially all of his time to corporation.

Case	*Taxpayer's Objective*	*Issue*	*Facts Cited By Court*
Richard Rubin vs. Commissioner 51 T.C. 251 (1968); remanded 429 F2d 650 (1970, 2d Cir.); 56 T.C. 1155 (1971); appealed 460 F2d 1216 (1972) aff'g TC	Taxpayer entered into an agreement to purchase the controlling interest of corporation A, whereby the taxpayer was required to render managerial consulting services to A. Taxpayer then formed corporation B which then entered into management consulting contract with A. The income earned by B under said contract was far in excess of what was paid taxpayer as compensation for his services.	Should all or part of the income earned by B be reallocated to the taxpayer.[17]	*1.* No employment contract entered into between taxpayer and corporation B for his services. *2.* Taxpayer continued to work for other companies in addition to his work for Corporation B. *3.* Corporation A often ignored corporation B and held taxpayer out personally as part of its management to third parties. *4.* Third parties often viewed taxpayer as an employee of corporation A, and often knew nothing of Corporation B. *5.* Corporation A wanted only the services of the Taxpayer and nothing else from Corporation B.

	Court Held	*Preventive Steps*
(Richard Rubin v. Commissioner, continued)	Taxpayer was channeling income generated directly by his services to a controlled corporation and that income of Corporation B which was generated by Taxpayer should be reallocated to him as the true earner.[18]	*1.* Have written employment contract between corporation and employee. *2.* Employee should, if possible, devote all his business time to corporation. *3.* Business should be conducted at all times in name of corporation.

OBSERVATION

Notwithstanding the frequent citation of these cases, the problem is more academic than real. The implication in these cases as well as the application of the "Disregard of Corporate Entity," assignment of income doctrine and Section 482 need not be a concern when the entire practice of a professional is transferred to the corporation and the corporation conducts itself as such. The Ach and Borge cases as well as the other cases cited in this chapter are prime examples of tax avoidance schemes which prompted the taxpayers to incorporate. Moreover, the taxpayers might have achieved their objectives in many of these cases had they operated their controlled corporation as a corporation rather than merely serving as their alter ego. Although the court in the Rubin case stated that tax avoidance is not necessary to trigger Section 482, the facts of that case are quite different than those that will be present in a professional corporation. The taxpayer in Rubin controlled two separate corporations and his services were rendered through one corporaiton to the other. In professional corporations, the services of the professional are not rendered to controlled corporations but to the community.

The following is a checklist on the steps the corporation should take to operate like a corporation. Follow these procedures, in addition to recommendations made elsewhere in this chapter, and the chance of a successful Internal Revenue Service attack upon the corporation on the above grounds will be greatly reduced, if not eliminated.

19-Point Checklist on How to Operate a Professional Corporation to be Treated as a "Corporation"

1. Elect officers and a Board of Directors, and adopt by-laws.
2. Open checking account in name of corporation.
3. Purchase corporate seal.
4. Issue stock.
5. Obtain federal and state employer identification numbers for corporation.
6. File all reports required by state and federal law.
7. File employer-employee tax returns — professional employees should be included in workman's compensation and unemployment returns as well as withholding returns.
8. Obtain malpractice and liability insurance in name of corporation.
9. Assign or redraft all leases or existing contracts to corporation.
10. Change all signs, letterheads, bills, cards to name of corporation.
11. List telephone in corporate name.
12. Obtain new Blue Shield number in name of corporation.

13. Order all equipment and supplies in corporate name.
14. Have regular meeting of the Board of Directors to consider corporate policy and to implement management decisions.
15. Minutes should be kept and maintained of all Board of Directors' meetings.
16. Execute employment contracts with all professional employees.
17. The Board of Directors should be given sole authority in making decisions relative to the affairs of the corporation. As an example, the Board of Directors should have the authority to:
    1. Hire professional employees for the corporation.
    2. Determine compensation to be paid employees — both lay and professional.
    3. Control the working hours of the employees, establish coverage policy, arrange vacation and convention time, and adopt policy in regard to reimbursement of business expenses.
    4. Assign patients or clients to various employees.
    5. Review and modify work product of employees.
    6. Significant purchases of equipment should be approved by Board of Directors.
18. Corporation should follow policy established in by-laws and by Board of Directors.
19. If corporation borrows money, see if this can be done without personal guarantee of shareholder employee.

If the above checklist can be summarized in one sentence, it would be *"All activities to be conducted by the corporation should be conducted in the name and for the benefit of the corporation."*

TAX AVOIDANCE UNDER SECTION 269

Section 269 of the Internal Revenue Code provides that if any person or persons acquire control of a corporation and the principal purpose for which such acquisition was made is evasion or avoidance of Federal income tax by securing the benefit of a deduction, credit or other allowance such deduction, credit or allowance may be disallowed by the Internal Revenue Service. Since the principal objective of most professionals in incorporating their practices is to adopt pension and/or profit sharing plans as well as other fringe benefits available to the corporation, Section 269 may be another avenue of attack by the Internal Revenue Service upon the professional corporation.

However, it is doubtful that Section 269 is applicable to the professional corporation context. The primary purpose of Section 269 was to prevent tax avoidance schemes through the acquisition of a loss corporation for the purpose of reducing the profits of the acquiring corporation,[19] and it is unlikely that this section can be extended to deny deductions to a corporation for contributions to its retirement program, although the adoption of a retirement plan might have been one of the motivating factors for incorporating.

Taking advantage of certain tax benefits which are *granted* by Congress should not be considered tax avoidance under Section 269.

This position even appears to be supported by the Internal Revenue Service,. In a ruling, the Internal Revenue Service indicated that the creation of a new corporation for the purpose of obtaining the benefits of Western Hemisphere Trade Corporation did not constitute tax avoidance under Section 269.[20] The same analogy can equally be applied to a new professional corporation which adopts a pension or profit sharing plan and other fringe benefits available to a corporation. This contention was further supported in an article by K. Martin Worthy, Chief Counsel of the Internal Revenue Service when he stated[21]

> Suppose it were determined as a factual matter in a given case that the principal purpose for which a professional corporation was formed was to secure the benefit of tax deductions for

contributions to qualified pension and profit sharing plans. Would Section 269 deprive the corporation of the sole reason for its being?

There are certain possible obstacles to applying Section 269 in this area. First, there will obviously be a factual question in each case as to whether the professional corporation actually was organized principally to obtain given tax benefits. In some of the litigated professional corporation cases involving the classification question, the courts have found as a fact that corporations were formed principally for nontax purposes. Secondly, even assuming that in a given case it did appear that a corporation was organized principally for the purpose of taking advantage of Code provisions relating to qualified pension and profit sharing plans, there is some question whether such a purpose would constitute "evasion or avoidance" of taxes for purposes of Section 269. These Code provisions do, after all, represent a deliberate granting of tax benefits to employers and employees. In IT 3757, 1945 CB 200, a case presenting a possibly analogous question, the Service ruled that the creation of a new corporation for the purpose of obtaining the benefits of Code provisions relating to Western Hemisphere Trade Corporations did not constitute tax avoidance within the meaning of Section 269.[22]

Thus, Section 269 should not prove to be a real problem to the practitioner. However, the section is still available to the Internal Revenue Service in the appropriate case, and therefore, the section should not be ignored. The following are several preventive steps which all practitioners should take to further minimize the threat of the problem.

Preventive Steps to Avoid Section 269

1. The minutes of the organizational meeting of the corporation should state non-tax reasons for incorporating, such as centralized management, limited liability of shareholders for acts committed by other shareholders, and ease in transferring shares.
2. The minutes of the Board of Directors authorizing the adoption of the pension and/or profit sharing plan should state non-tax reason for its adoption such as a statement to the effect that the adoption of the plan will provide incentive to employees to continue their employment with the corporation, and will serve to attract and hold new qualified employees to the corporation.
3. Operate the corporation as a corporation. Section 269 may arise in cases when the formation of the new corporation serves no business purpose or is in fact, a "sham." As previously discussed, this attack can be greatly minimized or eliminated by merely conducting the professional's practice in the name and for the benefit of the corporation.

PERSONAL HOLDING COMPANY

One area of prime concern to many practitioners is that the Internal Revenue Service may use the personal holding company provisions of the Internal Revenue Code[23] to impose a 70% penalty, in addition to the other federal taxes, upon the undistributed net income of the professional corporation.

In order to be classified as a personal holding company, two tests must be met:

1. At least 60% of the "adjusted ordinary gross income" for the taxable year is *personal holding company income*[24] and,
2. if at any time during the last half of the taxable year more than 50% in value of the outstanding stock is owned, directly or indirectly, by not more than five individuals.[25]

These provisions were originally enacted by Congress in order to prevent what is commonly referred to as the "incorporated pocketbook." It was common for taxpayers with substantial income from dividends, interest, rents and royalties to incorporate in order to obtain the lower corporate tax rate and thus avoid the higher personal tax. Subsequently, the definition of personal holding company income was broadened under Section 543 (a) (7) to include income which is generated from "personal service contracts."

Income will be classified as "personal services contracts" income when:

1. A corporation is required to furnish personal services.
2. Some person outside the corporation has the right to *designate by name or description* the individual who is to perform the services,

OR

3. The person who is to perform the services is designated, by name or description, in the contract, and
4. The person who performs the services under the particular contract owns more than 25% of the stock in the corporation.

If any of these elements is missing, then the definition is not satisfied and the penalty will not apply.

The critical issue is whether the designation of the person to perform the services must be made in writing or whether it may be implied. In large professional corporations, it is arguable that a patient or client has no right to designate the person who is to perform the services, since the patient may be seen by the physician who is on call or the client's work may actually be performed by a junior member of the firm. However, this argument becomes weak in a one-man professional corporation, since there is no other person who can perform the services, thereby creating an implied oral contract between the patient or client and the professional.

Although there is support for the contention that there can be an implied contract for personal services contract income,[26] the courts have consistently held that without a written contract specifically designating the person who is to perform the services, you do not have personal services contract income.

An example of a case in point is S. O. Glagget v. Commissioner,[27] whose facts are similar to those present in most one-man professional corporations. Mr. Clagget was a construction engineer who decided to incorporate his business, which was being conducted as a partnership. Mr. Clagget was the sole shareholder and employee, and all contracts which had originally been in his name in the partnership were redrafted and S. O. Clagget, Inc. appeared where his name originally appeared. In all other respects, the contracts remained the same. In essence, the corporation performed the same services as he did as a partner.

The court did not agree with the Internal Revenue Service that the personal holding company penalty should be applied under these facts to the undistributed net income of the corporation. The court held that, since Clagget as an individual was not specifically designated in the new contract to perform the services, then the personal holding company provision would not apply, even though it was expected by all parties that Clagget would in fact perform the services. "For amounts to constitute personal holding company income under Section 543 (a) (7), they must be paid under a contract designating that person to render the services."[28]

This case and the cases cited should be comforting to the professional who is conducting his practice in a one-man professional corporation. Nevertheless, even if it is subsequently determined that "implied" designation is sufficient for personal holding company status, Congressional intent seems to clearly indicate that this penalty is not applicable to professional corporations.

D. Alden Newland, in an excellent article,[29] stressed several convincing arguments why the personal holding company sections should not be applied to professional corporations. The reasons stated are as follows:

1. There is no contractual right between the patient or client and professional obligating the latter to perform services. "Even with a one-man professional corporation, it is clear that amounts received for professional services are not personal services contract income even though there is no one else to perform the services. This follows because, even though there is only one professional in a one-man professional corporation, the recipient of services does not have a contractual right under a particular contract to demand services ... It is apparent ... that Congress intended that there be 'mutuality of obligation' or consideration on both sides of a personal services contract by its repeated references to 'contracts' and 'particular contracts.' "[30]

2. There is no 'particular contract' between a patient or client and the professional as required by Section 543 (a) (7). "Generally services are performed on an 'as come' basis and there are no formal contracts."[31] A written contract between an entertainer and a studio is a 'particular contract.'

3. Services performed by architects, engineers and advertisers were specifically excluded by the House Committee Report, and there is a great similarity between services performed by these professionals and those performed by a physician, lawyer or dentist.[32]

4. Congress, in enacting the personal holding company provisions, was attacking the entertainers who were sheltering large sums of money from personal income taxes by incorporating. In other words, Congress was attacking the 'unique talent.' The services of a physician or lawyer are not 'unique' since they can be performed by others, whereas the 'unique' services of Bob Hope cannot be replaced by another entertainer.

5. Rev Rul 71-372 IRB 1971-38,8 held that a member of the New York stock exchange who chose to incorporate his business would not receive personal holding company contract income under Section 543 (a) (7), since the services of the member were not unique to any one particular broker. The ruling would appear to be equally applicable to the services performed by a professional.

Although the personal holding company provision of the Internal Revenue Code should not pose a real threat to the professional corporation, the problem should not be ignored by the practitioner. Fortunately, there are many steps which the practitioner can take to avoid or minimize this issue, which are listed in the following checklist.

FIVE STEPS TO TAKE TO AVOID PERSONAL HOLDING COMPANY PENALTY

1. Do not retain large sums of taxable income in the corporation. The penalty applies only to the undistributed net income of the corporation, and if the income is distributed or kept to a minimum each year, then the problem becomes academic. If there is no undistributed net income, there is no income upon which the penalty can be applied. In many professional corporations, especially small professional corporations, this will be the easiest and most effective method of avoiding the problem.[33]
2. In large professional corporations, try to arrange stockholding so that no more than 50% in value of the corporate stock is owned by five or fewer stockholders. If this is achieved, then the personal holding company provisions will not apply.[34]
3. If the stock arrangement suggested in point two is not possible, then (if corporation is large enough) arrange stock ownership so that no stockholder owns more than 25% of the stock. If the person designated to perform the services does not own more than 25% of the stock, then the penalty cannot apply.
4. Provide in the employment contract between the corporation and the shareholder employee that the corporation will have the right to designate the professional who will perform the services.
5. Be sure that no contract for services to be rendered by the corporation provides the name of the person who is to perform the services.

ACCUMULATED EARNINGS TAX

The corporate tax rate, in almost all cases, is lower than the individual tax rate of its professional shareholders, and in many cases, the shareholders will prefer to shelter the earnings of the corporation by allowing it to accumulate in the corporation, rather than to distribute it to themselves. If this is done indefinitely, the corporation runs the risk of the Internal Revenue Service imposing the accumulated earnings tax on its accumulated taxable income.

The Internal Revenue Code imposes an accumulated earnings tax on any corporation that is formed or availed of for the purpose of avoiding the income tax on its shareholders by permitting its earnings and profits to accumulate instead of being distributed.[35] Thus, the prohibited purpose which will trigger this penalty is the intent of the corporation to be used as a vehicle to shelter its income from the personal tax rate of its individual shareholders.

Evidence of such a purpose is when the earnings and profit of the corporation are permitted to accumulate beyond the reasonable needs of the business.[36]

In most professional corporations, especially in the corporation consisting of only a few shareholder employees, it will be quite difficult to justify the accumulation of large sums of money since the requirement for a large working capital is non-existent in most cases. However, there will be cases where the corporation will be required to accumulate money to meet its needs. This arises when money is needed to purchase expensive equipment or to purchase or build a medical building.[37] Extensive working capital may also be required in large architectural, engineering and medical clinics, which would justify the accumulation of large sums of money.

It has been questionable in the past whether accumulating funds to purchase the shares of a deceased shareholder constituted a reasonable business need. Professional corporations are different in this regard than the ordinary business corporation. All states require that stock in a professional corporation cannot be held by a person not licensed to practice the profession for which the corporation was organized, and some even require a mandatory redemption by the corporation in the event of the death of a stockholder. Therefore, it would now seem that accumulating funds for the purpose of redeeming the stock of a deceased shareholder as required by law would constitute a legitimate business purpose.

If imposed, the accumulated earnings tax is levied at the rate of 27½% of the first $150,000 of the accumulated taxable income and 38½% of the excess, which is in addition to the other taxes the corporation is obligated to pay.[38] All accumulated earnings are not subject to this tax. Only those earnings which are accumulated in excess of the reasonable needs of the business are subject to the penalty, which includes not only actual, current needs, but its anticipatory needs.[39] In addition, the first $150,000 of accumulated earnings is exempt whether its accumulation was reasonable or not.[40]

As a practical matter, this penalty should pose few problems to most professional corporations. Aside from the fact that most professional corporations will have no business reason for accumulating large sums of money, such accumulations are inconsistent with the objectives of the professional in incorporating his practice. The reason a professional incorporates is not to shelter part of his income in a corporation, but to make contributions to a retirement program in excess of what he is permitted as a self-employed individual under the Keogh plan. To accomplish this objective, most corporations are established whereby the base salary of the professional plus contribution to the retirement program and other fringe benefits to which he is entitled, is approximately equal to the earnings of the corporation. Thus, a small or negligible surplus is left in the corporation at the end of each year. In addition, since the maximum tax rate on earned income is now 50%, the advantage of sheltering the professional's income in the corporation is further reduced, and may be eliminated entirely, depending upon the amount which was intended to be accumulated each year.[41]

Nevertheless, the practitioner should not ignore this possible problem. If the corporation is not watched carefully, the accumulated earnings tax may become a real threat. The following are preventive steps to take to minimize this problem.

Six Preventive Steps to Avoiding the Accumulated Earnings Tax

1. Keep accumulated income to a minimum.
2. If money is being accumulated for expansion purposes, such as the purchase of a professional building or expensive equipment, then document this corporate intent in the appropriate minutes of the Board of Directors, stating the estimated cost of such purchase and the reasons for it.
3. In regard to prevention step number two, if a building or equipment is to be purchased, a better solution may be to have the shareholders themselves make such purchases. This will enable the corporation to keep its capitalization low, thus reducing the threat of an unreasonable compensation attack, and will enable potential shareholders to buy stock in the corporation at a lower price.
4. Avoid investing undistributed earnings in assets having no reasonable connection with the corporation's business. Thus, the corporation should not invest surplus earnings in securities, mortgages, oil ventures or real estate ventures.[42]
5. Pay out retained income not needed to meet business requirements in form of dividends to shareholders.
6. Do not accumulate money unless there is a business reason for doing so.

FOOTNOTES

[1]TIR 1019; Rev Rul 70-101, 1970-1 CB 278.

[2]The Internal Revenue Service will seldom limit its attack to one theory alone. Often, it will raise several grounds for attack and use them as the alternatives.

[3]Jackson v. Comm'r 233 F2d 289 (1956); Higgins v. Smith 308 U.S. 478 (1939); Gregory v. Helvering 293 U.S. 465 (1934); Moline Properties, Inc. v. Comm'r 319 U.S. 436 (1943).

[4]Moline Properties, Inc. v. Comm'r, See note 3; see also Nathaniel Cole *32 TCM 313 (1973)*. In this case, the well-known entertainer created a corporation through which his entertainment business was conducted. The Internal Revenue Service contended, inter alia, that corporation was a sham which served no purpose other than collecting amounts earned by Cole and disbursing these amounts in payment of Cole's expenses. The court did not agree and refused to disregard the corporate entity, since it performed substantial services designed to generate income, as well as incurring expenses and bearing entrepreneural risk. In the case of Pauline W. Ach, 42 TC 114 (1964) the taxpayer sold a profitable dress business at a low book value to her son's corporation which was consistently sustaining losses, in order to take advantage of the loss carryover provisions of the Internal Revenue Code. Although the court applied the principals of Section 482 in reallocating the income back to the taxpayer, the court refused to disregard the corporate entity, since it outwardly existed, there had been a genuine transfer of assets to it, it was used to conduct business, it had salaried employees, and it discharged all state and federal corporate obligations.

[5]Gregory V. Helvering, note 3; Comm'r v. National Carbide Corporation 167 F2d 304 (1948).

[6]53 TC 365 (1969).

[7](DC Wis.) 74-1 USTC ®9284; aff'g (CA7) 74-1 USTC ®9135

[8]In Floyd Patterson v. Comm'r *25 TCM 1230 (1966)* the taxpayer formed a corporation to handle the ancillary rights in connection with his boxing matches, but continued in many instances to enter into and sign for such rights personally. In addition, the corporation did not follow the most basic of corporate procedures — accounting principals were not followed, receipts reported on corporation tax returns were in fact deposited in taxpayer's personal account, expenses connected with corporation were deducted by taxpayer on his personal tax return, corporation minutes were not kept and stock was not paid for. The court ignored the corporation as a taxable entity, stating "... that the corporation merely served as an instrument by which income and expenses could be arbitrarily allocated to serve the tax interest of petitioner ... and therefore should not be recognized for income tax purposes."

In Johansson V. U.S. 336 F2d 809 (1964) the taxpayer formed a Swiss corporation which was to conduct his business affairs. The taxpayer, nevertheless, continued to conduct his affairs largely independent of the corporation. The court disregarded the corporation as a taxable entity holding "... had no legitimate business purpose, but was a device which was used by Ingemar Johanssen as a controlled depositary and conduit by which he attempted to divert temporarily his personal income, earned in the United States, so as to escape taxation thereon by the United States."

[9]Lucas V. Earl 281 U.S. 111 (1930) The court held that a husband could not shift the incidence of the income tax on his future personal earnings merely by contracting to pay part of them to his wife; Helvering v. Hurst 311 U.S. 112 (1940) The court held that a taxpayer who retained the ownership of a bond but gave an interest coupon to his son was taxable on the interest collected by the son; Helvering v. Eubank 311 U.S. 122 (1940) The taxpayer was liable for the income tax on renewal commissions earned by him as an insurance agent, the right to collect which had been assigned to another. The basic position of this doctrine is that the taxpayer has a right, present or expecting, to income which he had assigned to another.

A case in which this doctrine was raised, and in which the Internal Revenue Service lost, was the case of Nathaniel Cole; see note 4. The taxpayer in this case assigned to his comporation the rights to royalties on phonograph records which he would make in the future. The court rejected the assignment of income theory that, at the time the taxpayer had made the contract which he assigned, he had no vested rights to income, rather he was assigning a contractual right.

[10]Pauline Ach *Note 4*; Victor Borge 405 F2d 673 (1969); Richard Rubin 460 F2d 1216 (1972), see Ach, Borge and Rubin chart, this chapter, p. 45.

[11]See Note 10.

[12]See chapter 2 "How to Organize a Professional Corporation Tax-Wisely" section entitled "What Assets Should be Transferred to the New Corporation", p. 21.

[13]Richard Rubin *See Note 10*.

[14]See Note 17.

[15]Rev. Proc. 65-17, *1965-1 CB 833*.

[16]In order to apply Section 482, it must be shown that the taxpayer is conducting a separate trade or business to which income can be allocated. The cited cases clearly established the principal that the services of an employee constitute a trade or business separate from the trade or business of the corporation.

[17]In Rubin's first appearance in the Tax Court, the Court used the assignment of income doctrine which would have resulted in additional income to the taxpayer of $35,000 in one year and $50,000 in the rest. The Court of Appeals remanded the case back to the Tax Court with instructions to use Section 482 rather than the all or nothing approach of the assignment of income doctrine. The Tax Court, under Section 482, reallocated only $4400 and $23,500 for each respective year, which was affirmed by the Court of Appeals.

[18]The disturbing aspect of this case is that the Court of Appeals stated that it was immaterial whether the taxpayer was rendering the services before the corporation was organized, or whether the services were to begin with the formation of the corporation. The Court also stated that the tax avoidance motive is not necessary to apply Section 482. This appears to be a

significant expansion of this section as used by the courts in the Borge and Ach cases.

[19]"This statutory restriction was originally enacted in 1943, principally to curb a growing "market" for defunct corporate shells. These hollow entities were in demand because the World War II excess profits tax exempted a corporation's "normal" profits, based on its historic earnings or invested capital, and some owners of booming war businesses hoped to shield themselves against taxable "excess" profits by carrying on their activities through a corporation that in the past had enjoyed substantial earnings or invested capital. Other negotiable tax benefits were loss carryovers and potential deductions to be created by selling high bases assets (usually Section 1231 property) with low current values. ... Section 269 was enacted in 1943 on the Treasury's recommendation to provide a more specific statutory attack on these devices"; Bittker and Eustice, *Federal Income Taxation of Corporation and Shareholders* Second Edition, 1966, Section 13.21, see also Senate Report No. 627, 78th Congress, 1st Session, 1016-1017, 1944 CB973.

[20]IT 3757, 1945 CB 200, superseded by Rev. Rul. 70-238, IRB 1970-20, 8.

[21]"Internal Revenue Service Chief Counsel outlines what lies ahead for professional corporations" *32 JTAX February 1970.*

[22]See also Modern Home Fire & Casualty Insurance Company 54 TC 839 (1970).

[23]IRC §541-547.

[24]IRC §542 (a) (1).

[25]IRC §542 (a) (2).

[26]Rev.§ Rul. 69-299, 1969-1 CB 165; K. Martin Worthy *Note 21;* "... it seems questionable whether the mere fact that a designation is not in writing should render the statutes inapplicable. This is an area where the law may be further developed with the advent of professional corporations."

[27]44 TC 503 (1965).

[28]Ibid., See also Allen Machinery Corporation v. Commissioner 31 TC 441 (1958) and General Management Corporation v Commissioner 135 F2d 882 (1943) when the court in both cases held that personal holding company income is generated only when the contracts designate the person who is to perform the services.

[29]"Should Today's Professional Corporations be Liable for the Personal Holding Company Penalty Tax?" JTAX July 1972.

[30]Ibid., page 26.

[31]Ibid., page 27.

[32]H. Rept. No. 1546, 75th Congress 1st Session 6 (1937).

[33]This does not mean that there should be no taxable income left in the corporation at the end of each year, or that any surplus should be paid out in the form of bonuses. The corporation will certainly need money for working capital, and "stripping" the corporation at the end of the year by paying bonuses will certainly be a red flag for the unreasonable compensation problem (See Chapter 4, Planning for and Avoiding the Unreasonable Compensation Dilemma, Section entitled "Contingent Compensation and Bonuses" p.60. Instead of paying a large percentage of the surplus out in the form of a bonus, dividends should be declared as well as a bonus. What is to be avoided is the accumulation of large sums of money in the corporation for no business reason.

[34]This arrangement can only be made in corporations consisting of 10 or more shareholders.

[35]Section 532 (a).

[36]The burden of proof is upon the corporation to show that the earnings were not unreasonably accumulated, unless the corporation submits a statement as required by Section 534 (c), setting forth the facts on which it relies, showing that the earnings were not unreasonably accumulated. In the event of such corporate notification, the burden is then shifted back to the Internal Revenue Service. Even if the corporation is unable to carry its burden of proof that the accumulations were to meet the reasonably needs of the corporation, the corporation may still escape the tax if it can prove by the "preponderance of the evidence" that the purpose of the accumulation was not to avoid tax on its shareholders (Section 533 (a). However, this is almost impossible for the corporation to prove.

[37]In small corporations, it is probably better to have the shareholders purchase the equipment or building in their own names and lease it to the corporation. This will minimize the reasonable compensation problem and will maintain the stock at a low value, which will enable new shareholders to purchase stock without a hardship to them. (See Note 11, p. 17).

[38]§531.

[39]§537 (a) (1).

[40]§304 of the Tax Reduction Act of 1975 amended IRC §535(c) to increase minimum accumulated earnings tax credit from $100,000 to $150,000 for years beginning after December 31, 1974.

[41]The corporation tax rate on income in excess of $25,000 is 48%. It certainly makes little sense to accumulate money in the corporation at this rate rather than distribute it as salary to the shareholders and pay a tax at the maximum rate of 50%

[42]Regs. §1.533-1(a) (2) (ii).

4

PLANNING FOR AND AVOIDING THE UNREASONABLE COMPENSATION DILEMMA

The area of law which may prove to be the Achilles heel of professional corporations is the uncertain area of reasonable compensation. This is a difficult problem faced by every closely-held corporation, but it may prove even more difficult for the professional corporation since the income of the professional shareholder is high, the tests for reasonableness are vague and there are so few precedents relating to professional corporations upon which the practitioner is able to rely. In addition, the problem is made even more difficult since the burden is upon the taxpayer to prove that the compensation paid its officers or shareholder employees is reasonable[1] and it is impossible to obtain an advanced ruling from the Internal Revenue Service whether the compensation to be paid is reasonable.[2]

The consequences of having compensation disallowed upon the ground of being unreasonable will have serious effects upon the corporation. The disallowed portion may not be deducted by the corporation for its tax purposes. Thus, the disallowed portion will now become subject to "double taxation"; once by the corporation and again by the professional. Furthermore, dividends are not considered earned income subject to the 50% tax limit under Section 1348 of the Internal Revenue Code. In such an event, it is possible that the disallowed portion may be taxed to the professional at a rate up to 70%. In addition, contributions to qualified retirement plans are based upon compensation received by the participants and if part of the compensation is disallowed, then a pro rata reduction in the contribution to the retirement plan is required.[3]

There is no hard and fast rule by which reasonableness of compensation is determined by the courts. Each case is determined on its own peculiar facts and circumstances. However, the courts over the years have developed traditional factors which they consider in determining reasonableness. Some of the factors most often referred to by the courts are as follows:[4]

1. The Employee's special training, experience and ability to perform the work of the corporation;
2. His time and energy devoted to the corporation;
3. The nature of his duties and responsibilities;
4. The manner and timing in establishing bonuses or other amounts above base salary, including their relationship to shareholdings;
5. The dividend history of the corporation;
6. The compensation paid for comparable positions in comparable businesses, including the relevance of pre-incorporated salaries;
7. The percentage of employee compensation to gross profit and net income.

In most cases, the courts will choose to focus on the factors it considers relevant, often to the exclusion of any discussion of the others. As a rule, a determination is made by the courts by a combination of factors which it considers important under the circumstances. A case is rarely decided on one factor alone.

Generally, if the courts in applying the traditional factors found that the compensation was reasonable, then the corporation was entitled to deduct the entire amount classified as salary. However, recent developments in this area have been most disturbing. Some courts have abandoned the traditional approach to the problem and have held that although payments may be considered reasonable, it is not deductible to the extent that it is in reality a distribution of corporate earnings and not compensation for services rendered. This has been called the "fair return of invested capital" approach, and applies that payments received as compensation may in fact represent a return of invested capital.

Because of the seriousness and vagueness inherent in this problem, this chapter will examine the traditional factors established by the courts and the most recent cases in detail since the courts are primarily responsible for the guidelines we have. In addition, this chapter will provide drafting techniques and planning steps to take to prepare for and minimize the reasonable compensation problem. It can be said with sufficient certainty that with careful draftsmanship, planning and knowledge of the problem the practitioner should be able to protect the Achilles heel of professional corporations.

WHAT IS COMPENSATION

In determining whether compensation is reasonable, the courts include the total value of all benefits conferred upon the employee by the corporation. Thus, compensation includes base salary, bonuses, as well as contributions made to a qualified retirement plan for the benefit of the employee. In fact, a contribution to a retirement plan can cause an employee's compensation to be considered unreasonable,[5] and contributions are only deductible to the extent they constitute "a reasonable allowance for compensation for the services actually rendered."[6] One recent case held that contributions to a pension plan were not to be considered as part of compensation for the purpose of determining whether the compensation was reasonable.[7] However, no authority for this position was cited and it is highly unlikely that this position will be acquiesced to by the Internal Revenue Service or have any significant effect.

Other benefits which are considered of value which are included in compensation are the other fringe benefits which may be conferred upon the employee, such as group term insurance, disability income protection insurance, medical benefits and any other benefits which are available to the employee.

As a practical matter, however, most compensation disputes will involve the total of salaries, bonuses and retirement plan contributions. Other fringe benefits are generally considered too small to be of real concern to the Internal Revenue Service auditor.[8]

RELATIONSHIP OF PROFESSIONAL INCOME PRIOR TO INCORPORATION TO CORPORATE SALARY

What is most difficult to understand is the fact that the compensation received by a professional from the corporation may still be found to be unreasonable even though it is equal in amount to what he received as a partner in a partnership or as a sole practitioner. This is because the Internal Revenue Service views pre-incorporated income as not only representing the value of his services but also representing a return on equipment or other capital, the services of suboridinates, and even good will. The compensation received by the professional from the corporation represents none of these items and may only represent the individual's services to the corporatiion.[9] In fact, some courts have supported this view and have rejected a comparison of partnership income to corporate income, as a factor for determining whether corporate compensation was reasonable.[10]

Nevertheless, although significant reliance can not be placed upon pre-incorporation income, it certainly does provide us with an amount that would be required to hire the professional by a corporation in an arm's length transaction. Certainly, a man will not take a position with a company in which he assumes the same duties and responsibilities as when he was a sole practitioner or partner for less compensation. Therefore, there is a strong argument that the compensation the professional is receiving represents his fair value to the corporation when you compare his earning capacity as a sole practitioner to his corporate income.[11] In fact, many courts have found that the employee's salary prior to incorporating to be of considerable importance when determining whether his compensation is reasonable.[12]

Therefore, the practitioner, when establishing the professional's compensation in the minutes of the meeting of the Board of Directors should refer to the professional's income prior to incorporating as a means of establishing the professional's value or worth to the corporation.

RELATIONSHIP OF COMPENSATION TO BILLINGS

It has been commonly felt that if a professional receives a compensation package equal to his billings, then his compensation should be considered reasonable since his income equals his production.

There have been two significant cases decided on this point which involved professional corporations both of which held that reasonable compensation may equal 100% of billings.[13]

It can be inferred from these cases that compensation is reasonable to the extent it represents the services that the professional has actually rendered as represented by his billings or other services rendered which generates income; but is unreasonable as to payments made which are generated from other sources, such as rental and investment income. Thus, a professional corporation should avoid transferring rental producing income such as a professional building to a corporation or purchasing income producing securities, since the income generated cannot readily be distributed in the form of salary to the professional shareholders without having the distribution considered a dividend by the Internal Revenue Service upon an audit. Salary should be paid for services rendered, and distribution of investment income does not represent services rendered.

In addition, if a professional is to perform administrative and supervisory functions, as well as pure professional services, then these additional responsibilities should be documented in the corporate papers to justify the compensation which is being paid.

However, as will be subsequently discussed, relating billings to compensation is no guarantee that the professional's compensation will be considered reasonable by the Internal Revenue Service or the courts. Nevertheless, it certainly does provide a foundation in that the practitioner can demonstrate that his professional client is worth the salary he is receiving since it is equal to the income that he is generating.

EXPERIENCE, TRAINING AND ABILITY OF EMPLOYEE

One factor which courts often emphasize in considering the reasonableness of compensation is the experience, training and ability of the employee.[14] This is certainly one area where any professional can "score points" in his behalf. Therefore, the professional's educational background, special training, experience, awards and honors and any other factors which tend to support his ability should be inserted into the minutes of the meeting of the Board of Directors in which his salary is discussed and determined. This may be done by inserting his curriculum vitae into the records.

LONG HOURS, HARD WORK, FEW VACATIONS

Many professionals devote an inordinate amount of time to their practices. Frequently courts refer favorably to employees who devote 50 to 60 hours a week to their jobs, work weekends and/or nights, and rarely take vacations.[15] On the other hand, courts are critical where the employee works infrequently, or devotes much of his time and energy to other businesses.[16] Therefore, if the professional has long working hours, works odd hours and takes few vacations, these facts should be emphasized in the corporate minutes, particularly in relation to explaining bonuses and salary increases. If the professional has business and other activities outside the corporation, these facts also should be explained in the corporate minutes. The Board of Directors should grant approval for these activities and indicate that the salary level was established with consideration of these outside interests. If lectures, seminars or advanced training take up significant time, the minutes should also reflect the fact that these activities will improve the abilities of the employee and increase future corporate earning capacity.

DUTIES AND RESPONSIBILITIES OF EMPLOYEE

Another issue which courts tend to examine is the scope of duties and responsibilities assumed by the employee. Courts have commented favorably on the compensation of employees who were primarily responsible for the major business or development decisions, management of operations, supervision of subordinates, obtaining of customers and even advice and ideas.[17]

The practitioner should determine the existence of such extra duties and responsibilities, as well as the usual and normal duties which will be performed in the given practice. The extra duties are especially important where the salary of an employee appears high in relation to his billings. Thus, where a professional has supervisory or management responsibilities, or is instrumental in the training of subordinate professionals or nonprofessionals, or tends to bring in clients through social or business contacts, these factors should be in both the employment contract and the corporate minutes.

In *McClung Hospital, Inc. vs. Commissioner of Internal Revenue,*[18] the court upheld aggregate compensation for two supervisory doctor-shareholders equal to 100% of the aggregate billings without reduction for the expenses of treating their patients or for uncollectible accounts. Nonshareholder doctors received salaries equal to only 60% of their billings. The court justified the differential, and the compensation, on the basis of the administrative and supervisory responsibilities of the shareholders.

COMPENSATION PAID BY COMPARABLE BUSINESSES

Generally, one of the most important criteria where evidence in point is available is that of comparing the salaries of other professionals to the salary received by the employee whose salary is now being considered unreasonable by the Internal Revenue Service.[19] There is one of the only tests specifically set forth in the Regulations.[20] Moreover, where evidence concerning compensation of comparable employees is offered, courts generally emphasize this factor. The reason behind this may well be that this criteria offers concrete figures to justify a decision as opposed to many other criteria which are largely subjective. In fact, courts have consistently held that such evidence overcomes the presumption that the Internal Revenue Service's determination of what is reasonable compensation is correct. Unless the Internal Revenue Service introduces contrary evidence as to what comparable firms are paying, *it* may lose *the* case for failure to carry *its* burden of proof.[21]

The practitioner should note in applying this test on behalf of his professional client the following:

1. The salaries of unincorporated professionals is of limited value;[22]

2. Other criteria of reasonableness discussed elsewhere is this chapter must be used in establishing comparability. Thus, you would ask questions such as (a) Is the professional's background comparable to the other professionals in like corporations in terms of qualifications, responsibilities, effort expended, and contributions to the success of the corporation; and (b) whether the corporations are similar in types of practice, as well as in income, organization and operation, and capital and debt structure. In other words, the practitioner must compare the salaries paid for like services, by like enterprises under the same circumstances.

CONTINGENT COMPENSATION AND BONUSES[23]

In nearly all instances, the professional shareholder will wish to get most of the income of the corporation (other than amounts used for contributions to the retirement plan and for other fringe benefits) distributed to him in the form of compensation. Double taxation is avoided, the compensation received is subject to the 50% maximum tax on earned income, and any potential problems with personal holding company classification or accumulated earning taxes are eliminated.

However, it is generally not possible to anticipate corporate income precisely. Thus, it becomes necessary to supplement the basic salary with contingent compensation or a bonus. This poses problems with the Internal Revenue Service and the courts. The essential issue in reasonable compensation disputes is whether the amount in dispute is compensation or in fact a distribution of profits of the corporation in the form of compensation, which in fact is a dividend. Basic salary supplements are generally given at year-end and very clearly reduce the amount available for the payment of dividends. Supplements thus appear to more closely resemble a disguised dividend than does a base salary set at the beginning of the year when profits are not known. For example, the Internal Revenue Service and the courts are most skeptical of a year-end bonus declared when profits were known, and not given in accordance with any pre-existing incentive formula. The basis for this skepticism is that in a close corporation the recipient of the "bonus" will generally have control over whether and how much of the money that he knows is available he chooses to distribute as compensation or in the form of dividends. Awarding oneself a year-end bonus when no dividends have been declared makes the bonus particularly susceptible to attack.

The Internal Revenue Service has even shown hostility to contingent compensation plans based on corporate income which were established at the beginning of the year when profits were not known. The Internal Revenue Service's position, with which some courts have agreed, is that a shareholder-employee does not need a contingent compensation incentive to make him work harder to increase corporate income. The only expressed basis for this position has been that a shareholder already has sufficient incentive to work harder in light of his proprietary interest and its increased value with an increase in corporate earnings.

In order to have the Internal Revenue Service accept as compensation an amount above the basic salary, the practitioner should observe the following:

1. The total compensation of the professional should be set as close as possible to his expected net income before his total compensation package is paid.

2. The method for distributing bonuses or the formula for a contingent compensation plan should be established at the beginning of the corporation's taxable year before profits are known. The practitioner should consider setting production goals for the professionals, and if such goals are exceeded additional compensation will be paid. If bonuses or incentive compensation is paid out of unexpected profits or in no apparent pre-set basis, there is a greater risk of having the additional compensation considered a dividend distribution.

3. Avoid distributing all or nearly all the surplus of the corporation as bonuses or incentive compensation. A corporation's consistently negligible taxable income is an indication that the bonus system is based on the funds available rather that on services rendered. Thus, always leave some surplus in the corporation upon which taxes will be paid.

4. Avoid paying bonuses in exact proportions to the stockholdings of the recipients. Such a distribution resembles a dividend. The corporate records should provide, when paying bonuses or incentive compensation that such additonal compensation is being paid as a result of the recipient's increased workload, additional responsibilities and duties assumed during the previous year or increased productivity.

5. Avoid paying bonuses or incentive compensation just to shareholders. If there are other professionals employed by the corporation who are not shareholders and bonuses are paid, they should participate in the bonuses which are being distributed. This will be of great value in convincing the Internal Revenue Service and the courts that the year-end distribution was not a disguised dividend to the stockholder employees.

Bonuses

The Internal Revenue Service may classify a year-end bonus or year-end establishment of salary as a dividend, regardless of the total amount of compensation, especially where (1) all or nearly all earnings are thus absorbed by officer-shareholder remuneration, and (2) the bonus or salary is in proportion to the shareholdings.[24] Therefore, all bonuses, especially those voted at year-end without prior corporate authorization should be explained in the corporate minutes.[25] The increased remuneration should be labeled the result of hard work causing greater than anticipated corporate income.

In two recent cases the Tax Court upheld year-end bonuses despite the fact that they were determined without regard to any pre-set formula and appeared to be paid solely out of money available.[26] The basis of both decisions was the responsibilities and long hours assumed by the respective employees which contributed to the success of the corporation. It should be reiterated at this point that reasonable compensation criteria are very much interrelated; as previously discussed, the failure to pay any dividends makes it particularly unlikely that the Internal Revenue Service will accept a significant year-end bonus as compensation.

Contingent Compensation

Where possible, supplements to basic salary should be in the form of contingent compensation based on a formula established prior to the taxable year. The time at which the formula is established is of crucial importance.[27] A proper plan for contingent compensation can be justified as an incentive for employees which is designed to increase corporate income.

Important factors concerning contingent compensation are whether the total produced is reasonable in amount[28] and the formula employed can in fact act as an incentive.[29] The formula end result should reflect productivity rather than shareholdings.[30] Although the courts have in many cases approved contingent compensation plans based on a percentage of net income or profits,[31] such an arrangement closely resembles dividends. Therefore, the formula should be based on gross income. For example, the professional can receive 60-70% of the amount of billings for which he is responsible in excess of a specified amount. A supervising professional could receive compensation based on the productivity of his subordinates.

It should be noted that a number of recent important cases have cast doubt on the acceptability of incentive compensation plans for employees who are shareholders.[32] These cases contend that a proprietary interest is a sufficient incentive to make a shareholder work harder, and that increased personal income from the greater workload can come via dividends rather than compensation. One case, while agreeing with this reasoning, judged the compensation to be reasonable.[33] Other cases reject this reasoning, either explicitly or in their results.[34]

This reasoning is illogical and discriminatory against close corporations. If the shareholder-employee is treated as an employee in every regard-employment contracts, subject to Federal withholding, unemployment taxes, social security taxes - it is inconsistent to choose one area in which to disregard his employment status. In addition, it is discriminatory in that officers of public corporations will not have similar contingent compensation plans challenged. More importantly, in cases ruling against employee-shareholder incentives, there have been other factors adverse to the corporation, particularly the failure to pay any dividends.[35]

If the contingent compensation can be kept relatively small in proportion to basic salary and if the corporation distributes a reasonable dividend, the payment of contingent compensation should not be attacked.

RELATIONSHIP OF COMPENSATION TO GROSS AND/OR NET PROFITS

Courts frequently refer to the ratio of employee's compensation to gross and/or net income in either upholding or denying reasonability. However, there does not appear to be any discernible pattern of acceptable ratios.

It is clear than in personal service corporations, where the employee is principally responsible for the corporate income, a higher percentage of income can go towards compensation. However, in precisely this situation in *The Barton-Gillet Company* case,[36] the Tax Court held compensation was excessive which exceeded 19% of gross profit and 60% of net income. In a number of cases involving other personal service corporations, the courts have upheld salaries which exceeded 60% of net income,[37] some of which were between 75 to 100%,[38] or 19% of gross income.[39] The conclusion appears to be that a ratio of compensation to gross and/or net income will generally be examined together with other factors and will not be decisive in itself. For example, in *Barton-Gillet,* the taxpayer corporation failed to pay any dividends; in *Gladstone-Arcuni* and *Kay, Inc.*[40] where the courts approved compensation ratios even higher, significant dividends were paid in most of the taxable years.

REASONABLE BUT NONDEDUCTIBLE COMPENSATION

As previously discussed, the traditional approach taken by the courts in deciding reasonable compensation cases was to determine whether the payments were reasonable and purely for services rendered. If the answer to both these questions was answered in the affirmative, then the salary was generally held to be reasonable and therefore deductible to the corporation. However, some recent cases have departed from this customary method and have held that even if the salary paid an employee is reasonable in amount, a full deduction may still be disallowed if the employee is also a stockholder and he has not received a reasonable return on his capital investment in the corporation. This implies an imputed dividend may be declared by the courts and has been called the "fair return on capital approach".[41] On this theory, the alleged compensation is reduced by an amount representing a fair return on capital.

Traditionally, one of the factors which courts examine in determining whether compensation in a close corporation was reasonable is the dividend paying history of the corporation. The failure to pay any dividends or negligible dividends has often been given as a supporting factor by the courts in determining that the payments were unreasonable and in reality a disguised dividend.[42] These recent cases appeared to have given the traditional dividend test unprecedented importance.

In "Klamath Medical Service Bureau v. Commissioner",[43] one of the few cases dealing directly with a professional corporation, the court held that although the total of alleged compensation paid for services was reasonable in amount, it still disallowed the total deduction for all amounts paid as compensation to the shareholder employees on the ground that a portion of the compensation was intended as a distribution of profits rather than compensation for services.

Subsequently, the court of claims in "McCandless Title Service v. U.S."[44] citing Klamath set forth the proposition that is now known as the "fair return of invested capital" theory. The court took the position that although the compensation may be reasonable under all the circumstances, a deduction may still be disallowed if the employee is a shareholder and the corporation has failed to pay any dividends. This position was based on the theory that part of the compensation in the absence of dividends, is in reality a distribution of earnings. The court then held that a "return on equity capital equal to 15% of net profits (before salaries and Federal Income Tax) would have been reasonable ...."

The court offered no explanation for its choice of 15%, admitting that its task was difficult and that it has no "precise formula" to aid it in its determination.

Two subsequent well-known cases, "Barton-Gillet Co."[45] and "Nor-Cal Adjusters v. Commissioner"[46] gave weight to the fair return of capital theory when it cited McCandless and disallowed a portion of the alleged compensation paid to the stockholder employees, although there was no real dispute as to the reasonableness of the amount paid.

Notwithstanding these cases, there is still reason to believe that future results will not depend solely upon this new theory. More recent cases have either ignored Barton-Gillet and McCandless or narrowed their scope in their use as precedent.[47] It appears that future cases will be decided by the court using the traditional factors while giving more weight to the dividend history of the corporation.

WATCH THIS

The lesson to be learned by these cases is that it is crucial that the corporation declare dividends. If there is an unexpected surplus at the end of the year, the entire surplus should not be distributed as additional compensation. Use this surplus to pay dividends. The tax that will be paid on the nondeductible dividend distribution will be one of the costs of incorporating. In addition, the payment of dividends will shift the burden from the taxpayer to the Internal Revenue Service to prove that the dividends paid were too low.

Is Capital In Fact An Income Producing Factor in Professional Corporations

It is interesting to note that the Internal Revenue Service and the courts have taken a position in regard to whether capital is an income producing factor in service corporations that is completely contrary to the findings in the McCandless and Barton-Gillet cases.

In a number of cases the courts have held that the shareholder-employees providing the service which produce nearly all of the corporate income are entitled to the large part of that income. These courts have noted that capital was not a material income producing factor to the corporation.[48] The Internal Revenue Service itself has held that professional fees are earned primarily through the reputation and skill of the professional, not through the use of capital, even where there is a large investment in office equipment[49] or subordinate nonprofessional employees performing some of these services.[50] In addition, proposed regulations dealing with Section 1348 of the Internal Revenue Code relating to the 50% maximum tax on earned income, treat capital as a non-income producing factor in service corporations.[51]

Nevertheless, despite the above, the concept of return of investment capital has been raised and must be reckoned with. To reduce or minimize this problem the practitioner should do the following:

1. Keep the capitalization of the corporation as low as possible. If the professional sole practitioner or partnership has substantial equipment, consider keeping the equipment outside the corporation and leasing it to the corporation.
2. Declare dividends on a regular basis. This is a must.

Goodwill As An Income Producing Factor

The issue which may pose as a formidable problem to overcome is that goodwill may be considered as part of the capital of the corporation upon which a dividend may be declared or imputed.[52] Therefore, the problems presented are:

1. Is goodwill in fact transferred by the professional to the corporation when he incorporates;
2. If goodwill is transferred, how should it be valued; and
3. Is goodwill an income producing factor.

Goodwill is essentially that quality which attracts and retains clients to the business establishment. It can be argued that in a professional service organization all of those attractions which draw people to it as clients attach personally to the professional rendering the services and not to the business entity itself. Originally the Internal Revenue Service in cases involving the sale of professional practices, where capital gain versus ordinary income was a factor, supported this position and held that "Transferable goodwill does not attach to the business of a professional man or firm or to any business, the success of which depends solely upon the professional skill, ability, integrity and other personal characteristics of the owner."[53]

However, the courts, have consistently rejected this position and have held that a professional does have goodwill which can be sold to the purchaser of his practice. As the result, the Internal Revenue Service has, over a period of time, modified its position, while giving as little ground as possible from its original position.[54]

In spite of the Internal Revenue Service position, most commentaries on the subject agree with the courts and feel the goodwill of a professional is transferred to the new corporation when the professional incorporates. However, if the Internal Revenue Service raises the issue that a portion of the compensation paid should be declared a dividend based upon the return on invested capital theory, and goodwill being included as part of capital, then certainly the practitioner should counter this attack with the Service's own position that where a business is dependent solely upon the skill and personal characteristics of the owner, no goodwill is transferred. This is certainly the case in most small corporations and if goodwill is not transferred then it cannot be considered a part of capital upon which a return can be expected.

In addition, even if goodwill is considered transferred to the new corporation, one court has held that goodwill is not an income producing factor since the goodwill was a result of the personal efforts of the owners of the business.[55]

Assuming that goodwill is transferred to the corporation, what value should be given to it? Surely anyone who has attempted to sell a professional practice or has tried to finance the purchase of a practice using goodwill as collateral will answer "that goodwill is not worth very much."

The answer in most cases depends upon the particular corporation involved. Certainly a hospital based physician, such as a pathologist or radiologist, does not have very much, if any, goodwill in his practice, since his entire income is generated from rendering services to patients of the hospital. His reputation and skill are not known to the patients nor do they seek admission to the particular hospital because of a particular radiologist or pathologist. On the other hand, an internist or dentist does certainly rely upon his reputation to attract patients to his office.

As a general rule, this author feels that goodwill in a health oriented practice is a very small part of the entire practice. In most cases, it is a situation of supply and demand, and not in reality dependent solely upon the individual's reputation. Nevertheless, *Medical Economics* magazine[56] addressed itself to the value of goodwill and does provide some basis upon which the practitioner can begin.

> Opinion on the precise value you can put on goodwill varies among management consultants. Some figure it on the basis of practice gross, taking goodwill as an amount

approximately equal to the gross receipts of the practice during the most recent three months. Some consultants figure it at a lower figure, basing their valuation on net. ... Using the first formula, a practice grossing $60,000 would have a goodwill valued at $15,000. ... Assuming a $40,000 net, would have goodwill valued at $10,000.

In view of the above, the Internal Revenue Service position on goodwill being transferable, congressional intent that capital is not an income producing factor, one court holding that goodwill is not an income producing factor, this author feels that the threat of having a dividend imputed on goodwill will not pose, except in extreme cases, a serious burden or cost to the professional corporation as one might think.

15 POINT CHECK LIST FOR AVOIDING UNREASONABLE COMPENSATION PROBLEMS

1. Fix anual compensation at a level which will very closely equal the expected net income to be earned by the corporation.
2. Use employment contracts and corporate minutes to document the factors which were used to arrive at compensation to be received by the employee.

   (a) State that compensation paid by corporation is equal to amount earned by employee prior to joining the corporation.

   (b) State that compensation is based upon the skill, experience and knowledge of the practitioner in his specialty. Insert curriculum vitae into records of minutes.

   (c) State that compensation is based upon the duties and responsibilities to be assumed by the employee.

   (d) If employee has outside activities, state that such activities will not materially interfere with his duties as an employee of the corporation.
3. Compensation should not exceed employee's gross billings. If it does, state that employee is being compensated for supervisory and/or administrative duties as well as for personal services.
4. Corporation should not invest in income producing investments. Will be difficult to distribute earnings on investments as compensation.
5. If additional compensation is to be paid above base salary, established criteria for paying bonuses at the beginning of the year before profits are known. Consider establishing incentive compensation formulas.
6. Don't establish incentive compensation on per cent of net profits.
7. If bonuses are paid, state that it is being paid for extra duties assumed by employee or for additional hours worked by employee which was not required of him under the terms of his employment agreement, and as a result, the income of the corporation has increased.
8. Avoid any sudden increases in salary or frequent changes in salary without justifying such changes in the minutes of the Board of Directors.
9. Avoid paying all corporate surplus as bonuses.
10. Avoid paying bonuses in exact proportion to the stockholdings of the recipients. Pay bonuses on production of employees.
11. If bonuses are paid, pay bonuses to employees who are not shareholders as well as to shareholder employees.
12. Keep bonuses or contingent compensation payments small in relation to the base salary.
13. Keep capital of the corporation as low as possible. If professionals have substantial equipment,

consider leasing it to the corporation rather than transferring it.

14. Pay dividends. This is crucial.
15. If dividends are not paid in any year because of lack of funds, this should be stated in the board of directors minutes and that it is the hope of the corporation to be able to declare dividends in the following year.

ALTERNATIVE PREVENTIVE STEPS

In addition to the above steps outlined in the checklist, there are two other alternatives available to the practitioner in coping with the reasonable compensation problem, which are as follows:

1. Have employee reimburse corporation for compensation considered unreasonably by the Internal Revenue Service.
2. Adopt Sub-Chapter S status.

Reimbursement Agreements

One method of protecting the corporation from double taxation in the event that compensation is considered unreasonable, is to provide in the employment agreement that the employee will agree to repay the corporation for any amount he receives as compensation which is disallowed by the Internal Revenue Service. Agreements of this kind have been approved by the Internal Revenue Service and have been recognized by the courts.[57]

Many practitioners believe that the principal advantage of such reimbursement agreements is that they will deter attempts by revenue agents to disallow salaries. If the employee is in a high tax bracket, his deduction upon reimbursement will often produce a greater tax refund than the additional tax due upon the corporation's loss of a deduction, thus making it counter productive for revenue to pursue the attack.[58] However, the insertion of such language may have a reverse effect. In two recent cases, the courts held that reimbursement language was an implied admission that the salary may be unreasonable.[59] Thus, instead of diminishing the problem, such language may enlarge it.

In addition, another disadvantage of the use of such an agreement is that the professional may not have the funds available to repay the disallowed compensation to the corporation. In many cases, it will be better, as a practical matter, to have the corporation pay the tax on the disallowed portion rather than repay it.

Tax Option Corporations

A professional can elect sub-chapter S status under Sections 1371 through 1378 of the Internal Revenue Code, which will enable the corporation to be taxed as a partnership. Therefore, corporations making such an election will greatly minimize, but not eliminate, the reasonable compensation problem.[60] The significant drawback from making such an election is that the contributions to the retirement plan are limited to the H.R. 10 limitation under the Tax Reform Act of 1969. However, with the increase of Keogh limits to $7500, sub-chapter S will now be a useful vehicle for those practitioners who have already incorporated and are contributing within the H.R. 10 limits to their retirement plan and for those practitioners who are considering incorporating who do not want to contribute more than $7500.

FOOTNOTES

[1]Botany Worsted Mills v. United States 278 U.S. 282(1929).

[2]Rev. Proc. 62-32 1962-2 CB 527

[3]I. Goodman "Development of Limitation on Deductions Under Pension and Profit Sharing Plans" Feb. 14, 1972; Rev. Rul. 67-341, 1967-2 CB 156.

[4]East Tenn. Motor Co. v U.S. 453 F2d 494 (1971).

[5]I. Goodman "Establishing A Successful Retirement Program" March 12, 1971, Questions & Answers, Question No. 3.

[6]Regs. 1.404(a)-1(b).

[7]Edwin's, Inc. v. U.S. 73-1, USTC Para. 9169. (1973).

[8]Commissioner v. Lincoln Electric Co. 176 F2 815 (6th Cir. 1949).

[9]Eaton, "Operation of a Professional Corporation" 28th N.Y.U. Federal Tax Institue (1970); Horsley and Dray "Compensating Officer-Stockholders of professional corporations; an analysis" JTAX March, 1971; I. Goodman "Legislation Developments of the Federal Tax Treatment of Pension and Profit Sharing Plans" March 2, 1971, Questions & Answers, question No. 2; Regs. 1.162-7 (b) (3).

[10]Kennedy Name Plate Company 6 TCM 622 (1947) aff'd 170 F2d 196 (9th Cir. 1948).

[11]Appeal of Woodcliff Silk Mills, 1 BTA 715, (1925); Home Packing Company 12 TCM 1217 (1953).

[12]Num Specialty, Inc. v. U.S. 257 F. Supp.1, (1966); N.A. Woodworth Co., 4 TCM 418 (1945); Stern-Slegman-Prins Co. v. U.S. 79 F2d 289 (1935).

[13]Klamath Medical Service Bureau v Commissioner 29 TC 339 (1957) Aff'd 261 F2d 842 (9th Cir. 1958); McClung Hospital, Inc. v. Commisioner 19 TCM 449 (1960).

[14]In the following cases, the court considered experience, training and/or general ability to be a factor in upholding reasonableness:
Hammond Lead Products, Inc. 28 TCM 54 (1969), aff'd 425 F2d 31 (7th Cir. 1970); J.J. Glenn 29 TCM 833 (1970); L.R. Schmaus Co., Inc., 26 TCM 959 (1967), rev'd on another issue, 406 F2d 1044 (7th Cir. 1969); L.J. Ruck, Inc., 28TCM 63 (1969); Sparks Nugget, Inc. 29 TCM 318 (1970); Scott, Krauss News Agency, Inc. 23 TCM 1007 (1964); Thomas Machine Mfg. Co., 23 TCM 1630 (1964); Klug & Smith Company 18 BTA 966 (1930); Kay, Inc., 8 TCM 911 (1949); Faucette Company, Inc. 17 TC 187 (1951); Bedford Sportswear, Inc., 13 TCM 634 (1954); Brown-Forman Distillers Corporation v. United States, 132 F. Supp. 711 (Ct. Cl. 1955); Mahaska Bottling Co., 21 TCM 1530 (1962); King, Quirk & Co., Inc. 20 TCM 1429 (1961); Pennsylvania Containers, Inc. 22 TCM 1235 (1963).

[15]L.R. Schmaus Co., Inc. Ibid,; Gilles Fozen Custard, Inc. 29 TCM 311 (1970); California Vegetable Concentrates, Inc. v. C.I.R. 10 TC 1158 (1948); Gladstone-Arcuni Inc. v. Commissioner 21 TCM 1016 (1962); Glenshaw Glass Company, Inc. v. C.I.R. 55 U.S.T.C. P. 9308, 1955; Firefoam Sales Company v. Commissioner 6 TCM 406 (1947); Anthony Mennuto et al. v. C.I.R., 56 TC 910 (1971); Mahaska Bottling Co., Ibid.; Dixo Company, Inc. 27 TCM 644 (1968); Bush Hog Manufacturing Co. 42 TC 713 (1964); Thomas Machine Mfg. Co., Ibid.

[16]W. C. Hudlow, Jr., 30 TCM 894 (1971); Salem Packing Company 56 TC 131 (1971); Logan Lumber Company 23 TCM 735 (1964), aff'd 365 F2d 846 (5th Cir. 1966); Bev Anderson Chevrolet, Inc. 26 TCM 338 (1967); Atlanta Biltmore Hotel Corp. 22 TCM 1266 (1963), aff'd 349 F2d 677 (5th Cir. 1965).

[17]W. C. Hudlow, Jr., Ibid., (obtain customers, business decisions); Barton-Gillet Comapny 29 TCM 679 (1970) aff'd per curiam 442 F2d 1343 (4th Circuit 1971), (ideas, personal salesmanship); V.H. Monette & Co., Inc. 45 TC 15 (1966), aff'd 374 F2d 116 (4th Cir. 1967) (solicited accounts); S. & B. Realty Co. 54 TC 863 (1970) (supervision); Ivers Department Store 71-2 U.S.T.C. Para. 9611 (1971) (advice); Dahlem Foundation, Inc. 54 TC 1566 (1970); Bringwald, Inc. 334 F2d 639 (Ct. Cl. 1964); Pennsylvania Container's, Inc. Note 14; In the following cases the courts were very critical of the failure of the employee to perform, or even to have, significant specific duties: Issac Engel Realty Co., Inc 22 TCM 1372 (1963); Alicia Ruth, Inc. 28 TCM 262 (1969); Craigs Drug Stores, Inc. 28 TCM 1104 (1969); Atlanta Biltmore Hotel Corp., Note 16.

[18]See Note 13.

[19]In the following cases the court noted that like firms were paying comparable salaries for like services:
Ward Trucking Corp. 24 TCM 217 (1965); Van's Chevrolet, Inc. 26 TCM 809 (1967); Young Auto Parts 27 TCM 778 (1968); Gordy Tire Co. 296 F2d 476 (Ct. CL. 1962); G.H. Ehrlich 30 TCM 317 (1971); Salem Packing Co., Note 16; J.J. Glenn, 29 TCM 833 (1970); Appelton Electric Co., 26 TCM 1043 (1967); Manu-Mine Research and Development Co. 26 TCM 1259 (1967); Rust-Oleum Corporation v. Ernest J. Sauber 1 A.F.T.R. 2d 994 (N.D. Ill. 1958); Savko Brothers Col, Inc. 22 TCM 1014 (1963), aff'd 338 F2d 956 (6th Cir. 1964); Appeal of Woodcliff Silk Mills, Note 16.In the following cases, the court noted that like firms were not paying comparable salaries for like services:
H.G. Hatt 28 TCM 1194 (1969); Griffin & Co., Inc. 389 F2d 802 (Ct. Cl. 1968); Harolds Club 22 TCM 969 (1963), aff'd 340 F2d 861 (9th Cir. 1965).

In the following cases, the court noted with disfavor in findings against the taxpayer the absence of proof of comparable salaries: Northlich, Stolley, Inc. 368 F2d 272 (Ct. Cl. 1966); Craigs Drug Store, Inc., Note 17; Barton-Gillet Co., Note 17; R. Guzowski 26 TCM 666 (1967); Hampton Cor. 23 TCM 899 (1964) aff'd per curiam, 65-2 U.S.T.C. Para. No. 9611 (9th Cir. 1965).

[20]Regs. §1-162-7(b)(3).

[22]Supra. "Relationship of Professional Income Prior to Incorporation to Corporate Salary" p. 58.

[23]Contingent Compensation is herein defined as a supplement to a base salary determined in accordance with a pre-established formula. A bonus is herein defined as a supplement to a base salary established without regard to a prior, specific formula.

[24]In Pacific Grains, Inc. v. Commissioner of Internal Revenue, 399 F2d 603 (9th Cir. 1968), the court held that substantial bonuses paid just prior to the end of each taxable year at issue, apparently to avoid unreasonable accumulations, constituted

dividend; in Nor-Cal Adjutsters, 30 TCM 837 (1971), the court disallowed bonuses given only to shareholder-employees, the amounts being determined on purely the basis of the availability of cash and percentage of shareholdings, not on the basis of client billings ("a more appropriate gauge of what he deserved"). Likewise, in W.C. Hudlow, Jr., Note 16, the court disallowed a bonus system whereby the President was given a relatively small base salary plus substantial bonuses apparently based on the level of corporate profits. The court noted with disfavor the facts that the only employee receiving bonuses was the President shareholder, the bonuses were not paid pursuant to any long-established incentive formula, and that the President devoted much of his time to other corporations.

[25]Bluefries-New York, Inc. v. Commissioner 5 TCM 58 (1946).

[26]Skyland Oldsmobile, Inc. v. Commisssioner 31 TCM 47 (1972); G.H. Ehrlich, Note 19.

[27]Brown-Forman Distillers Corporation v. United States, Note 14; Weaver Airline Personnel School, Inc. v. Bookwalter 218 F. Supp. 599 (W.D. Mo. 1963); Home Packing Company v. Commissioner, Note 11.

[28]American Allsafe Company, Inc. v. Commissioner 13 TCM 95, 101 (1954); Hammond Lead Products, Inc. v. Commissioner, Note 14; Watertown Abattoir Co., 22 TCM 258 (1963); Hoffman Radio Corporation v. Commissioner of Internal Revenue 177 F2d 264 (9th Cir. 1949).

[29]Home Packing Company v. Commissioner, Note 27; American Allsafe Company, Inc. v. Commissioner, Note 28; Charles Schneider & Co., Inc. v. Commissioner 32 TCM 555 (1973).

[30]Am-Plus Storage Battery Company v. Commissioner of Internal Revenue 35 F2d 167 (7th Cir. 1929); Anthony Mennouto, et al. v. Commissioner, Note 15; Craigs Drug Stores, Inc., Inc., Note 17.

[31]K.D. Smith 24 TCM 899 (1965); Thomas Machine Mfg. Co., Note 14; Watertown Abattoir Co., Note 28; California Vegetable Concentrates, Inc. v. Commissioner of Internal Revenue 10 TC 1158 (1948).

[32]The Barton-Gillet Company, Note 17; City Chevrolet Company v. Commissioner 228 F2d 894 (4th Cir. 1956); Irby Construction Company v United States 290 F2d 824 (Ct. Cl. 1961).

[33]Giles Industries, Inc. v. United States, P-H Para. 58,023 (1973) (Ct. Cl. Commissioner Report).

[34]Superior Pattern & Manufacturing Company v. Commissioner 18 TCM 343 (1959); Skyland Oldsmobile, Inc. v. Commissioner, Note 26; G.H. Ehrlich, Note 19; Weaver Airline Personnel School, Inc. v. Bookwalter, Note 27; Watertown Abbatoir, Note 28; Thomas Machine Mfg. Co., Note 14; K.D. Smith, Note 31.

[35]Barton-Gillet Company, Note 17; Charles Schneider & Co., Inc. Note 29; Pacific Grains, Inc., Note 24; Nor-Cal Adjusters, Note 24.

[36]Note 17

[37]Gladstone-Arcuni, Inc. v. Commissioner, Note 15; Shafer Electric Co., Inc. v. Commissioner 5 TCM 603 (1946); Savko Brothers Co., Inc., Note 19; Griswold Rubber Co., Inc. 24 TCM 184 (1965) employer salaries totaling over 60% of net income were approved in non-personal service businesses.

[38]Kay, Inc. v. Commissioner, Note 14; Firefoam Sales Company v. Commissioner, Note 15.

[39]Weaver Airline Personnel School, Inc. v. Bookwalter, Note 27.

[40]See Footnotes 37 and 38.

[41]McCandles Tile Service, 422 F2d 1336 (Ct. Cl. 1970); Barton-Gillet Co., Note 17; Horsley and Dray, "Compensating officer-stockholders of professional corporations; an analysis" JTAX March, 1971.

[42]Pacific Grains, Inc., Note 24; B. Perlmutter 44 TC 382, aff'd 373 F2d 45 (10th Cir. 1967); Logan Lumber Co., Note 16; Jones Brothers Bakery, Inc., 411 F2d 1282 (1969); Nor-Cal Adjusters Note 24.

[43]Note 13.

[44]Note 41.

[45]Note 17.

[46]Note 24.

[47]In Skyland Oldsmobile, Inc. v. Commissioner, Note 26, a base salary plus a large year-end bonus (not determined by any fixed formula) paid to the owner-employee was upheld despite the failure to pay dividends in any of the three taxable years. The court noted the traditional grounds of long hours, considerable duties, and clear responsibility for corporated success-McCandles, Barton-Gillet and Nor-Cal Adjusters were not mentioned. In G.H. Ehrlich, Note 19, and Anthony Mennuto, Note 15, the court made no mention of whether dividends had been paid or not, rather focusing on the traditional tests of long hours and productivity. In Office Communications Company, Inc. v Commissioner, 31 TCM 33 (1972), the court allowed the salary of the President-sole shareholder despite the fact that this produced a net loss for the year. The court presented the key test as the value of the employee's services to any unrelated employer under similar circumstances. In Dahlem Foundations, Inc., Note 17, the court, without much discussion, found the salaries reasonable by applying "the traditional tests to facts and circumstances of the case..." In Equipment Rental Co., Inc. v. United States of America, (W.D. Ky. 1973), 73-1 USTC Para. 9475, the court instructed the jury that first consider whether the alleged compensation was paid because of ownership of the business or services rendered; the jury was told that a factor to consider win this regard was the corporation's dividend history and that the absence of dividends was only "some evidence" that the supported compensation constituted a dividend. The court went on to state that if the jury believed that the compensation was in fact for personal services, it should then determine whether the compensation was reasonable in amount. Giles Industries, Inc. v. United States, Note 33. The Internal Revenue Service argued that under any circumstance, 15% of profits (before federal taxes and salaries in dispute) were not deductible on the basis of the formula employed in McCandless. In his report the Court of Claims Commissioner rejected this reading of McCandless for the following reasons:
(1)McCandless admitted that there is no precise formula, e.g., 15%, for determining a reasonable dividend. The facts of the particular case are determinative of what is reasonable. (2)In McCandless there were two officer-shareholders, each owning 50% of the stock and correspondingly receiving 50% of the profits; dividends were never paid. (3)In Giles, three of four officers were shareholders, while two of five shareholders were not officers (although wives of officers); compensation was not proportional to

shares held; compensation was only 27.6% of profits (pre-tax and pre-salaries in dispute). Most importantly 6.85% of shareholders' original investment was paid in dividends, a larger percentage than paid by similar companies. It is interesting that the dividend referred to was forced on the taxpayer due to the Internal Revenue Service disallowance of the claim that this amount was a loan to the President and the largest shareholder.

[48]Gladstone-Arcune, Inc. v. Commissioner, Note 15; Klug & Smith Company v. Commissioner, Note 14; Shafer Electric Co., Inc. v. Commissioner, Note 37; Kay, Inc. v. Commissioner, Note 14; Firefoam Sales Company v. Commissioner, Note 15; Alexander & Garrett v. United States, 21 F2d 547 (S.D. Ga. 1927); Weaver Airline Personnel School, Inc. v. Bookwalter, Note 27; Spinner, Inc., 63-1USTC Para. 9168 (1963).

[49]Rev. Rul. 57-141 CB 1957-1, 14 "Inasmuch as the amount of capital employed has only an incidental affect on the amount of profits derived from professional fees, the growth of the profession being dependent primarily on the reputation and technical skill of a doctor, dentist or other professional taxpayer, it is held that such capital is not a material income-producing factor in the taxpayer's business."

[50]Mem. 3802, IX-1 CB, 121 (1930).

[51]Moore "Capital as a material income-providing factor for 1348 purposes: An analysis" JTAX June, 1973.

[52]Worthy "IRS chief counsel outlines what is ahead for professional corporations" 32 JTAX February, 1970.

[53]Rev. Rul. 57-480 1957-2 CB 47.

[54]Rev. Rul. 60-301 1960 CB-2, 15, held that even if the firm name is transferred to purchaser of the business, if business is dependent *solely* upon the skill and other personal characteristics of owner, no goodwill is transferred; in Rev. Rul. 64-235, 1964-2 CB, 18, the Service held"...the Service will no longer take the position that, as a matter of law, a one-man professional practice cannot have salable goodwill...the extent to which the proceeds of a sale can be allocated to goodwill will be determined on the facts rather than by whether the business is, or is not, dependent solely upon the professional skill or other personal characteristics of the owner." Ruling then held that no goodwill is sold if entire practice is not sold; in Rev. Rul. 70-45 1970-1 CB 17, the Service held that there can be a partial transfer of goodwill when a professional admits new partners.

[55]American Lawyers Co. 21 BTA 370 (1930).

[56]Medical Economics "As of right now, what is your practice worth?" December 20, 1971.

[57]Vincent E. Oswald 49 TC 645 (1969).

[58]Anderson "Compensation in Professional Corporations — A Survery of Opportunities and Obstacles" 18th Practical Lawyer, March, 1972.

[59]Schneider & Co., Inc. 500 2d 148 (Ca-8) 1974, aff's TCM 1973-130, cert. den.; Saia Electric, Inc. TCM 1974-290; Rizzo and Carey "Salary reimbursement agreements: How they are used today; drawbacks; future Problems" 43JTAX 72 (1975).

[60]For discussion on sub-chapter S corporations, see chapter 2 "How to Organize a Professional Corporation Tax-Wisely" section entitled "Tax Option Corporations (sub-chapter S)" page 32.

5

DRAFTING THE EMPLOYMENT CONTRACT

It is most important when organizing a professional corporation consisting of two or more professional employees to thoroughly discuss and decide the various aspects of the working relationship of the professionals to each other and to the corporation. The success of the corporation will often depend upon the ability of the parties to develop a harmonious working relationship. Therefore, careful draftsmanship and planning at the organizational stage of the corporation will help avoid unnecessary disputes which could arise between the parties, and even result in the dissolution of the corporation.

Therefore, one of the most important corporate documents is the employment contract. This instrument should represent the intent of the parties, and should be so drafted that the parties will be readily able to determine their obligations and responsibilities to the corporation and the corporation's obligation to them.

In addition, the employment contract provides another opportunity to further distinguish between the corporation as the employer and the professional as the employee. For this reason, an employment contract is even important in the one-man professional corporation.

The following is an 18-point checklist of the issues which should be considered by the professionals when formalizing their relationship with each other and with the corporation. This chapter will discuss these issues in detail.

18-Point Checklist of Issues to be Answered by Employment Contract

1. Will the employee be expected to devote all of his time to the business of the corporation
2. Will the employee be permitted to assume duties and responsibilities outside the corporate business
    A. What outside activities will be permitted

   B. Will said outside activities materially interfere with the duties the employee has been hired to perform
   C. Will the income generated from such outside activities be the income of the employee or the corporation
3. What authority will the corporation have over the employee
4. How should the employee's salary be paid
5. What happens if earnings of corporation are not sufficient to pay employee his salary
6. What method should be used to increase the employee's base salary
7. Should an employee be paid his salary while disabled
8. If an employee is paid his salary while disabled, for what period of time should it be continued
9. How should disability be defined
10. Should disability income protection insurance be used to provide disability benefits
11. Should the stock held by a disabled employee be redeemed after a certain period of time
12. Should an employee be entitled to severance pay upon the termination of his employment
13. If an employee is entitled to severance pay, how should it be determined
14. Will disability income benefits affect the amount of severance pay
15. How will the corporation treat expenses incurred personally by its employees on the business of the corporation
   A. Should the corporation reimburse the employee directly for said expenses
   B. Should the corporation require that the employee incur said expenses as a condition of his employment
   C. Should the employees transfer their automobiles or equipment, either by sale or a part of the initial capitalization to the corporation
16. What events should cause the termination of the employment contract
17. How should convention and vacation time be arranged
18. Should the employment agreement provide restrictive covenant provisions

EMPLOYMENT RELATIONSHIP

One of the first issues which must be decided is whether the employee is expected to devote his entire time and energy to the business of the corporation, or whether he will be permitted to participate in outside business or charitable affairs. Generally, the decision is based upon whether the outside activities will interfere with the duties to be assumed by the professional in his capacity as an employee. If the answer is no, the outside activities are usually permitted. Nevertheless, there are various other factors which must be considered and no one rule can be applied in all cases.

Charitable and Teaching Activities

Charitable and teaching activities of an employee will normally enhance the reputation and prestige of the corporation in the community. Therefore, such activities are usually permitted to be performed by the employee, provided they do not interfere with the duties he is required to perform for the benefit of the corporation.

Services Rendered on a Fee for Service Basis

If the fees generated by an employee who is performing professional services outside the business of the corporation on a fee for service basis, or who subsequently desires to engage in such activity, are considered the income of the corporation, such activities will generally be permitted, provided, of course, that such activities do not deter from the professional's primary duties and responsibilities.

Normally, most professionals will wish to have the outside income paid to the corporation. In this manner, more money is available to be contributed to the retirement plan. At times, however, it may be impossible or inadvisable to have the income paid to the corporation, either because of the policy established by the payor or because of the fringe benefits the employee might lose if he lost his employee status. For example, the professional may be paid a small salary by a hospital for consulting services. As a result of this employment relationship, he may be entitled to certain fringe benefits, such as health insurance. If this employee status was changed, and the income was paid directly to the corporation, he would not longer be entitled to this fringe benefit, since he has become an independent contractor and, as such, is not entitled to benefits given to employees. Thus, the employee will have to pay for his own health insurance. Therefore, in such cases, it is often advisable to continue to have the income paid directly to the employee.

If the income cannot or should not be made payable to the corporation for the reasons stated above, the minutes of the Board of Directors discussing the salary of the employee and the employment contract should acknowledge the fact that the employee will be performing services outside the business of the corporation which will not materially interfere with his duties to be performed for the corporation and that the income derived from such services will belong to the employee personally rather than to the corporation. However, if a one-man professional corporation is involved, it is important that the outside activities are a very small part of the entire practice which is incorporated.[1]

CORPORATE AUTHORITY

It is most important to take advantage of every opportunity to distinguish the corporation as the employer and the professional as the employee. The employment contract affords such an opportunity. The agreement by itself recognizes the employment relationship between the professional and the corporation. Nevertheless, this image should be further strengthened by providing language in the agreement to the effect that the corporation shall have complete control over the employee in regard to the scheduling of work hours, the right to supervise and review the work of the employee, and generally establish policy affecting the manner of performing the duties to be assumed by the employee. In addition, the personal holding company problem can be minimized if the contract provides that the corporation will have the power to refuse or accept any patient for treatment and the right to allocate patients among its employees.[2]

SALARY

Time Payment of Salary

The cash flow of a corporation may fluctuate, and therefore, it may be difficult for some corporations, especially in small professional corporations, to pay the base salary of an employee on a regular fixed basis. In employment contracts in which the corporation is obligated to pay the professional's base salary in fixed installments, it is not uncommon for the corporation to pay the professional's net salary and lack the sufficient funds to pay the withholding taxes at the appropriate time and thereby incur a penalty. In addition, the professional often becomes quite concerned that his employment contract is locking him into a fixed annual salary which must be paid even though the income of the corporation may not be sufficient. This fear of being required to meet this fixed obligation may even deter a professional from incorporating or may place unnecessary anxiety upon him. To eliminate this unnecessary problem, the author provides in the employment agreement in the section regarding employee's salary the following language: "That the annual base salary of the employee will be paid at such time and in amounts as the treasurer shall deem appropriate in his discretion in view of the earnings of the corporation."

Although every attempt should be made to pay the employee's base salary in convenient installments, the above language will permit the treasurer to postpone payments if the income of the corporation is not adequate. In such an event, the postponed payment may be made in the following week or month. In the event the income of the corporation is not sufficient to pay the total salary of its shareholder employee, the difference between the salary paid to the employee and his required salary should be considered a debt of the corporation and paid to the employee when the earnings of the corporation permit. Thus, if the employee's base salary is $58,000 and in 1974 he only receives $52,000, then the $6000 difference is a liability of the corporation and should be paid in 1975 if possible. Thus, in 1975 the employee will receive $64,000.

Increases in Compensation

The employment agreement should specify the basis upon which the payment of bonuses or additional compensation will be made to the employee. Not only will this provide an incentive to the employee, but it will also help avoid a dividend label being placed upon the bonus by the Internal Revenue Service. As was discussed in the previous chapter,[3] it is easier to substantiate the payment of a bonus as a reasonable additional payment for services rendered, based upon a formula or policy adopted by the corporation before profits are known rather than declaring a discretionary bonus after profits have been determined. Therefore, if the reasonable compensation problem is to be minimized, the practitioner must give careful consideration to this issue when drafting the employment contract.

DISABILITY INCOME

Period of Disability

Determining the period of time and amount a disabled professional employee's salary should be continued is one of the most perplexing problems facing the professional corporation when negotiating the employment contract.

The answer will often depend upon the nature of the practice in which the corporation is involved. In practices where the corporation renders its services directly to the public, the period that disability income will continue will usually be longer than in a corporation that is rendering services to a hospital for a percentage of the gross fees. In the first case, there is often a time span between when services are rendered and when payment is received. Therefore, the corporation will continue to receive income generated by the employee from the services he rendered prior to his disability. This is certainly not the case when a physician, such as a pathologist or radiologist, is paid in the early part of the month following the month in which he performed the services. In this case, there are no accounts receivable which are ever outstanding. Therefore, any disability income which is paid is derived from the income earned by the disabled employee's associates and not from the services rendered by the employee prior to his disability.

The acceptance of the premise that the corporation may receive income which was generated by a disabled employee for which he should be compensated, provides a basis upon which the disability compensation provisions can be determined. The length of time disability income will continue and in the amount they will be paid is usually based upon the estimated amount of accounts receivable generated by the employee prior to his disability and the length of time in which they can be expected to be collected. In corporations rendering services to the public, it is not uncommon to have income paid to an employee over a period of time, which decreases in amount at certain stated intervals. For example, full pay for the first two months of disability, one-half pay for the next two months of disability, and one-quarter pay for the next two months. In corporations rendering services to a health institution, an employee may have one month of disability at full pay and one month at one-half pay.

Again, there can be no set answer which can be applied to every case. The professionals of each corporation must examine their own particular situation and decide for what time period and in what amounts they wish to continue the salary for an associate who has become disabled.

Definition of Disability

The definition of disability is obviously important, since it determines when disability income payments begin. Normally, disability is defined as the inability of the employee to perform the majority of the duties for which he was employed. To provide for a more stringent definition of disability, such as disability as defined for social security purposes, will certainly prevent most professionals from collecting disability benefits, which is certainly not the intent or objective of the corporation.

The Use of Disability Income Protection Insurance

One of the more important nonretirement fringe benefits is the ability of the corporation to provide its employees with disability income protection insurance,[4] and certainly the use of such insurance is an important consideration in determining the disability income provisions of an employee's employment contract.

The first consideration is whether disability income payments which are required to be made should come in its entirety or in part from disability income protection insurance proceeds. If one accepts the premise set forth above that a disabled employee, in most corporations, is merely receiving payments which represent income he generated prior to becoming disabled, then the answer will be no. Generally, the author feels that this is the correct approach, and that disability income protection insurance proceeds should not be considered part of the total amount due the employees in the event of his disability. Therefore, it is possible for an employee to receive full disability benefits from the corporation and, in addition, the proceeds from the insurance policy.

However, since the purpose of disability income protection insurance is to replace lost income it is often preferable to have the disability insurance benefits commence at that moment the corporation ceases to pay the employee disability income under his employment contract. Thus, if the employee is receiving payments from the corporation for six months, then there would be a six-month waiting period before insurance benefits will begin. If the corporation feels that it may not be able to afford to continue disability payments for an extended period of time, then the payment period of the corporation should be reduced, and the disability income protection insurance benefits commence earlier.

Cumulative Disability vs. Consecutive Disability

Another important consideration which can cause a great deal of difficulty if not provided for in the employment contract, is whether periods of disability should be considered cumulative or consecutive. The choice will produce completely different results in most cases.

For example, assume the disability period is defined as full pay for the first two months of disability and one-half pay for the next two months of disability and thereafter no compensation is paid. If the period of disability is considered consecutive, then the following situation could result. An employee may become disabled for a period lasting two months and then return to work. A short time later, he becomes disables and is out of work for another one month. In this case, the employee will receive three months full pay because his return to work broke the consecutive period of disability.

However, if disability was considered cumulative in the above situation, then the employee would only have been entitled to one-half pay when he became disabled for a second time.

Therefore, it is crucial that the employment contract provide whether periods of disability are to be cumulative or consecutive; otherwise, in situations similar to the one discussed above, serious difficulties may arise if the disabled employee claims that he is entitled to full disability pay for a period of time considerably longer than contemplated or expected.

Redemption of Stock from Employee in Event of Prolonged Disability

It is quite possible that a shareholder employee may become so seriously ill that he will never be able to resume the duties and responsibilities he performed for the corporation prior to his disability.

Therefore, serious consideration should be given for providing in the employment contract a provision requiring the redemption of the stock of a disabled employee of the corporation after a certain stated period of time of disability.

Such a provision will insure that only individuals who are able to perform the services for which the corporation was organized will be shareholders. A disabled stockholder has all the rights as such; namely, to be notified of meetings of the shareholders, to be entitled to any dividends distributed by the corporation in proportion to his shareholdings in the corporation and to vote for corporate officers and upon other corporate decisions requiring shareholders' consent. Certainly it is more desirable for individuals having such rights to be actively engaged in the business of the corporation. Otherwise, practical legal difficulties may arise where the disabled stockholder's presence is required at meetings or his signature is required on certain corporate documents.

In addition, stock that is held by a stockholder who is disabled in a professional corporation dilutes the interests of the other stockholder employees, which will make it more difficult to sell or attract a new associate to the corporation.

If a disabled shareholder recognizes the burden he may place upon the corporation by his ownership in the stock of the corporation and agrees to sell his stock back to the corporation, there will be no problem. However, it may be difficult for an individual who has been active all his life to accept the fact that he will no longer be able to work at his chosen profession. As a result, he may feel that his ownership in the stock of the corporation still makes him an active part of the corporation, or that his disability is only temporary and he will be returning to work in the near future, and therefore, feels that there is no reason why his stock should be redeemed. It is the purpose of providing for the mandatory redemption of stock to prevent such a situation from occurring.

The period of disability which must elapse before the mandatory redemption provisions take effect should be decided by the shareholders when forming a corporation. There is no correct time span, and the period of time which makes the individuals secure is the appropriate one to adopt. As a general rule, many corporations usually provide that the corporation has the right, unless it decides otherwise, to redeem the stock of the disabled participant immediately after his disability income payments cease.

SEVERANCE PAY

An important issue which must be resolved is whether a professional employee will be entitled to severance pay upon his termination of employment, and if he is, the method of determining the amount of such benefit. If we proceed upon the same assupmtion as we did in regard to diasability income, namely, that the corporation will receive income which was generated by the employee prior to his disability, then we can equally conclude that the purpose of severance pay is to give to an employee an amount which equals the fair value of the services he has rendered prior to the date of his termination of employment for which he has not yet been compensated. The issue then becomes one of determining the value of the benefit conferred upon the corporation and in computing the amount to which the employee should be entitled.

The issue is further clouded, however, when the employee is also a shareholder. In this instance, we become concerned with a very important collateral issue of determining a value for the stock of the employee which will be redeemed by the corporation and more specifically, whether accounts receivable should be included as part of the value of the stock.

The method of valuing the stock will directly affect the amount which is available for severance pay. If the value of the stock includes accounts receivable, the benefit conferred upon the corporation will be paid back to the employee shareholder when his stock is redeemed. If accounts receivable are not included in the value of the stock, then the corporaiton should compensate the employee in an amount equal to his share of the accounts receivable expected to be collected by the corporation after the termination date. Thus, once the value of the benefit conferred upon the corporation is determined, it becomes a question of whether the employee should be compensated by including the value of said benefit in the value of the stock which will be redeemed or by paying the value of said benefit in the form of severance pay to the employee.

For the reasons subsequently discussed in detail,[5] it is more desirable to pay out the accounts receivable attributed to the services of the employee in the form of severance pay, rather than as part of the value of the employee's stock.

Normally, if a non-shareholder employee terminates his employment, he will only receive the income accrued but unpaid as of the date of termination. However, if a severance benefit is provided, it will either be determined in the same manner as a shareholder employee or in an arbitrary amount determined by the Board of Directors.

Determining the Amount of Severance Pay

Normally, the shareholder employee will be entitled to his proportionate part of the corporation's outstanding accounts receivable as of the date of his termination. Although there are various methods of determining the employee's proportionate share of accounts receivable, one of the most common methods is as follows:

1. Determine the value of the accounts receivable of the corporation as of the end of the month in which the employee's employment was terminated. Normally, there is a cut-off point in which accounts receivable older than a certain age will not be included on the basis that they probably will not be collected.
2. From the amount computed above, the outstanding accounts payable are subtracted.
3. A determination is then made as to the anticipated collectability of the accounts receivable after complying with items 1 and 2. This is accomplished by multiplying the result in item 1 by a percentage which represents the anticipated amount which will be collectable. For example: 80%.
4. A determination is then made to what portion of the result in item 3 the employee will be entitled. This is done by multiplying item 3 by a fraction, the numerator of which represents the employee's compensation and the denominator of which represents the compensation paid to all other professionals employed by the corporation.

The Relationship Between Disability Income and Severance Pay

In some cases, an employee's employment may terminate as a result of illness or other disability which prevents him from being able to perform the services for which he was employed. In this situation, the employee probably received disability income payments from the corporation for a certain stated period of time. Since the purpose of the disability income payments made by the corporation to the employee was to compensate the employee for services rendered for the benefit of the corporation for which he has not yet been compensated, the employee would receive double benefits if he were to receive a full severance pay benefit as computed above, since severance pay is based upon the same premise as disability income pay. Thus, to avoid double payments, the employment contract should provide that if the employee has received disability income payments, then this amount will be subtracted from the amount otherwise due the employee under the section regarding severance pay.

VACATION

The parties must agree as to the vacation period to which the employee will be entitled. In this regard, it must be decided whether time spent at professional conventions and seminars will be considered part of vacation time, and it must be decided whether vacation time is to be cumulative.

There is no set answer to the above questions. The policy adopted by the corporation will obviously depend upon the philosophy of the parties themselves. As a general rule, this author has found that most corporations provide that convention time will not be considered part of vacation time, and that annual vacation time is not carried over to future years, unless otherwise decided by the Board of Directors.

RESTRICTIVE COVENANTS

Whether or not to provide restrictive covenants in the employment contract may be the most difficult issue to resolve and may cause bitter feelings for all parties if not handled with understanding. In many states such clauses are considered in restraint of trade and therefore invalid. It is in the states which permit "reasonable" restrictive covenants in which we became involved with the problem.

The purpose of the covenant is to prevent an employee from competing with the corporation in the event he leaves the employ of the corporation. On the other hand, the employee does not want to find himself in a situation where he must move his home to another city or town because he is prohibited from practicing in specified geographical area because an employment relationship did not prove satisfactory to one or both parties.

Keeping in mind the purpose of a restrictive covenant, the following discussion may provide possible solutions to the problem.

During the first year of employment, the employee will often not have the opportunity to develop a strong following among the patients or clients of the corporation. Therefore, the author will rarely provide for a restrictive covenant if employment is terminated during this period. The corporation will usually have little to fear in losing a significant number of patients to the departing employee and the employee will not be penalized because the relationship dissolved, for whatever reason, during this trial period.

It can be argued that the mere presence of a new professional in the area will cause the corporation to lose clients or patients and therefore the restrictive covenant should be inserted into the agreement. However, such competition would arise at any time a new professional with the same specialty moves into the area. Since the employee will provide no more of a threat to the corporation that if he had opened his practice in the same area in which the corporation is located without having been associated with the corporation.

However, the above is not true when the employee has been employed with the corporation for many years and has treated many of the same patients on numerous occasions. In such cases, the patients often seek the services of one particular professional in the corporation, and if the employee leaves the employ of the corporation, he will be able to attract many patients or clients away from the corporation. Whether the employee should be restricted from practicing in the area in which the corporation is located should depend upon the reason for the termination.

If the employee voluntarily terminates his employment, without cause, then it is reasonable, in the author's opinion, to provide that the employee will not be able to practice within an area in close proximity with the corporation. However, if the corporation has terminated the employee's employment, without cause, the employee should not be penalized because of incompatability or because his skill is below what was expected from him. In such situations, a possible alternative solution is to have the departing employee pay the corporation a certain established fee for the privilege of being able to practice in the same locality as the corporation. If the employment relationship is terminated by the mutual consent of all parties, then there should be no restrictive covenant.

WATCH THIS

If restrictive covenants are to be enforced by the courts in states where they are legal, they must be reasonable both in distance and in the term of the covenant.

TERMINATION OF EMPLOYMENT

Every employment contract should provide for the method of termination prior to the expiration of the term of the agreement. The following are the most customary events causing termination of the employment agreement:

1. Whenever the employee is disqualified to practice the profession for which he was employed to perform.
2. Whenever the corporation and the employee shall mutually agree in writing to terminate the agreement.
3. Upon the death of the employee.
4. Upon the disability of the employee to perform the services for which he was employed for a certain stated period of time.
5. Upon prior notice by either party to the other of his intention to terminate the employment relationship. The time span between the date of notice and the effective date may be thirty, sixty, ninety, or any time period the parties feel is equitable.

In situations where a new associate is employed, he may be concerned when his employment may be terminated on short notice. This is especially true when the new associate has moved his family and himself to a new location to take the new position. A fair solution to this problem is to provide that during the first year of employment, the employment contract may be terminated at any time upon prior notice from one party to the other within a stated period of time. Thereafter, the employee's employment may not be terminated until the end of the succeeding year's employment, and will continue for the year following unless prior notice is given by the corporation to the employee of its intention to terminate. In this way, both parties have an opportunity to develop their working relationship during the first year, and surely if the parties are incompatible for any reason, such problems should be noticeable within the first year. In the first year, the employee has the risk that the employment relationship may not develop as he had hoped. Thereafter, the employee is protected from unexpected termination and has security for the following year, while the corporation will still have the right of termination. In this way, both parties' interests are adequately protected.

HOW TO HANDLE BUSINESS EXPENSES

The policy adopted by a corporation in handling the business expenses of its professional employees incurred by them in the course of their employment is of prime importance, since proper planning will eliminate possible sources of friction among the professional employees. The most frequent expenses which a professional will incur personally are: automobile, home office, entertainment, attendance at professional conventions, and dues in professional societies.

Prior to incorporating, the sole practitioner or partner in a professional partnership would deduct personally the above expenses which he incurred, irrespective of what expenses or the size of the deduction which his partners were claiming for the same items on their returns. Incorporating changes this simplified approach.

In one-man corporations there is usually no problem in establishing a corporate policy in regard to the treatment of expenses. However, in corporations consisting of more than one professional, problems may arise since the professional employees may all drive automobiles of different values, some may or may not take a deduction for a home office, and the expenses incurred for entertainment and convention attendance may differ. In such cases, a policy must be devised whereby all employees are treated fairly.

This section will address itself to two areas:

1. How to handle the business expenses in a one-man professional corporation.
2. How to handle business expenses in corporations consisting of more than one professional employee.

One-Man Professional Corporations

In one-man professional corporations, the professional and his advisor have the luxury of being able to select the most advantageous method of handling business expenses incurred by the employee without concern as to how said method will affect any other individual.

Generally, there are three alternatives available in handling home office, entertainment, convention, and other miscellaneous professional expenses, which are as follows:

1. The corporation reimburses the employee directly for such expenses.
2. The employee is required to incur such expenses personally as a condition of his employment, and deducts them on his personal income tax returns as an unreimbursed business expense.
3. The corporation pays for some of the expenses and the employee pays for others.

In many cases, the corporation will elect to reimburse the employee directly for all expenses incurred during a certain period of time, and the corporation issues a check to the employee for the appropriate amount.

However, many practitioners feel that the corporation should not reimburse the employee directly, since more funds will be available to be contributed to the retirement plan if the employee paid these expenses personally and deducted them on his own income tax return. That is, if all expenses total $4500 per year, and the employee pays the amount personally, then the corporation will have an additional $4500 to divide between additional salary for the employee and additional retirement plan contributions. The additional salary will have no adverse income tax consequences to the employee since he will be able to offset said increase by a $4500 deduction for unreimbursed business expenses.

It is the author's opinion that such a policy should not be adopted for a one-man professional corporation for these reasons:

1. *Lack of Corporateness* - The most important aspect of running a professional corporation is that all business activities be conducted in the name of the corporation. This is especially true for a one-man professional corporation. Therefore, since the employee is now conducting his profession in the name of the corporation and not personally, business expenses incurred by him in the course of his business should certainly be the responsibility of the corporation rather than of the employee. The corporation, by assuming the responsibilities of the expenses of its employees, provides another example of the "corporateness" of the professional corporation.

2. *Unreasonable Compensation Problem* - If the employee assumes personally certain business expenses, then his annual salary will be increased, which will certainly not assist in reducing the unreasonable compensation problem. Obviously, the higher the income, the greater the risk of an unreasonable compensation attack.

3. *Employee Reporting of Reimbursed Expenses on Personal Tax Return* - It is much easier for the employee to be reimbursed for expenses incurred during the course of his employment rather than deduct them on his personal tax return. If the employee accounts to the corporation, he will not have to report the reimbursement of these expenses on his income tax return. If expenses are not reimbursed, then he must properly itemize the expenses he is claiming with the appropriate supporting evidence. In addition, some expenses may be lost if he elects the standard deduction on his return.[6]

The above reasons for not favoring the assumption of business expenses by the employee personally certainly apply to corporations consisting of more than one professional, although to a lesser extent in regard to item one. Nevertheless, circumstances may be such, where good judgment dictates that the employee assume these expenses. In such cases, it should be provided in the employee's employment contract that such expenses are to be incurred and paid by the employee personally as a condition of his employment. This language will assure that the employee will be entitled to deduct the amount of such expenses. Otherwise, it may be presumed by the Internal Revenue Service that the employee voluntarily assumed these expenses, which will result in a lost deduction to the employee.

Automobile

There is another method in which automobile expenses may be handled, other than the employee being directly reimbursed by the corporation or by the professional incurring such expenses personally. Another alternative is that the automobile can be transferred to the corporation as part of the contribution to capital or sold to the corporation by the employee. The author however, sees no particular advantages in having the corporation own the automobile, and there are several disadvantages, which are as follows:

1. *Sales Tax* - In states which have a sales tax, many require such a tax to be levied when the car is either transferred as part of the corporate capitalization or sold to the corporation. Thus, the corporation may find that it will have to incur an additional expense it did not contemplate.

2. *Constructive Dividend for Personal Use of Automobile* - If the employee uses the corporate-owned automobile for personal use as well as business use, then the Internal Revenue Service may impute a dividend to the employee equal to the value of the automobile which was used for personal pleasure. A dividend is a non-deductible expense to the corporation and taxable to the employee. If personal use by the employee is contemplated, then the employment agreement should recognize such personal use by the employee and that value of such use will be considered additional compensation. This should avoid the double tax effect.[7]

3. *Accelerated Depreciation Test* - If the employee has been using accelerated depreciation for his automobile, he cannot continue such method of depreciation when he transfers the car to the corporation. Thus, in some circumstances where the employee has been using the faster depreciation method, it is advisable for the employee to continue to own the automobile personally, and continue to depreciate it under the applicable method he has adopted.

4. *Recapture of Depreciation* - A tax-free transfer of an automobile to the corporation under Section 351 of the Internal Revenue Code will not generate the depreciation recaption provision under Section 1245 of the Internal Revenue Service. However, if the automobile is sold, such provision will be activated. Therefore, before such a sale is, in fact, consummated, the effect of these sections should be analyzed carefully.

6. *Reasonable Compensation Problem* - As was discussed in the previous chapter,[8] the Internal Revenue Service has imputed dividends to shareholder employees based upon the "fair return of capital" doctrine. As a result, most practitioners recommend a low capitalization for the corporation. Transferring or selling an automobile to the corporation is not in line with this recommendation.

Generally, automobile expenses are treated in the same manner as other expenses. That is, the employee is reimbursed for his expenses in operating and maintaining his automobile. This expense includes depreciation.

For example, assume a professional has been deducting 85% of his automobile expenses on his personal return as a business expense. Assume that the depreciation expense equaled $1200 per year. When the professional incorporated, he would be reimbursed the $1200 by the corporation, which represents the depreciation on the automobile, and 85% of his other operating expenses.

WATCH THIS

In many cases, the employee has fully depreciated his automobile. In such a situation, it is often better to be reimbursed by the mileage method. By this method, the employee may be reimbursed up to 15 cents a mile.[9] The mileage method should also be used when the employee drives many miles on corporate business and the depreciation value of the automobile plus other anticipated operating expenses will be less than what can be obtained under the mileage method. Therefore, the practitioner should make a comparison between the different methods available in order to select the greatest savings to the professional.

OBSERVATION

Many professionals feel that if the corporation owns the automobile, they will now be able to take a 100% deduction for its use through the corporation. Nothing could be further from the truth. The corporation is entitled to deduct the cost of the automobile to the extent it is in fact used on corporate business. To the extent it is not, it will be treated as additional compensation or as a dividend to the employee. Certainly, a dentist who merely drives his automobile to the office and returns home cannot now expect to deduct the entire cost of operating the automobile because he has incorporated and the corporation now owns the car. The corporation is going to have to substantiate that the automobile is being used entirely on the business of the corporation in order for the corporation to obtain a 100% deduction for the maintenance and operating expenses.

Corporations Consisting of More than One Professional Employee

Almost everything discussed which applies to the one-man professional corporation also applies to the professional corporation consisting of more than one professional employee. However, there is one significant difference. This difference is that the employees of a multi-employee group may have different personal expenses. For instance, the automobile driven by the professional may have different values, one employee make take a home office deduction, whereas his colleague doesn't, or one employee may attend professional conferences located at various parts of the country, whereas his associate may not travel so extensively. Therefore, although it might be preferable for the "corporateness" of the corporation to reimburse each employee for all expenses incurred in the furtherance of corporate business, irrespective of the differences in amounts each employee would be reimbursed, as a practical matter, such a policy may cause resentment on the part of the employees. Certainly, the employee who drives an inexpensive economy car is not going to like supporting his associate's Cadillac, or financing his attendance at a professional conference some two thousand miles from their office when he only attends the local conventions.

In these situations, each employee could be required to incur such expenses personally and deduct them on their personal income tax return. However, there are alternative solutions. One solution would be to have the corporation reimburse the employees an amount for each item of expense which represents the smallest amount which all employees claimed on their income tax return for the year prior to incorporating, and have the employees incur the excess as a condition of their employment.

For instance, assume that in a corporation consisting of three professionals, each employee claimed $1400, $1900 and $2250, for automobile expenses respectively. In such a case, the corporation would reimburse each employee $1400 and any amount in excess of this figure would be required to be incurred by each employee personally as a condition of his employment. Thus, the employee maintains his deduction and the corporation maintains a more "corporate" image.

The same would apply for the other common expenses, and in the event one employee claimed no deduction for a particular expense, such as home office, then the corporation would make no reimbursement to any employee for that expense.

Another alternative is to create an expense account from which each employee will be reimbursed. For example, under this method, the corporation may establish an expense account of $3000 for each employee, from which he may submit an account for expenses incurred and receive reimbursement, irrespective of the amount claimed for the same expense by his colleagues. If total expenses exceed this amount, then they will be incurred personally by the employee, and no reimbursement will be made. If an employee only has $2500 in expenses, then the $500 difference will be considered additional compensation to the employee.

REIMBURSEMENT OF EXPENSES

The employment contract should provide that in the event any reimbursement for expenses to an employee should be disallowed as a deduction to the corporation, and such determination has been acceded to by the corporation, the employee will reimburse the corporation the amount of such disallowed deduction. As an alternative to making a direct reimbursement, the agreement may provide that the amount due the corporation under this clause may be withheld in installments from the employee's future salary payments.

The purpose of this provision is to avoid the ''double taxation'' burden which will result if the disallowed portion is not reimbursed. That is, the disallowed expense is included in the corporation's income and is then treated as a dividend to the employee. If the expense is reimbursed to the corporation, then only the corporation will be taxed.

A provision of this kind has been acquiesced to by the Internal Revenue Service.[10] However, repayment must be mandatory and cannot be voluntary. Thus, the requirement for repayment must be inserted in the employment contract.

In addition to reimbursing the corporation for disallowed expenses, reimbursement has also included compensation which has been held to be unreasonable by the Internal Revenue Service and thus non-deductible to the corporation. This author has been reluctant to expand the reimbursement requirements to disallowed compensation since the affected employee may not have the financial ability to repay the amount disallowed and in view of recent cases that have held that reimbursement language may be an implied admission that the compensation was unreasonable.[11]

FOOTNOTES

[1]See chapter 3 ''Operating the Corporation to Avoid Internal Revenue Service Problems'' section entitled ''Assignment of Income and Section 482 '' p. 43.

[2]Ibid., section entitled ''Personal Holding Company'' p. 49.

[3]See chapter 4 ''Planning and Avoiding the Unreasonable Compensation Dilemna,'' section entitled ''Contingent Compensation and Bonuses'' p. 60.

[4]See chapter 7 ''How to Take Advantage of Non-Retirement Fringe Benefits,'' section entitled ''Wage Continuation Plan and Disability Income Protection Insurance'' p. 115.

[5]See chapter 6 ''How to Avoid Tax Pitfalls in Expanding, Contracting and Liquidating the Professional Corporation,'' section entitled ''How to Value the Stock'' p. 92.

[6]Regs. 1.274-5(c); See P-H Professional Corporation Guide ''How Professionals and their Corporations Cope with the Tax and Business Realities of Expense Accounts'' Paragraph 12,111.

[7]CCH Professional Corporation Handbook Paragraph 1049.

[8]Note 3, section entitled ''Reasonable But Nondeductible Compensation'' p. 62.

[9]Rev. Rul. 71-412 1971-2 CB 170.

[10]Rev. Rul. 69-115, 1969-1 CB 50; see also Vincent G. Oswald 49 TC 645 (1968).

[11]See chapter 4 ''Planning for And Avoiding the Unreasonable Compensation Dilemma'' Section entitled ''Alternative Preventive Steps'' p. 66.

6

HOW TO AVOID TAX PITFALLS IN EXPANDING, CONTRACTING AND LIQUIDATING THE PROFESSIONAL CORPORATION

With the increase in the number of professional corporations, most practitioners will at some time be required to render advice on the following problems:

1. How should a professional be admitted as a shareholder.
2. How should a departing shareholder's stock be redeemed.
3. How should the professional corporation be dissolved.

There are numerous different methods available to accomplish the above situations, and each has its own particular tax consequences. Furthermore, the problem of expansion, contraction and liquidation should be planned for at the organization stage of the corporation. With the proper planning at this level and the careful evaluation of the facts when the particular occurrence arises, the practitioner will be able to devise the most suitable method which will produce the best tax consequence for the parties involved.

This chapter will discuss the various aspects of how to expand, contract and liquidate a professional corporation, pitfalls to avoid, and provide guidelines to use to accomplish the desired result with the most favorable tax consequences.

EXPANDING THE CORPORATION

The problem of expanding the professional corporation may arise in several different situations, which are as follows:

1. The hiring of a professional by the corporation as an employee.

2. A non-shareholder professional employee who now wishes to buy an equity interest in the corporation.
3. An unincorporated professional with an independent practice who desires to join together with an incorporated professional.
4. When an incorporated professional wishes to merge his practice with another incorporated professional.

Hiring New Professional Employees

The hiring of a professional employee by a professional corporation is the easiest form of expansion and, other than the normal considerations which must be decided in drafting the professional employee's employment contract,[1] there are no tax considerations which must be solved by the practitioner. As will be readily observed, the same ease of hiring a new employee is not equally applicable in the other three situations mentioned above.

Admitting a New Shareholder

In many professional practices, especially in medicine, it is not uncommon for the senior man to make his associate a 'partner' after two or three years of association. Very often, the new partner will pay only a nominal price for his interest, and at times, he may not be required to pay anything for his partnership interest. Generally, if all the new partner receives is an interest in the partnership profits and not the partnership capital, there will be no taxable event when he becomes a partner.[2]

However, the same principal is not applicable when a professional in a corporate practice wishes to make his associate a shareholder in his corporation. There are various methods of transferring stock to a new man, each with its own tax consequences, and there may be a taxable event depending upon the method which is used.

The problem thus confronting the practitioner, which will be subsequently discussed, is twofold:

1. How shall the new associate acquire stock in the corporation to achieve the best possible tax results, and
2. How should the stock which the new associate is to purchase be valued?

Methods for Acquiring Stock

1. *The corporation can give the stock to the new associate* - In this event, the corporation will probably be considered as having transferred stock to the professional in consideration of services rendered, and he will report as income the value of the stock he has received on his personal income tax return.[3] The corporation in such a case is entitled to deduct the value of the stock transferred on its returns.[4] However, if the stock has considerable value, the new professional may find himself with a substantial tax liability for the year in which he receives the stock without adequate funds to pay the tax. Alternatively, the issuance of stock might be considered a gift by the other shareholders to the new professional,[5] in which case, the other stockholders may find themselves liable for a gift tax. Neither result is particularly desireable.

2. *Corporation can sell the stock to the professional* - If the corporation sells Treasury or unissued stock, there will be no taxable gain to the corporation,[6] nor any taxable event to the shareholder. If a high value is placed on the stock, then the shareholder may find it financially difficult to buy into the corporation. Two possible solutions to the problem are to one, have the new shareholder, where state law permits, give his promissory note for the stock, or, two, to take a reduction in pay until his stock is paid for.

3. *The other shareholders can sell their stock to the new associate* - In this event, the shareholders selling their stock to the new associate will incur a capital gains tax to the extent the consideration they

receive exceeds their basis in the stock.[7] If the value of the stock has increased considerably over the shareholder's basis, they may find themselves with a considerable tax liability to pay.

4. *The corporation can sell the stock to the new associate for less than adequate consideration* - If the corporation sells the stock, there will be no taxable event to it, but the purchasing associate will be taxed on the difference between the fair market value of the stock and the price he paid for it as ordinary income.[8] In addition, the stockholders should not sell their stock to the new professional in exchange for services to be rendered in the future. In such a case, the corporation will not be able to deduct the value of the services since it did not incur the expense, and the shareholders will not be entitled to any deduction since the payment of stock as compensation was not paid in their trade or business.[9]

WATCH THIS

If the corporation has elected subchapter s status, then it is imperative, if the election is to remain effective, that the new shareholder file his consent to the election within thirty days of becoming a stockholder.[10]

OBSERVATION

The most appropriate method for the sale of stock in a professional corporation is to have the new associate purchase it for its fair market value from the corporation. In this manner, there will be no taxable event to either the existing shareholders, the corporation, or to the new shareholder. In addition, it will avoid the adverse tax consequences created upon the sale of stock for less than adequate consideration and upon the sale of stock by the existing shareholders at a price which substantially exceeds their basis in the stock. Thus, the corporation must determine the fair market value for its stock. The different methods of valuing stock and how the method adopted will affect the ease by which a new associate will be able to purchase stock in the corporation are discussed in the following section.

How To Value The Stock

There are various methods of determining the value of stock in a closely-held corporation, and each method may result in a completely different value. If the method of valuation is reasonable or determined in an arms-length transaction between two unrelated shareholders, the method of valuation will generally be acceptable to the Internal Revenue Service. Thus, the parties have some flexibility in establishing a fair value which will best meet their objectives.

Some of the most common methods of variation are:

1. *Agreed Dollar Value* - By this method, the parties establish a value of stock based upon what they consider the fair value of stock to be at a particular period of time.
2. *Value Determined by Appraisers* - In this case, the value is based upon the average yearly net earnings for a certain number of prior years, which is then capitalized at a stated interest percentage.
3. *Book or Fair Market Value Method* - The book value method provides that the value of the stock will be determined by the net value of the business assets as shown by the corporation's books. Under the fair market value method, a fair value is determined for the assets as opposed to their current basis after depreciation. In either method, it must be decided whether ''business assets'' for purposes of valuation includes accounts receivable and good will.

OBSERVATION

If the method of valuing the stock which is adopted creates a high value, the problem then confronting the new associate is whether he has the financial ability to purchase the stock. To facilitate the ease by which a new professional is able to ''buy into'' the corporation, this author advocates adopting the book value method, since it will always produce the lowest value for the stock. In furtherance of this objective of keeping the purchase price of the stock as low as possible, accounts receivable should not be considered in determining the value of the stock.[11] Accounts receivable should instead be paid out in the form of deferred compensation under the shareholder's employment agreement.[12] Furthermore, although there has been much discussion as to whether or not a professional practice has good will,[13] the author does not place a value on good will in computing the value of the stock. Not only will this position facilitate the admission of new members by reducing the value of the stock, but it will assist the corporation in minimizing the threat of the Internal Revenue Service computing a dividend based upon the "fair return of invested capital" theory.[14]

In addition, it should be kept in mind that not only will the value placed upon the stock affect the price to be paid by a new associate upon his admission as a shareholder, but it will establish the value of the stock in the event of his withdrawal. Thus, if the shareholder pays a high price upon his admission as such, the corporation will be required to pay a high value for his stock upon his withdrawal. This can place an unexpected financial burden upon the corporation or remaining shareholders. This can be avoided by placing a low value on the stock. Thus, if the new associate pays a nominal price, he will receive a nominal amount upon his departure.

The Effect Capitalization Will Have on the Value of Corporate Stock

The method by which the corporation is capitalized will have a direct effect upon the value of the stock. If the original incorporators transfer property having a high value to the corporation in exchange for stock, then obviously, the value of the stock for purposes of resale of redemption is increased. In such a case, a shareholder who has transferred expensive equipment to the corporation is not going to be willing to transfer his equity interest in the equipment for less than adequate consideration. The problem thus arises as to where the new shareholder is going to obtain the funds to purchase the stock at its fair market value.

Thus, the capitalization of the corporation should be kept as low as practically possible, and the problems which arise in admitting new shareholders can be effectively minimized if not entirely eliminated.[15]

How To Merge an Incorporated Practice With an Unincorporated Practice

The problem facing the practitioner when two professionals, one of whom is incorporated and the other of whom isn't, wish to join together and practice within the existing corporation is to determine by what method the merger should take place in order to achieve the best possible tax results. Generally, the parties themselves will view the transaction as merely a transfer by the unincorporated professional of his practice to the incorporated practice in exchange for a certain percentage of the stock (assume for purposes of this discussion that the unincorporated professional receives 50% of the stock). However, the answer is not so simple in terms of the tax consequences.

The Internal Revenue Code provides that a transfer of property in exchange for stock will be tax free only if the transferor has obtained control of the corporation immediately after the exchange. Control in this case means that the transferor owns 80% or more of the outstanding stock of the corporation.[16] Since the unincorporated professional will only receive 50% of the stock, the exchange will not quality under §51 of the Internal Revenue Code and will result in a taxable event.

To avoid this result, it has been suggested that the incorporated professional contribute additional property to the corporation, in which event both professional transferors would own 100% of the stock and thus qualify this transaction as a tax-free exchange. Unfortunately, the Treasury has already considered such a possibility, and has effectively precluded such a solution by providing that if the transfer of property is solely for the purpose of qualifying the exchange, then its transfer will not be considered for purposes of §351.[17] However, if the parties can demonstrate that the additional contribution of property by the incorporated professional served business purposes other than to qualify the transfer, it will be treated as a tax-free exchange under §351. Certainly the incorporated professional would be required to contribute more than a nominal amount of property in order to qualify the transaction.

If the transfer by the unincorporated professional is considered a taxable exchange, then he may have a substantial gain to report in his personal return in that year. The character of the gain will be determined by the type of assets which are transferred. For instance, if good will is transferred, then the gain will be considered a capital gain. However, any gain resulting from the transfer of depreciable property may be ordinary income under the recapture of depreciation rules.[18] Furthermore, the professional might also be subject to the recapture of investment credit rules which will also result in ordinary income. In addition, if accounts receivable are transferred, ordinary income will arise to the extent they exceed the accounts payable.

Thus, the results of a taxable exchange may produce disastrous results for the unincorporated professional. The next question is obvious—what can be done to avoid a taxable exchange? The following are suggested possible solutions.[19]

1. Incorporate the Unincorporated Professional and then Merge the Two Corporations

Although the Internal Revenue Code provides that a merger under state law will be tax free,[20] only about one-half the states specifically provide that professional corporations may merge and the other states are silent on the subject. As a practical matter, however, state law should not be a stumbling block to using a merger as a possible solution to this problem.

However, it is possible that the Internal Revenue Service may treat the two events as a step transaction, in that the incorporation of the unincorporated practice served no business purpose other than to avoid an otherwise taxable event, and thus should be ignored.[21] Thus, caution would advise obtaining an advance ruling from the Internal Revenue Service if this route is going to be followed.[22]

2. The Unincorporated Professional Remains as Such and Forms a Partnership with the Corporation

Although this can be legally structured, it certainly provides no tax benefits to the unincorporated professional since he will still not be eligible for the fringe benefits which are only available to the corporate employees. Thus, as a practical matter, this solution is not really a solution at all.

3. Both Professionals Would Form a Second Corporation, to Which They Would Transfer Their Practices in Exchange for Stock.

Although this would be an acceptable solution for purposes of avoiding a taxable exchange, most state laws prohibit the ownership of stock in a professional corporation by anyone other than an individual who is licensed to practice that profession. Thus, a professional corporation will not be able to exchange its assets for the stock in another professional corporation or hold stock of another professional corporation, since it is not an individual. This is the case even though the corporation is comprised of individuals who are licensed professionals and even if the transferring corporation immediately liquidated and transferred the stock to the licensed shareholder. When state laws do not place such a restriction on stock ownership, this would be a practical solution.

OBSERVATION

It is apparent from the discussion that there is no legal problem for an unincorporated and incorporated professional to join practices in one entity. The only stumbling block is that the unincorporated professional may pay an expensive price for the merger. It would appear that a suitable alternative to the above suggested solution would be to have the unincorporated professional retain his furniture, fixtures and equipment, accounts receivable and accounts payable outside the corporation and purchase stock in the corporation he wishes to join. He would then continue his practice through the corporation, the accounts receivable arising from his practice prior to the merger would be collected by him personally, and he would then lease his personal property to the corporation. This, of course, is facilitated if the value of the corporate stock is low. In this manner, there will be no taxable event. Although the corporation might have an initial cash flow problem since the accounts receivable are not being transferred, this would appear preferable than having the unincorporated professional sustain a substantial tax in a taxable exchange.

How to Merge Two Incorporated Practices

The merger of two incorporated practices presents the fewest problems as far as §351 is concerned since there is no state prohibition against such a merger[23] and the Internal Revenue Code specifically provides that a merger under state law will be tax free.[24]

However, there is another sizable problem which must be resolved. Namely, how should the retirement plan of the acquired corporation be treated? If the merged corporation is required to terminate its plan and distribute its assets to the participants who are now employed by the surviving corporation, the participants will treat the distribution as ordinary income since there hasn't been a separation of service[25] which would prevent the use of the more favorable averaging provisions for lump sum distribution.[26] This is certainly a disastrous result for the professional as well as the lay employees. Not only will they pay taxes on their regular compensation for the year in which the merger occurs, but they will also include as income their entire retirement accounts. The tax savings which prompted the professional to incorporate will probably be substantially reduced if not entirely eliminated by this result.

To avoid this result, the retirement plan should contain language to the effect that the participants of the merged corporation's retirement plan may transfer their interests to the surviving corporation's plan, or if the surviving corporation has no plan, then it can continue the merged corporation's retirement plan.[27]

Unfortunately, all problems are not solved by merely providing that plan assets may be transferred by an acquired corporation retirement plan to the retirement plan of the surviving corporation. There are a host of other considerations which arise and which must be resolved in order to avoid any undesirable results.

For instance, the acquiring corporation's retirement plan must be comparable to the merged corporation's retirement plan, otherwise the latter's plan will be considered terminated and all accounts will vest in the participants.[28] A transfer from a pension plan to a pension plan and from a profit sharing plan to a profit sharing plan is considered comparable whereas a transfer from a pension to a profit sharing plan or vice versa is not considered comparable.[29] In addition, the contribution level, benefits, vesting schedule, and eligibility requirements of the surviving corporation's retirement plan must be comparable to the acquired corporation's retirement plan. Otherwise, the latter's retirement plan will be considered partially terminated, and benefits will vest to the extent the plan is partially terminated.[30]

Although the termination or partial termination of one plan will not result in the participants having to report taxable income in the year their benefits vest, it will cause a more rapid vesting of benefits than originally comtemplated or desired by the professional employees.[31] Furthermore, if a target benefit or fixed benefit pension plan is considered terminated or partially terminated, then the limitation of benefits under Regs. § 1.401-4(c) (2) (iii) may apply, causing the professional of the acquired corporation to lose a portion of his pension account.[32]

Thus, careful planning and thought must go into any planned merger of two professional corporations, and the practitioner should obtain a determination letter as to the consequences of the assumption of one plan by another.[33]

Miscellaneous Problems

In addition to the tax problems which are created in expanding the professional corporation, there are numerous non-tax considerations. For example, employment contracts will have to be reviewed and amended, stock redemption plans must be reviewed or adopted, and the appropriate changes made, the medical reimbursement plan should be reviewed as well as other fringe benefit programs which are available to professional as well as lay employees.

In brief, the existing corporation must coordinate its objectives with the objectives of the entering professional, and the appropriate and necessary documents must be prepared to reflect their new relationship.

CONTRACTING THE PROFESSIONAL CORPORATION

All state statutes provide that stock can only be owned by individuals who are licensed to practice the profession for which the corporation was organized. Thus, if a professional shareholder becomes disqualified to practice his profession or dies, redemption of his stock is required. Otherwise, the stock will be held by non-licensed stockholders. If there is no agreement among shareholders themselves or with the corporation providing for the purchase of a professional's stock upon his disqualification or his death, the required disposition of the affected professional's stock will usually be governed by state statute which may establish the price, method, and terms of the sale.

On the other hand, if a shareholder terminates his employment for any reason other than death or disqualification, there is no legal requirement that said professional's stock be redeemed or otherwise disposed of. However, in order to assure the smooth operation of the corporation, there should be an agreement providing for the redemption or purchase of a withdrawing stockholder's stock.[34]

WATCH THIS

Not only will such an agreement provide for the orderly disposition of the stock of a departing shareholder, but in the event of a shareholder's death, the agreement will establish the value of the stock for federal estate tax purposes.[35]

Here are three ways by which a professional can sell his shares in the corporation.

1. He can sell his shares directly to the corporation.
2. He can sell his shares to the other shareholders of the corporation.
3. He may sell the stock to another licensed professional who has no relationship with the corporation.

Generally, the last alternative is the least desirable for the remaining stockholders, since they do not want an outsider to own shares in the corporation, and the least practical for the departing shareholder, since he will find the market for his shares almost non-existent. Therefore, in reality, this question becomes one of whether the stock should be sold to the remaining shareholders or be redeemed by the corporation. This is also the same issue facing the corporation in the event of a shareholder's death or disqualification.

Thus, the questions confronting the practitioner are to determine the most appropriate method of redeeming or purchasing the stock of a shareholder in the event of his termination of employment for whatever reason and to determine the value of said stock.

Stock Redemption vs. Cross Purchase

There are two basic stock purchase agreements which can be used to redeem the stock of a departing shareholder. One is known as a stock redemption agreement whereby the corporation is obligated to purchase the shares of the affected professional, and the second is known as a cross purchase agreement whereby the stockholders obligate themselves to purchase the stock of a terminated employee, usually on a pro rata basis.[36]

The following chart illustrates the basic characteristics of these two agreements.

STOCK REDEMPTION & CROSS PURCHASE AGREEMENTS

A COMPARISON

Stock Redemption Agreement	*Cross Purchase Agreement*
1. Corporation uses its own funds to purchase the stock of the departing shareholder.	1. Remaining shareholders personally purchase the shares, usually on a pro rata basis.
2. If agreement is funded with insurance, corporation owns insurance and receives proceeds upon death of shareholder to purchase his stock.	2. If agreement is funded by insurance, each stockholder keeps insurance on the other stockholders' lives and each stockholder receives the proceeds of insurance in the event of the death of one of them, which is then used to purchase the stock of the other.
3. Premiums paid for insurance to fund agreement are not deductible as an ordinary business expense.[37]	3. Premiums paid for life insurance by the individual shareholders are not a deductible expense.[38]
4. The premiums for insurance paid by the corporation will not be considered taxable income to the shareholders of the shareholders if the corporation is the sole owner and beneficiary of the policies.[39]	4. The proceeds of insurance will not be taxable to the shareholders.[40]
5. The proceeds of insurance will not be taxed to the corporation.[41]	5. The purchase price paid for the stock is not a deductible expense.
6. The purchase price paid for the stock is not a deductible expense to the corporation.	

Generally, the stock redemption agreement will be the best method for purchasing the stock of a departing shareholder. The reason for this is its simplicity as compared to the cross purchase arrangement. For example, if insurance is used as a funding medium in a stock redemption agreement, it is only necessary for the corporation to purchase as many policies as there are shareholders. However, if a cross purchase method is used, then each shareholder must buy a policy on the life of every other shareholder. If there are only two shareholders, there will be no problem. However, if there are three shareholders, it will be necessary to purchase six insurance policies, and if there are four shareholders it will be necessary to purchase twelve insurance policies. This obviously can become extremely cumbersome as well as expensive. In fact, the expense may be so prohibitive that this agreement may never be able to be used by some corporations.

Furthermore, if a cross purchase agreement is used, and insurance is used as a funding medium, the shareholders will be required to purchase the insurance with their after-tax dollars. Thus, if the professional is in the 50% tax bracket, he will have to earn $2.00 for every dollar he spends on insurance. In almost all cases, it will usually be less expensive to purchase the life insurance through the corporation, since the corporation will be in either the 22% or 48% tax bracket and, usually, the former.

It will be an unusual case when the corporation's tax bracket is greater than the professional's. However, if that should be the case, then the cross purchase agreement will cost less to fund.

Nevertheless, there are some distinct advantages to using the cross purchase agreement. First, the question of whether or not funds can be accumulated in the corporation for the purpose of purchasing the stock of a departing shareholder constitutes a reasonable business need in order to avoid the penalty tax on unreasonable accumulation under Internal Revenue Code § 531 is avoided.[42] Second, the question of whether the redemption can be considered a dividend to the selling shareholder under Internal Revenue Code § 302 is completely avoided, and third, the remaining shareholders who purchase the shares of the departing shareholder will receive a stepped-up basis to the extent of the consideration paid for these shares, which will reduce their tax in the event they might sell the stock prior to their death. In a stock redemption agreement, the cost basis of the stock of the remaining shareholders remains the same.

OBSERVATION

The problem of unreasonable accumulations, dividend treatment to shareholders upon the redemption of their stock, and the danger of the collapsible corporation provisions of Internal Revenue Code § 341 are more academic than real to most professional corporations, especially if the value of the stock is kept low. Thus, for purposes of simplicity and ease, most practitioners will, in most cases, find the stock redemption agreement the vehicle to use in redeeming the stock of a withdrawing shareholder.

How To Value The Stock

The same methods of determining the purchase price of stock to be paid by a new shareholder are equally applicable in valuing the stock in stock purchase agreements.[43] This author, as stated previously, is of the firm opinion that the value of the stock should be kept as low as possible. In furtherance of this objective, this author uses the book value of the corporate assets without consideration to good will or accounts receivable. The departing shareholder's share of accounts receivable is then distributed in the form of deferred compensation.[44] A redemption based on this method will produce the following results.

1. *Will avoid a liquidity problem* - If the value of the stock is high, then the corporation will be required to produce the funds necessary to effectuate the redemption. This may prove quite difficult and create a severe liquidity problem, especially if redemption is required of a shareholder's stock who is departing for reasons other than death. In the event of death, the liquidity problem can be avoided by purchasing life insurance. Thus, it is usually easier to purchase the stock of a withdrawing shareholder if the value of the stock is low.

2. *Creates deduction for corporation* - Corporate payments made by a corporation in redemption of its stock are not a deductible expense. Thus, if accounts receivable are included in the value of the stock, the corporation loses a deduction for that portion of the payments made which represents the value of the accounts receivable. However, if accounts receivable are paid out under a salary continuation or deferred compensation agreement, the corporation can deduct such payments.

3. *Minimize reasonable compensation problem* - A buy-sell agreement entered into arms-length negotiation which eliminates good will from the value of the stock may serve to reduce the possibility of a dividend being imputed by the Internal Revenue Service upon the "fair return of capital" theory.[45] If good will is eliminated from capital, then the capital of the corporation is reduced and the size of the dividend which may be imputed upon the capital of the corporation is also reduced.[46]

4. *Avoid unreasonable accumulation problem* - If the value is low, there will be no need to accumulate large sums of money in order to fund the redemption agreement, thus eliminating the penalty upon unreasonable accumulations.

5. *Reduce danger of collapsible corporation provisions*[47] The purpose of § 341 is to prevent the conversion of what would otherwise be ordinary income into capital gain. If accounts receivable are included in the value of the stock to be redeemed by the corporation, then ordinary income will be converted into capital gain, since the withdrawing professional will treat any gain as a capital gain. Thus, if the collapsible corporation provisions of the Internal Revenue Code are applied by the Service in such a case, the sale will result in ordinary income to the withdrawing shareholder. The danger can be avoided by paying the accounts receivable out as deferred compensation and by keeping the purchase price as low as possible.[48]

6. *More money will be available for retirement plan contributions* - If the value of the stock is high, some provisions must be made for funding the corporation's obligation to redeem the stock, whether through insurance or by other means. Money which is used for these purposes reduces the amount of money available for retirement plan contributions.

HOW TO LIQUIDATE A PROFESSIONAL CORPORATION

It may be necessary to liquidate a professional corporation for various reasons; the parties may become disenchanted with the corporate form of conducting their practices, and wish to carry on their practices as a partnership, the corporate shareholders may become incompatible and desire to practice separately, or alternatively, in the event of the death or retirement of a professional in a one-man professional corporation, it will become necessary at that time to dissolve the corporation.

There are various methods by which a corporation can be liquidated, and each has its own particular tax consequences. Furthermore, the tax results may differ if the practice is continued after liquidation as a partnership or as a sole practitioner, as opposed to a complete discontinuance of the practice after dissolution.

There are three basic methods by which a professional corporation can be liquidated. The following chart sets forth their characteristics and the tax consequences to the corporation and the shareholders. Certain liquidating problems confronting the practitioner are subsequently discussed in more detail.

§331 - Taxable Liquidation	*§333 - Tax Free Liquidation*	*§337 Liquidation*
1. Shareholders exchange their stock for the assets of the corporation. Shareholders are considered as having sold a capital asset and thus, are entitled to capital gain treatment.[49]	**1.** Under this section a shareholder's gain on liquidation will be recognized only to the extent of the greater of the corporation's earnings and profits or the sum of any cash, stock or securities received on liquidation.[54]	**1.** This section provides that if a corporation adopts a plan of complete liquidation and within a 12-month period of time distributes all of its assets (less assets retained to meet claims), it will not recognize gain or loss from the sale or exchange of property within said 12-month period. Previously, if the corporation sold its assets, it would be taxed on any gain and when the assets were distributed, the shareholders would be taxed again. Thus, double taxation resulted. This section eliminates this problem.
2. The shareholder's gain or loss is the difference be-	**2.** Certain requirements must be met if the benefits of	**2.** This section is non-elective and if the require-

tween the adjusted basis of his stock and the fair market values of the property which he received on liquidation.	this section are to be achieved: **A.** Election to be treated under this section must be made by "qualified electing shareholders."[55] Qualified electing shareholders must own at least 80% of the total combined voting stock of corporation to have effective election.[56] **B.** The liquidation must be made pursuant to a plan of liquidation.[57] **C.** Election must be filed with IRS within 30 days of adoption of the plan of liquidation.[58] **D.** The distribution must be a complete redemption of all stock and the transfer of the property must be made within one calendar month.[59]	ments are met, then gain or loss arising on the sale will not be taxed. If it is desirable for the corporation to recognize loss or gain, then the sale should take place prior to the adoption of the plan of liquidation.
3. Good will may be taxed to shareholders. **4.** Shareholder's assumption of liabilities on transferred property will reduce the gain. **5.** Shareholder basis for property received is the fair market value of the property which they received.[50] **6.** Corporation does not usually recognize gain or loss upon liquidation. However, income may be realized in the following situations:[51] **A.** Accounts receivable may be taxed to the corporation as ordinary income prior to their distribution to shareholders. **B.** Income may be realized under recapture of depreciation provision of Internal Revenue Code[52] **C.** Income may be realized under recapture of investment credit provision of Internal Revenue Code.[53]	**3.** Good will will not be taxed upon liquidation to the shareholders.	**3.** Corporation will recognize income in the following situations: **A.** Under the recapture of depreciation provision **B.** Under the recapture of investment credit provisions **C.** Upon the sale of installment obligations.

D. Income will be recognized if installment obligations are distributed.

4. The basis of the shareholder's stock becomes the basis of the property received on liquidation reduced by any money received and increased by any gain recognized.[60] Basis is allocated among assets received in proportion to the fair market value.[61]

5. Treatment of subsequent gain or loss by shareholders upon sale of distributed assets will depend upon whether or not the assets are capital assets and whether their disposition is considered a sale and exchange.[62]

6. Corporation will not usually recognize gain or loss upon liquidation. However, income may be realized in the following situations:

A. Under the recapture of depreciation provisionf of Internal Revenue Code.

B. Under the recapture of investment credit provisions of Internal Revenue Code.

C. When installment obligations are distributed.

7. Accounts receivable will probably not be included in the corporation's income, although the point is not clear.

D. Property that is sold which was previously expended will give rise to ordinary income.[63] This will affect corporations who purchase a substantial amount of supplies.

E. Accounts receivable which are distributed to the shareholders will most probably be taxed to the corporation as ordinary income.

F. If accounts receivable are sold by the corporation, then its reserve for bad debts will be treated as ordinary income.[64]

4. If good will is distributed to shareholders, they will be taxed on value. §337 will not apply to:

A. Liquidation of collapsible corporations

B. Liquidation is Under § 333.

5. Shareholder's basis for property received in liquidation will equal its fair market value at the time of distribution.[65]

How To Prepare For and Minimize the Problems in Liquidating a Professional Corporation

Accounts receivable

Even though the Internal Revenue Code sets forth the general position that a corporation will not recognize gain or loss upon liquidation,[66] a professional corporation which distributes its accounts receivable to its shareholders in a liquidating distribution will probably be required to treat the value of the receivables as ordinary income by the Internal Revenue Service.[67] Otherwise, apart from the collapsible corporation problem, the shareholders will be able to convert what would otherwise be ordinary income to the corporation into capital gains. This is accomplished by the fact that the corporation will avoid tax on the receivables by distributing them in complete liquidation and the shareholder will pay only a capital gains tax on the difference between the fair market value of the property received in distribution, (which will include accounts receivable) and his adjusted basis for his stock.

It is not certain whether receivables will be required to be taken into income by the corporation in a § 333 liquidation. However, since the receivables will be treated as ordinary income by the shareholders, the corporation should not also be required to take them into income." The courts might regard § 333 liquidation as being more closely analagous to the tax free incorporation of a business under § 351 and not require their inclusion in the liquidating corporation's final return.[68]

If accounts receivable are attributable to the income of the corporation in a § 333 liquidation, the consequences of such inclusion will be much more severe to the shareholders than under a § 331 liquidation. There will be double taxation in both cases, but under § 331 the shareholders will include the value of the accounts receivable in computing their capital gain whereas under § 333 they will report them as ordinary income when collected.

Thus, when planning the liquidation of a professional corporation, the practitioner should consider the possibility of the corporation being required to take into income their accounts receivable and take the appropriate steps to minimize the possible adverse tax consequences. Some possible solutions are:[69]

1. Postpone the liquidation until most of the receivables have been either collected or sold. In this manner, it might be possible to spread the income derived from the receivables over two corporate taxable years. Otherwise, the corporation would be required to treat the entire value of the accounts receivable as income on its final income tax return, which could result in a substantial tax if the amount which had to be reported exceeded the surtax exemption causing the excess to be taxed at the rate of 48%.

2. If possible, pay out as much of the receivables as additional compensation which can be substantiated as reasonable. This may be difficult if the purpose of the corporation's existence is mainly to collect its receivables and no additional services are being rendered for the corporation.

3. Pay out the accounts receivable in the form of deferred compensation to the shareholder employees.

4. Pay off as many of the corporate liabilities as possible.

Good will

The most serious problem which may confront the professional corporation upon liquidating is if the Internal Revenue Service asserts that the shareholders received good will as well as other tangible assets in the liquidating distributions. Since the transfer of good will from one entity to another assumes the transfer of the earning capacity from one to the other, the problem of whether good will is distributed upon liquidation will usually arise only when the business is continued in another form and not when it is completely discontinued.[70]

Although there is much support for the contention that good will does not attach to the business of a professional person or firm which depends solely upon the skills and ability of the owner, most courts have taken a contrary position.[71] Thus, if a high value is placed upon good will by the Service, the shareholders may find themselves faced with a substantial capital gains tax. Or even worse, ordinary income may be realized if the corporation is classified as a collapsible corporation.

Therefore, if the practice is intended to be continued in another form and the liquidating corporation has very little accumulated earnings and profits and cash or securities, then it would appear that a liquidation under § 333 will avoid this problem. In addition, the buy-sell agreements should provide for a low valuation for the stock which specifically excludes good will. If the value for the stock includes good will for redemption purposes, it will be almost impossible to convince the Service that there is no good will for liquidating purposes.[72]

Recapture of depreciation

If depreciable property is part of the liquidating distribution, the corporation may realize ordinary income under the recapture of depreciation provisions of the Internal Revenue Code.[73] The effects of recapture, however, may not be that severe depending upon the corporation's tax rate. In addition, the tax paid will reduce the shareholder's capital gain on the liquidation by the amount of extra tax the corporation paid on the recaptured income, since the money paid in taxes would have been distributed to the shareholders, thus increasing his capital gains tax.[74]

However, the recapture provisions may have a much more severe effect in a § 333 liquidation. The net income after paying taxes on the recaptured income is included in the earnings and profits of the corporation. Thus, the shareholder's reportable ordinary income is increased by the increase in the corporation's earnings and profits. If the recaptured income is high, then the shareholder's tax may make a liquidation under § 333 imposible.[75]

The solution to this problem can be stated in one sentence. Keep the assets of the corporation to a minimum. If there is no expensive equipment or real estate in the corporation upon which substantial depreciation deductions can be taken, then there can be no serious recapture problem upon liquidation.

Collapsible corporations

Although it is not considered a serious danger by many tax advisors,[76] the collapsible corporation problem poses a potential threat in a corporate liquidation as well as when the stock of a withdrawing shareholder is redeemed. However, it is felt that since the liquidating corporation will be required to be taking into income its accounts receivable, the Service will not pursue the collapsible corporation attack against a liquidating corporation since ordinary income is not being converted into capital gain.[77]

Nevertheless, the practitioner can prepare for and minimize the problem by keeping the stock of the corporation as low as possible by avoiding large accumulation of corporate earnings and profits and by keeping the taxable assets to a minimum amount.

Guidelines On How To Select The Best Method Of Liquidation

The method most appropriate to use in liquidating a professional corporation will be determined by the corporation's assets at the time the liquidation will take place and whether the shareholders intend to practice their professions after the corporation is dissolved. The following charts represent several corporate fact patterns and the most suitable section of the Internal Revenue Code to use under those conditions. It must be remembered, however, that these fact patterns are only basic illustrations whose purpose is to give the practitioner a place to begin in finding the appropriate method of liquidating the corporation. Factors such as good will, effects of recapture of depreciation and investment credit, outstanding accounts receivable, and the assets which are being distributed must all be considered and will directly affect the decision of which section to liquidate the corporation.

When to Use §331

Facts	*Reason*
1. Shareholders of dissolving corporation have no interest in continuing their practices in another form.	Tax will be minimized since good will will probably not be a factor since practice is not being continued. Furthermore, if corporation has substantial earnings and profits, cash or securities, the shareholder will receive these assets at capital gain rates.
2. Corporation has equipment with high value but low basis. Shareholders intend to continue practice in another form and seek a stepped up basis for corporate assets.	Shareholder's basis in corporate assets will be its fair market value at time of liquidation. Thus, greater depreciation deduction is created at the cost of a capital gains tax. (Corporation may report ordinary income under recapture of depreciation and investment credit provisions of Internal Revenue Code.)
3. Corporation has substantial earnings and profits, cash and securities. Shareholders wish to continue practice in unincorporated form.	Earnings and profits, cash and securities will be taxed at capital gains rate as compared to ordinary income treatment if corporation was liquidated under §333.

When To Use §333

1. Corporation has substantial good will and minimal cash, stock or securities and earnings and profits. Shareholders intend to continue practice in another form.	If good will is a factor, then the value of the good will will escape tax which would have been reported under § 331.
2. Corporation has appreciated property with low adjusted basis with minimal earnings and profits, cash or securities. Recapture of depreciation and investment credit not a factor. Shareholders wish to avoid tax on difference between fair market value of property and its basis.	This is the primary time this section will be utilized.
3. Corporation has substantial property and minimal earnings and profits, cash and stock or securities. Shareholders do not intend to continue practice and wish to sell property on installment method.	Installment method cannot be utilized under § 331 and § 337.[78]

When To Use §337

Corporation has property with high value, and it desires to sell these assets while incurring only one tax.	§ 337 is used in situations where the liquidating corporation wishes to sell its assets to an outsider. Gain will not be taxed at both the corporate and shareholder level.

Effect Capitalization of Corporation Will Have On Corporation

Most of the tax problems which are presented in liquidating the professional corporation arise because of the substantial assets which are present in the corporation thus creating a higher value for the corporate stock. Thus, if the assets of the corporation are kept to a minimum, the problems of avoiding or postponing taxable gain and recapture of depreciation and investment credit are minimized or even eliminated. Therefore, in cases where a low value can be placed upon the stock, it will make little difference whether the liquidation comes under § 331 or 333 since the tax to the shareholder under § 331 will probably be minimal.

Thus, when initially capitalizing the corporation, property having a substantial value should not be transferred to the corporation but retained personally by the incorporatinng professionals and leased to the corporation. Any additional needs by the corporation for substantial equipment should be satisfied by the purchase of such equipment by the professionals, who lease it to the corporation.

FOOTNOTES

[1]See Chapter 5 "Drafting the Employment Contract." p. 70.

[2]Regs. 1.721-1(b)(1).

[3]Regs. S1.61-2(d)(4).

[4]Rev. Rul. 62-217 1962-2CB59.

[5]Regs. S1.351-1(b)(1).

[6]IRC §1032.

[7]IRC §1002.

[8]Regs. S1.62-2(d)(2)(i).

[9]CCH Professional Corporation Handbook Paragraph 2104.

[10]Regs. §1.1372-3(c).

[11]"It is obvious that, the lower the actual value of the shares, the less significant are the practical and tax problems which arise in connection with ownership changes. Also, it is easier for a purchaser of the shares to pay what they are worth. ... Keeping down the value of the stock is, in turn, one of the reasons for not including receivables in valuating the stock under a buy-sell or redemption agreement." Eaton, "Professional Corporations and Associations" Matthew Bender, Volume I, §13.01(2), p. 13-4-13-4. 1.

[12]"Quite commonly, the receivables are omitted in computing the value of the stock and are instead reflected in the amount paid as deferred compensation or as a death benefit.

"Within the perameters of practicality and tolerable tax impact, this author reiterates his general preference for minimizing the price (and value) of the stock and picking up the slack, if any, in the form of deferred compensation." ibid, §13.04(2), p. 13-24 and 13-26, respectively.

[13]See Chapter 4 "Planning for and Avoiding the Unreasonable Compensation Dilemma" Section entitled "Good will as an Income Producing Factor" p. 64.

[14]Ibid., Section entitled "Reasonable but Nondeductible Compensation," p. 62; "This is a factor (referring to good will) to be considered in framing the buy-sell agreement. If there is no good will that is being paid for by the shareholders..., your buy-sell agreement does not give the government ammunition to argue and contend that there is good will. If you do not provide for good will, I think you are making it easier to avoid the unreasonable compensation issue ... It is only by reason of the introduction of the good will factor that the parties acknowledge in the buy-sell agreement that the government is even able to make a case." *Schreiber* "How to Save Taxes and Increase your Wealth with a Professional Corporation" The MacMillan Company 1970 Part II, p. 5.

[15]This position is well stated in Schreiber, *Ibid.,* in a section entitled "Do Not Overcapitalize" part 1, page 22.

"... Cautious planning points toward avoiding transfers into the professional corporation of large amounts of capital assets. The capital of the professional corporation should be limited to what the corporation needs to function and operate properly.

The creation of large capital values in the corporation might hinder the admission of new shareholders in future ...

Furthermore, the high capital value would make it difficult or expensive for the new shareholder to pay for his shares...

However, if the costly capital assets were not owned by the professional service corporation, but rather were owned by a separate corporation or partnership comprised of some or all of the members of the service corporation ... the new shareholder could purchase shares in the service corporation for a more modest amount ..."

[16]IRC §351(a).

[17]Regs. §1.351-1(a)(ii);

[18]IRC §1245.

[19]See Prentice-Hall Professional Corporation Guide "How to Expand a Professional Corporation." Paragraph 12,484.

[20]IRC §361 and §368(a)(1)(A).

[21]Rev. Rul 70-434 CB 1970-2, 83.

[22]A Prentice-Hall commentary (PCG Paragraph 12,484) feels that chances of obtaining a favorable ruling are quite good. "The overall transaction really doesn't jeopardize the fisc. Hence, the taxation of paper income in such a setup would not seem to be justified. No one is getting away with anything. No ordinary income escapes taxation or is converted to capital gain by the transaction. It really only amounts to a change in the form of doing business. And, once the transfer takes place, things will go on as usual — the receivables will be treated as ordinary income by the corporation and payables will be deductible by it. So, since there is no economic gain or tax avoidance, the ruling ought to be forthcoming."

[23]See CCH Professional Corporation Handbook, Paragraphs 4054 and 4055.

[24]See Footnote 20; For a complete discussion, see Prentice-Hall, Professional Corporation Guide "How to Reorganize a Professional Corporation" Paragraph 12,501.

[25]Rev. Rul. 72-440 IRB 1972-38; Rev. Rul 73-413 IRB 1973-41,10.

[26]IRC §72(n)(4).

[27]For sample language see Miller, Professional Corporations - 1974 PLI 1974, page 185.

[28]Rev. Rul. 67-213 IRB 1967-27.

[29]*Ibid.*

[30]Rev. Rul. 69-24 IRB 1969-4; see chapter 9, Qualifying the Retirement Plan section entitled "Effect if Corporation Reduced the Benefits Payable under a Retirement Plan, p. 166.

[31]Rev. Rul. 55-368, CB 1955-1, 40; Rev. Rul. 55-427, 1955-2 CB 27.

[32]See chapter 9, Qualifying the Retirement Plan section entitled "Premature Termination-defined benefit and target benefit pension plan" p. 163.

[33]See Bodner "Consolidations of Qualified Plans: How are they Treated; What are the Dangers?" JTax October, 1973, p. 242.

[34]See chapter 5 "Drafting the Employment Contract" section entitled "Redemption of Stock from Employee in the Event of Prolonged Disability" p. 74.

[35]These conditions must be satisfied in order for the buy-sell agreement, whether stock redemption or cross purchase, to establish the value of the stock for federal estate tax purposes.

1. The estate must be obligated to give the right of first refusal to buy the stock of the deceased professional to the corporation or remaining shareholders. (Commissioner v. Bensel 100 F2d 639 (3rd Cir. 1938)

2. The agreement must provide that a departing shareholder must first offer his stock to the corporation or remaining shareholders at no more than the agreed price before he will be permitted to sell his stock to outsiders. (Regs. S20.2031-2(h))

3. The price which is established for the stock must be fair and reasonable. [Regs. S20.2031-2(h)].

[36]The agreement, whether stock redemption or cross purchase, does not have to obligate the corporation or remaining shareholders to purchase the stock of a withdrawing shareholder. It is possible to merely give the right of first refusal to the corporation or remaining shareholders which, if not exercised, the departing shareholder can then offer his shares to other licensed professionals. However, most agreements will provide for a binding obligation to purchase and sell on both parties.

[37]Regs. §1.264-1.

[38] §264(a)(1).

[39]Casale v. Commissioner *247 F2d 440 (1957)*, Prunier v. Commissioner, *248 F2d 818 (1957)*.

[40]§101(a)(1).

[41]*Ibid.*

[42]See chapter 3 "Operating the Corporation to Avoid Internal Revenue Service Problems" section entitled "Accumulated Earnings Tax" p. 52.

[43]See section "How to Value Stock" this chapter, p. 86.

[44]See chapter 5 "Drafting the Employment Contract" section entitled "Severance Pay" p. 75.

[45]See *Note 13*.

[46]See Williams and Mathews "Effective Estate Planning for Shareholders of Professional Corporations" Estate Planning, Autumn, 1973, pages 26,27; Gibbs "Getting out of a Professional Corporation: Preparing for the forthcoming Problems" 34 JTax March, 1971 pages 124,125.

[47]§341.

[48]See Note 46.

[49]IRC §331(a)(1).

[50]IRC §334(a).

[51]IRC §336.

[52]IRC §1245,1250.

[53]IRC §47.

[54]The shareholder's ratable share of earnings and profits will be taxed to him as "dividends," and the remainder of the gain will be taxed as a capital gain to the extent of the cash or securities the shareholder received. (S333(e)).

[55]IRC §333(c).

[56]IRC §333(c)(1).

[57]IRC §333(a)(1).

[58]IRC §333(d).

[59]IRC §333(a)(2).

[60]IRC §334(c).

[61]Regs. S1.334-2.

[62]Osenbach v. Commissioner 198 F2d 235 (4th Cir. 1952).

[63]Rev. Rul 61-214, 1961-2 CB 60.

[64]West Seattle National Bank v. Commissioner 288 F2d 47 (9th Cir. 1961).

[65]§334(a).

[66]§336.

[67]Williamson v. United Stated 292 F2d 524 (Ct. Cl. 1961); Kilbourn, "Post Liquidating Problems, Corporate and Individual" 28 NYU Institute 701, 709 (1965).

"In cases in which the income is earned prior to liquidation and the amount can be estimated on a reasonable basis, the distribution in complete liquidation will result in a realization of income to the corporation at that time. It will be included in the final return of the corporation covering the short period ending on the date of distribution. It is not necessary to decide, therefore, whether the corporation's existence continues after that date."

[68]CCH Professional Corporation Handbook, Paragraph 2109; Eaton Professional Corporations and Associations, Matthew-Bender, Paragraph 13.03(2) pages 13-17.

[69]Ibid.

[70]Hertz "Liquidation of a Corporate Business in Kind" 26 NYU Tax Institute, pages 969-982 (1968); CCH Professional Corporation Handbook, Paragraph 2110.

[71]See *Note 13*.

[72]See Note 14.

[73]IRC §1245, 1250.

[74]Hertz, Note 70 , p. 972; Prentice-Hall Professional Corporation Guide "Professional Corporation and Recapture of Depreciation" Paragraph 12,401.

[75]Ibid.

[76]Eaton "Professional Corporation and Association", Matthew Bender section 6.07(7) pages 6-61.

[77]Gibbs, Note 46; CCH Professional Corporations Handbook Paragraph 2109.

[78]IBP, Professional Corporations, Associations and Partnerships Paragraph 6525.21.

7

HOW TO TAKE ADVANTAGE OF NON-RETIREMENT FRINGE BENEFITS

The most underrated and overlooked benefits of a professional corporation are the non-retirement fringe benefits. Although the primary advantage of a professional corporation is the ability to adopt a qualified retirement plan without H.R. 10 limitations, the corporation may provide additional fringe benefits which may save the professionals up to thousands of dollars in taxes.

The most significant non-retirement fringe benefit available to employees of a professional corporation are as follows:

1. Medical reimbursement plans
2. Wage continuation plans
3. Tax free death benefits
4. Group term insurance plan

This chapter will discuss these fringe benefits in detail, how they can save the professional up to thousands of dollars in taxes, how to take advantage of them, and how to draft the appropriate language adopting said plans.

MEDICAL REIMBURSEMENT PLANS

One of the most important non-retirement fringe benefits available to the professional after incorporating is the medical reimbursement plan. Under such a plan, the corporation can reimburse its employees for medical expenses incurred by them, their spouses, and dependents. The payments made are deductible to the corporation[1] to the same extent as rent, salaries, and office supplies, and the amounts received by the employees are not includable *in* their income for tax purposes.[2]

An individual taxpayer who itemizes his deductions on his personal income tax return is only able to deduct those medical and dental expenses which exceed 3% of his adjusted gross income.[3] In computing this deduction, drug expenses in excess of 1% of adjusted gross income are included in medical expenses subject to the 3% limitation.[4] However, health insurance premiums are deductible in an amout equal to one-half the cost of the policy of $150, whichever is less. The balance is then added to the other medical expenses subject to the 3% limitation.[5]

Thus, almost all professionals because of their high income will only be able to deduct a negligible portion of their medical expenses.

Example

Professional:	adjusted gross income	$42,000
	health insurance	950
	medical and dental expenses	530
	drugs	170
	Total	$ 1,650

Based upon the following computations, out of a total of $1,650 of medical expenses, the professional will only be able to deduct $220 on his personal income tax return, resulting in a loss of $1,430 of unused medical expenses.

Medical and Dental Expenses (not compensated by insurance or otherwise) for medicine and drugs, doctors, dentists, nurses, hospital care, insurance premiums for medical care, etc.		
1 One half (but not more than $150) of insurance premiums for medical care. (Be sure to include in line 10 below)......................	150	00
2 Medicine and drugs............................	170	00
3 Enter 1% of line 15, Form 1040	420	00
4 Subtract line 3 from line 2. Enter difference (if less than zero, enter zero)	0	
5 Enter balance of insurance premiums for medical care not entered on line 1	800	00
6 Enter other medical and dental expenses:		
a Doctors, dentists, etc.......................	225	00
b Hospitals....................................	170	00
c Other (itemize—include hearing aids, dentures, eyeglasses, transportation, etc.) ➧		
eyeglasses	85	00
hearing aid	50	00
....		
....		
....		
....		
....		
....		
....		
....		
....		
7 Total (add lines 4, 5, 6a, b, and c)...........	1330	00
8 Enter 3% of line 15, Form 1040	1260	00
9 Subtract line 8 from line 7 (if less than zero, enter zero)	70	00
10 Total (add lines 1 and 9). Enter here and on line 35...➧	220	00

If the professional in the above example had been incorporated, the corporation could have paid for all of his medical expenses. Thus, one can readily observe that a medical reimbursement plan may well save hundreds of dollars in taxes by shifting previously non-deductible medical expenses to the corporation.

What Medical Expenses Can Be Covered by the Plan

All expenses for medical care which can be deducted by the professional on his personal income tax return under § 213 of the Internal Revenue Code, notwithstanding the percentage limitation, may be reimbursed to him under a medical reimbursement plan. Such medical expenses include the following items.[6]

Medical Care

Payments to physicians, surgeons, dentists, optometrists, chiropracters, osteopaths, chiropodists, podiatrists, psychiatrists, psychologists, and Christian Science practitioners.

Payments for hospital services, therapy and similar services, laboratory, surgical, obstetrical, diagnostic, dental, X-ray fees, nursing services (including nurses' board), and ambulance hire.

Medicines and Drugs

Medicines and drugs legally obtained and generally recognized as medicines and drugs even if they do not require a prescription. This does not include expenditures for toothpaste, toiletries and cosmetics.

Vitamins, iron supplements, etc. prescribed or recommended by a doctor, unless these items are taken to preserve general health without their having been prescribed or recommended by a doctor.

Insurance

Medical insurance premiums

Medical insurance premiums do not include:

a. Premiums paid on policies providing reimbursement for loss of earnings or for the accidental loss of life, limb, sight, etc. or

b. A policy that guarantees a specified amount each week (not to exceed a specified number of weeks) in the event of hospitalization as a result of sickness or injury.

WATCH THIS

Medical plans may cover medical expenses by the professional's dependents as well as himself and his spouse. A ''dependent'' for medical expense provisions means a person described under Section 152 of the Internal Revenue Code, provided the professional provides more than one-half of the dependent's support even though the professional may not be able to treat the individual as a dependent on his personal income tax return. Thus, a person will be considered a dependent even though his income may exceed $750 per year.

Discrimination is Permitted

What is remarkable about medical reimbursement plans is that there is no equivalent for the non-discriminatory requirements which prevail for qualified retirement plans under Section 401 of the Internal Revenue Code.[7] In fact, the Treasury regulations specifically provide that ''. . . A plan may cover one or more employees, and there may be different plans for different employees or classes of employees.''[8] Therefore, all employees need not be covered by the plan, nor is it required that all classes of employees receive the same benefits. Thus, the corporation may select those employees it wishes to benefit under its plan.

Transportation	*Meals and Lodging*	*Miscellaneous*
Payment for transportation primarily for and essential to medical care. This includes: **a.** Amounts paid for bus, taxi, train or plane fares, or ambulance hire; and **b.** Amounts paid for gas, oil, parking fees, etc. or alternatively, six cents for each mile your car is used for medical purposes. When using the standard mileage rate, parking fees and tolls may also be deducted.	Payment for meals and lodging furnished by a hospital or similar institution as a necessary incident to medical care is a medical expense if the patient's condition is such that the availability of medical care is the principal reason for his presence there. If an individual is in a nursing home or a home for the aged because of his physical condition, and the availability of medical care is a principal reason for his being there, the entire cost of maintenance (including meals and lodging) may be included in medical expenses.	Payments for artificial teeth, eyeglasses, hearing aids and crutches.

WATCH THIS

Even though a corporation may discriminate as to who will be eligible to participate in the medical reimbursement plan, there are two requirements which must be met before the tax benefits can be obtained. These requirements are:

1. There must be a plan in existence; and,
2. the plan must be for employees.[9]

It is in this area that most of the litigation has arisen. The Internal Revenue Service's primary attack is that there is no plan in existence, and, alternatively, if there is a plan, this plan is for the benefit of the stockholders and not for the benefit of the employees. If the Service is successful, then the payments made by the corporation will not be deductible and will, in many cases, be taxable as dividends to the shareholder employee who received the benefit.[10]

REQUIREMENTS FOR A PLAN

There must be a plan in existence at the time an employee's illness begins. Fortunately, the Treasury regulations have been quite liberal with respect to what constitutes a plan. The plan may be insured or noninsured, the plan is not required to be in writing, and the employee's rights under the plan do not have to be enforceable, if, when the employee became sick or injured he was covered by a plan, program, policy or custom of which notice or knowledge was readily available to him.[11] Thus, a plan may be "informal" in that it has been established by company policy to pay the medical expenses of its employees, provided, however, that the employees who are covered have reasonable notice or knowledge that they are covered by the plan.

> ...in order for there to be a plan, the employer must commit himself to certain rules and regulations governing payment; these rules must be made known to his employees as a definite policy; it is not enough that he merely lets it be known that payments may be made to

deserving employees if they are absent from work for illness. The employer's rules, adopted or crystallized by policy or custom, may offer varying treatment for employees, but the rules must be determinable before the employee's sickness arises.[12]

PLAN FOR EMPLOYEES

A medical reimbursement plan may discriminate in favor of certain employees, and the corporation may provide different plans for different employees or classes of employees. However, the plan must benefit those individuals covered by the plan in their capacity as employees rather than in their capacity as shareholders. When a corporation adopts a plan which covers all employees (which includes non-shareholders), or covers some non-shareholder employees, the plan will generally be considered a plan for employees. It is only when the plan covers shareholder-employees or excludes members of the same class of employees who are not shareholders, that the Internal Revenue Service may carefully scrutinize the plan to see if, in fact, it is really a plan for the employees.

This does not mean that a plan cannot cover just the share-holders of the corporation. It has been well established that stockholder employees may well constitute a natural category of employees sufficient to indicate that the plan is for employees rather than shareholders.[13] However, the shareholders must form a class of employees that can be rationally segregated from the other employees, on criteria other than being shareholders of the corporation. If the shareholders do constitute a separate group of employees, it is important that other employees who may also comprise the same group as the shareholders, are also covered, and receive the same benefits under the plan. Thus, in where a plan which only covers professional employees, there are five professional employees in the corporation, four of whom are shareholders, the fifth professional should be covered. The plan should not be restricted to shareholder professionals. This would be stong indication that the plan was not a plan for employees.[14]

The following chart represents six of the most cited cases in this areas which will provide the practitioner with a working tool in determining what does or does not constitute a "plan for employees."

THE WINNERS

Case	*Employees Covered*	*Number of Employees Not Covered*	*Plan Provisions*	*Plan Existed*	*Plan For Employees*
Bogene, Inc. T.C. Memo 1968-147 (1968)	**1.** Plan specifically named the two shareholder officers of the corporation and their dependents as covered employees. **2.** The two covered employees were equal shareholders.	48	All medical expenses incurred by covered employees and their families were to be reimbursed.	**1.** Plan adopted at meeting of Board of Directors and reduced to writing in Board minutes. **2.** The two covered employees knew of the plan's existence and its terms and benefits. **3.** Benefits and coverage under plan were not discretionary on Board of Directors. Plan was specific in terms of coverage and benefits.	**1.** Both covered employees were full-time employees receiving equal compensation. **2.** All employees of same class, to wit, officers, were being treated equally. No one in same class was excluded or receiving different benefits. **3.** Either covered employee could receive benefits greater than the other. **4.** No relationship between the possible benefit to be received and the employee's stock interest in the corporation. **5.** Corporation maintained a group health insurance program covering all employees.

Case	*Employees Covered*	*Number of Employees Not Covered*	*Plan Provisions*	*Plan Existed*	*Plan For Employees*
E. B. Smith T.C. Memo 1970-243 (1970)	**1.** Officers of corporation were covered. **2.** Officers of corporation consisted of husband and wife, who were also the sole shareholders of corporation.	12 Employees - All but one were seasonal.	All medical expenses were to be reimbursed to covered employees.	**1.** Plan was adopted in 1963 and reduced to writing in 1966. **2.** Plan was known to covered employees. **3.** Payments were not made in ad hoc basis, i.e. payments not in discretion of Board of Directors.	**1.** Two shareholder employees were the key management employees of corporation **2.** They both devoted their working hours to corporate business. **3.** No other employees were excluded who performed the same duties as performed by the covered employees.

Case	*Employees Covered*	*Number of Employees Not Covered*	*Plan Provisions*	*Plan Existed*	*Plan For Employees*
A. R. Seidel T.C. Memo 1971-238 (1971)	**1.** Officer - Stockholders and their dependents were covered. **2.** Corporation consisted of two shareholder officers who were the only employees of the corporation.	0	**1.** Reimburse covered employees for their reasonable medical expenses. **2.** Pay premiums for accident, death and dismemberment group insurance. **3.** Pay premiums for group insurance plan for life, accident, medical and hospital insurance. **4.** Plan subsequently amended to cover all medical expenses of officer-shareholders and their dependents.	**1.** Plan reduced to writing in minutes of Board of Directors meeting. **2.** Terms of plan were known to covered employees. **3.** Coverage and benefits were specified-coverage and amount of reimbursement were not discretionary in Board of Directors.	**1.** Each covered employee devoted his entire time to business of corporation. **2.** When plan was adopted one employee had a history of illness that indicated that he would receive greater benefits under plan. This was strong evidence that the covered employees would not be benefited in proportion to their stock interest in the corporation, but as employees.

THE LOSERS

Case	*Employees Covered*	*Number of Employees Not Covered*	*Plan Provisions*
A.B. Larkin v. Commissioner 48TC 629 (1967)	**1.** Plan covered those employees whom the officers decided should be covered. **2.** In practice, the plan only benefited the two related shareholders of the corporation, their father, and another long-term employee, but on an unequal basis.	Approximately 24, of which 1/3 were full-time, 1/3 seasonal, and 1/3 part-time.	Employees to be covered under the plan and the benefits to be received by a covered employee were to be determined in the discretion of the officers of the corporation.

Plan Not For Employees			
1. No written evidence of plan other than a short sentence which appeared in the minutes of a Board of Directors meeting. **2.** The availability of benefits was not communicated to the employees until the decision was made to include them in the plan.	**3.** There was no indication that the payment of benefits was related to the performance of services. Father was entitled to same benefits as his sons, although his salary was substantially smaller. **4.** There was no indication that the non-shareholder employee who received benefits under the plan did so during the first several years of the plan's existence.	**5.** Payments were made to dependents of shareholder employees who were not covered by the plan, but there was no evidence of payments to dependents of covered non-shareholder employee. **6.** Coverage and benefits paid were made on an ad hoc basis.	**7.** There were no uniform benefits or treatment for covered employees.[15] The court pointed out that Blue Cross insurance was provided for the shareholder employees and not for the non-shareholder employee. In addition, there was no description of the limits of the benefits which the court felt was strong evidence that the plan was not for the benefit of employees.

Case	*Employees Covered*	*Number of Employees Not Covered*	*Plan Provisions*	*Plan Not For Employees*
S. Levine 50 T.C. 422 (1968)	**1.** President was specifically covered and all other employees were covered. **2.** There were four shareholder officers in the corporation, who consisted of a father, mother, and their two sons.	0	Plan provided that the president would be entitled to draw sick pay for the duration of his illness, and all other regular employees who might become ill would also be entitled to sick pay. Benefits for both the president and other employees would not exceed $100 per week.	**1.** The employees other than the officers did not see the minutes of the meeting adopting the plan, or any written rules or regulations pertaining to sick pay benefits. **2.** Employees other than officers were told orally that they would be entitled to sick pay. **3.** No evidence that non-officer employees were told that they would receive benefits for a continuous period of time extending many months or years. **4.** Sick pay was only paid to non-officer employees for short periods of time, the longest period only being two weeks. **5.** President received $100 a week for a three-year period even though he performed no services. **6.** Plan was adopted after President became seriously ill. **7.** Court concluded that corporation would never have made such continual payments to any other employee as it did to the President, and that the payments were made to the President in his capacity as a shareholder, rather than an employee. Thus, no plan for employees.

Case	*Employees Covered*	*Number of Employees Not Covered*	*Plan Provisions*	*Plan Not For Employees*
Edward T. Smithback T.C. Memo 1969-136 (1969)	**1.** President and his family were covered. **2.** President was the sole shareholder of the corporation and the only full-time employee.	Three part-time employees were not covered.	All medical expenses of covered employee and his family were to be paid by corporation.	**1.** Plan was not reduced to writing until two years after its adoption, and then only a brief reference was made to it in the minutes of a Board of Directors meeting. **2.** Evidence was introduced that the primary reason of the president in incorporating his business was to adopt a medical reimbursement plan. The court felt that this was a tax-avoidance purpose which would only benefit the president as a shareholder rather than as an employee. Therefore, the court concluded that the plan was not a plan for employees.

After reading the above cases, the practitioners can readily observe the same facts being cited by the courts in determining whether a particular plan was or was not for the benefit of employees. The facts most often cited by the courts are summarized in the following charts.

"The Losers"-What Went Wrong	*"The Winners"-What Was Right*
1. All covered employees of corporation did not see plan or know its terms or provisions.	*1.* Plan was often reduced to writing or its terms and provisions were known by the covered participants.
2. Coverage under plan was not defined - determined in discretion of Board of Directors.	*2.* Coverage was definite - was not left to discretion of Board of Directors.
3. Benefits under plan were not definite - amount of benefits was left to discretion of Board of Directors.	*3.* Benefits under plan were definite amount of benefits not discretionary.
4. No relationship between services rendered and benefits received.	*4.* There was no exclusion of any employee within the class of employees covered.
	5. Benefits were not paid in relationship to stockholdings in corporation.

OBSERVATION - PLANS FOR ONE-MAN CORPORATIONS

The Treasury regulations specifically provide that a plan may cover only one employee.[16] However, since the Smithback decision, commentators have seriously questioned whether a corporation can adopt a medical reimbursement plan which will only benefit its sole shareholder employee even though he may be the only employee of the corporation.

The author is of the opinion that such an interpretation is too extreme. It appears that the most important reason why the plan was not considered a plan for employees was that the primary purpose of the adoption of the plan was for tax avoidance purposes, which could only benefit the employee in his capacity as a shareholder and not as an employee. In addition, the corporation had other part-time employees who were not covered by the plan, and the plan was not reduced to writing until two years after its adoption. Thus it is quite possible that the court might have reached a different conclusion if:

1. The plan was reduced to writing immediately after its adoption.
2. No evidence was introduced that the primary purpose of incorporating the taxpayer's business was for tax avoidance purposes, to wit, adopting a medical reimbursement plan, and;
3. The other employees of the corporation were covered by the plan.

It would appear that one way to avoid the Smithback result when there are employees rather than the sole shareholder is to cover all or some of the other employees of the corporation. Benefits could then be based upon a percentage of compensation.

In addition, the author is of the opinion that different plans can be established for the sole shareholder employee and for the other employees. Therefore, if the sole shareholder is covered by a plan in his capacity as a member of a specified class of employees, such as those employees who are licensed to practice medicine, and the other employees are covered in a category entitled "all employees who are not licensed to practice medicine," then both plans together should be considered a plan for the benefit of employees, even though the only employee who is licensed to practice medicine is the corporation's sole shareholder.

The same rationale should be applicable to corporations consisting of no other employees other than the sole shareholder. If the plan covers the sole shareholder in his capacity as a member of a specified class of employees, and the plan is specific as to benefits and coverage, then there is no reason why the benefits of the medical reimbursement plan should not be available to a one-man professional corporation.

The Seidel case is an excellent example in support of this position. The corporation in that case adopted a plan that covered the two employees who were also the sole stockholders of the corporation. The court held that this was a plan for employees since the two shareholder employees were being benefited in their capacity as employees. There is no reason why corporations consisting of only two shareholder employees should be able to adopt a medical reimbursement plan and a corporation consisting of only one shareholder employee cannot.

Since tax avoidance was mentioned in the Smithback case, it might be helpful when drafting the minutes of the Board of Directors meeting adopting the plan to provide non-tax reasons for its adoption, such as, to attract new employees to the corporation by providing benefits offered by other corporations.

Drafting Techniques

As a practical matter, a corporation consisting of two or more professionals would be well advised to place a limit on the medical expenses which will be reimbursed to each professional. This will prevent one professional from receiving large payments in the event of a serious illness or accident which the corporation may not be able to afford or be willing to assume. Thus, when drafting the plan, a maximum limit should be placed on benefits which should closely approximate the normal and usual medical expenses of the professionals. This limit can be expressed in terms of a percentage of compensation or be a stated dollar figure.

The following is a seven-point checklist of how to draft a medical reimbursement plan.

Seven Point Checklist On How to Draft a Medical Reimbursement Plan

1. The plan should be in writing.[17]
2. Specify those employees who are covered by the plan.[18] Coverage in the plan should not be left to the discretion of the Board of Directors.
3. Specify the benefits to which covered employees will be entitled. Benefits should be clearly defined and should not be left to discretion of the Board of Directors as to what benefits a particular employee shall be entitled.[19]
4. Notify each covered employee of his participation in the medical reimbursement plan.
5. Inform each covered employee of the benefits to which he will be entitled in the event of accident or illness.
6. Do not exclude or discriminate against any employee who is part of the category of employees who are covered by the plan.
7. If there are employees other than shareholder employees, then some or all of these employees should be covered by the plan even though the benefit to which they may be entitled may be less than the shareholder employee's benefits.

The following is a sample plan for the officers of a corporation. The plan can easily be converted into a plan for all employees by merely deleting the word officer and inserting the word employee. Of course, each practitioner will want to alter the plan to meet his own particular situation.

MEDICAL REIMBURSEMENT PLAN
OF THE
OFFICERS OF XYZ, P.C.
I

1. Effective, 19 , XYZ, P.C. (hereinafter referred to as the "Company") will reimburse at least quarterly any officer of the Company, who is employed by the Company on a full-time basis, for all expenses incurred by such officer for the medical care (as defined in Section 213(e) of the Internal Revenue Code of 1954, or as hereafter amended) of such officer, his spouse and his dependents (as defined in Section 152 of the Internal Revenue Code of 1954, or as hereafter amended).
2. Reimbursement to, or the payment on behalf of any one officer including his spouse and his dependents, shall not exceed (use either A or B):
   A. X% of the officer's compensation.
   B. $X per fiscal year of the company.
3. *An officer* - shall be considered as employed on a full-time basis for the purpose of this Plan if he customarily works at least ten months in each year and thirty hours in each week.
   Expenses for medical care - as so defined in Section 213(e), include all amounts paid for hospital bills, doctor and dental bills, drugs, and premiums on accident or health insurance, including hospitalization, surgical, and medical insurance.
   Dependents - as so defined in Section 152, includes any member of such officer's family over one-half of whose support is furnished by such officer.

4 The Company may, in its discretion, pay directly any or all of the above defined expenses in lieu of making reimbursement therefor. In such event, the Company shall be relieved of all further responsibility with respect to that particular medical expense.

5. Any officer applying for reimbursement under this Plan shall submit to the Company, at least quarterly, all hospitalization, doctor, dental or other medical bills, including premium notices for accident or health insurance, for verification by the Company prior to payment. A failure to comply herewith may, at the discretion of the Company, terminate such officer's right to said reimbursement.
6. Reimbursement or payment provided under this Plan shall be made by the Company only in the event and to the extent that such reimbursement or payment is not provided for under any insurance policy or policies, whether owned by the Company or the officers, or under any other health and accident plan. In the event that there is such a policy or plan in effect, providing for reimbursement or payment in whole or in part, then to the extent of the coverage under such policy or plan the Company shall be relieved of any and all liability hereunder.
7. It is the intention of the Company that benefits payable under this Plan shall be eligible for exclusion from the gross income of the officers covered by the Plan, as provided by Section 105 of the Internal Revenue Code of 1954, as hereafter amended.
8. Any person hereafter becoming an officer of this Company, employed on a full-time basis, shall be eligible for the benefits provided under this Plan.
9. A copy of this Plan shall be given to all present and future officers of this Company, who are employed on a full-time basis.
10. This Plan shall be subject to termination or amendment at any time hereafter by affirmative vote of the Board of Directors of the Company; provided, however that such termination or amendment shall not affect any right to claim reimbursement for medical expenses under the provisions of the agreement, arising prior to said termination.
11. In the event that there should be a disallowance for federal or state income tax purposes of any of the deductions taken by the Company for the purposes set forth hereinabove, then and in that event, the amount disallowed shall be considered additional compensation to the employee.

WAGE CONTINUATION PLAN AND DISABILITY INCOME PROTECTION INSURANCE

A professional corporation, in addition to adopting a medical reimbursement plan for the benefit of its employees may adopt a wage continuation plan whereby the corporation agrees to pay an employee his salary or a portion thereof in the event of his inability to perform the services for which he was employed as a result of his sickness or illness. Benefits under such a plan may be provided by insurance or it may be self-insured.[20] As a general rule, most professional corporations will fund such a plan by purchasing disability income protection insurance policies which results in the following benefits never available to the self-employed practitioner.

1. The payments made by the corporation for disability income protection insurance are a deductible expense,[21] provided the benefits are not made payable to the corporation.[22]
2. The payments made by the corporation for disability income protection insurance are not included in the gross income of the employee.[23]

Thus, for the first time, a professional is able to shift the cost of purchasing his disability income protection insurance to the corporation which, as a self-employed practitioner or as a partner in a partnership, was not a deductible expense.[24]

However, there is one disadvantage when the corporaiton purchases disability insurance for its employees. After a 30-day waiting period, proceeds exceeding $100 a week will be taxable to the employee.[25] As a self-employed practitioner, the entire proceeds received by the professional from such insurance were completely tax free.[26] Nevertheless, as will be subsequently discussed in more detail, this is not a fatal disadvantage, and most professionals will prefer to reduce their out-of-pocket cost for this insurance by purchasing it with before-tax dollars.

Requirement For a Plan

The term 'wage continuation plan' means an accident or health plan as defined by Reg. §1.105-5.[27] Thus, all discussion regarding "is there a plan" and "is it for the benefit of employees" in the previous section on medical reimbursement plans is equally applicable to wage continuation plans. Therefore, although the corporation may provide disability income protection insurance for its key employees, who may also be its only shareholders, it must be purchased to benefit them as employees and not in their capacity as shareholders if the tax benefits are to be obtained.

Should Disability Insurance be Purchased through the Corporation

As previously mentioned, the proceeds from a corporation-purchased disability income protection policy will be taxable to the disabled professional to the extent that proceeds exceed $100 per week after the first 30 days of disability. Nevertheless, most professionals will still be better off by having the corporation pay for the premiums. There are two reasons for this , which are as follows.

1. In most instances, disability will be for a short period of time. Therefore, the tax the professional will pay on the proceeds will be, in almost all cases, far less than the tax savings generated by having the corporation pay for the premiums.
2. Even if disability is for a long period of time, the tax on the proceeds will not be that large since the major source of the disabled professional's income will be derived from the insurance policy, which will be reduced by the professional's itemized deduction and exemption (which generally will remain the same as prior to disability) and disability income exclusion.

Example:

Professional- Married, three children, is disabled on January 1, 1974 and is unable to return to work until January 1, 1975. Disability income protection policy provides $2000 a month income to the professional, commencing after the first thirty days of disability.

Assume no other sources of income, total income of professioanal is $22,000 (11 months x $2000), and that his itemized deductions and exemptions total $10,000. The professional's tax liability for calendar year ending December 31, 1974 will be $1,228, computed as follows.

Adjusted gross income	$22,000
Itemized deductions and exemptions	10,000
Disability income exclusion $100 a week x 48 weeks	4,800
Taxable income	$ 7,200
Tax	$ 1,228

In many cases, the ability to deduct the cost of the professional's insurance premium for just two years will result in a greater tax saving than the tax incurred on the proceeds in the event of disability for an extended period of time.

Needless to say, if disability occurs during the first year the premiums are paid by the corporation, or if disability continues for many years or if the professional is disabled for life from practicing the profession for which he has been trained, then the professional would have been better off had he continued to pay for disability insurance premiums personally rather than have the corporation assume the payments. Nevertheless, since most periods of disability are of a short duration, most professionals will choose to 'risk' the chances of serious disability and elect to shift the cost of the insurance premium from after-tax dollars to the corporation.

However, serious disability does occur to many people during their working lives, and many professionals wish to prepare for this possible event. In such cases, it would be advisable to have the corporation pay for part of the premium and the professional for the remainder. In the event of disability, the professional's tax liability on the proceeds would be reduced to that portion which represents the corporation's payments.[28] Alternatively, the corporation could pay for the professional's disability insurance which commences benefits after a short waiting period, and the professional could maintain a personally-owned policy whose benefits commence after a long period of disability. In the event of illness for a short period of time, the professional will be covered by the corporation-purchased insurance, and in the event of extended disability, he will receive benefits from two policies, but the proceeds from the personally-owned policy will be tax free.[29]

Another consideration in deciding whether or not the corporation should pay for the insurance premium on the amount of disability insurance the professional may wish to continue personally is the specialty of the professional. If the professional uses his hands, such as a dentist or surgeon, then an accident to his hands may render it impossible for the professional ever to perform the services for which he was trained. Since a serious accident is not necessary to render a surgeon incapable of operating, and the chances for such an injury are greater than a serious heart attack or stroke which will render the professional disabled for life, it is often advisable to have such a professional continue a large portion of his disability income protection insurance. In cases where the professional will have to incur a serious illness to render him unable to perform the services for which he was trained for an extended period of time, it is often advisable to have the corporation pay for the majority of the diasability insurance protection for the professional.

Nevertheless, there are no set rules which are applicable in all cases, and the choices will ultimately have to be made by the professional after considering the alternatives and their consequences.

Disability Insurance - What Kind, How Much, and When Should Benefits Begin

Disability income protection insurance is just as important to the professional as his life insurance. Without both, financial disaster may strike. Therefore, the author feels that the professional's minimum needs should be covered by a non-cancelable, guaranteed renewable insurance policy providing benefits in the event he is unable to practice the profession for which he was trained. That is, if a dentist is no longer able to perform dental services, he will be entitled to benefits even though he may be able to teach or assume some other occupation. The professional can then supplement this foundation with group disability coverage which may be available through his professional societies.

The professional should have sufficient coverage to be able to maintain a reasonable standard of living. Disability insurance will never be able to replace the professional's salary dollar for dollar, but a person earning $50,000 a year cannot, in almost all cases, live comfortably on disability income of $1,000 a month. In such cases, the professional would be well advised to increase his protection.

Disability insurance benefits should normally commence after the corporation ceases to pay the professional his salary under his employment contract.[30] In addition, the longer the waiting period the less expensive the cost of providing the insurance protection. Thus, proper planning can provide the professional a continued cash flow for the period of his disability.

The following is sample language that can be used in adopting a wage continuation plan.

WAGE CONTINUATION PLAN FOR OFFICERS OF XYZ, P.C.

1. Effective , 19__, XYZ, P.C. will continue the wages of any officer who is employed by the company on a full-time basis during any period in which the officer is absent from work as the result of personal injury or sickness. An officer shall be considered employed on a full-time basis if he customarily works at least ten months in each year and thirty hours in each week.

2. It is the intention of the company that this wage continuation plan shall be governed by the provisions of the Internal Revenue Service Regulations §1.105-4.

3. It is hereby recognized that the earnings of the corporation may not permit the continuation of the employee's salary for an indefinite period of time. Therefore, in furtherance of the objectives of this plan, the corporation is hereby authorized to purchase a disability income protection insurance policy for each officer providing benefits up to $______ per month; or alternatively, the corporation may assume the cost of each officer's personally-owned disability income protection insurance providing up to $______ in benefits per month.[31]

TAX-FREE DEATH BENEFIT

The Internal Revenue Code provides that a corporation may pay a $5000 death benefit to the employee's beneficiary or estate which will not be subject to taxation, provided such payment was made by reason of the death of the employee.[32] Although this is a small fringe benefit when compared to all the other fringe benefits made available to the professional, the professional is able, nevertheless, to provide a tax free benefit to his wife or other beneficiary, which is not available to him as a self-employed practitioner.[33] In addition, the payment made by the corporation is a deductible expense.[34] In the case of a one-man professional corporation, this will result in a reduction in the value of the corporation by $5000 for estate tax purposes.

This tax-free benefit is available whether or not:

1. The payment is made to the estate of the employee or to any beneficiary (individual, corporation, or partnership)
2. It is made directly to the beneficiary or held in trust.
3. It is made pursuant to a contractual obligation of the employer.
4. The payment is made in a lump sum or in installments.

If the Professional, prior to his death, had a nonforfeitable right to receive the death benefit while living, the $5000 will be taxed to the beneficiary.[35] However, it is not difficult to insure that the employee's interest in the death benefit is forfeitable. This can be accomplished by providing that no benefits will be payable to an employee who retires prior to his specified retirement date without the corporation's consent[36]. This condition is also satisfied if the employee's right to the benefit is forfeitable upon severance or termination of employment with the corporation.[37]

The following is sample language which is commonly used by the Board of Directors in adopting a plan providing for the payment of a $5000 death benefit to an employee's wife or beneficiary as a result of his death.

Death Benefit Resolution

VOTED:

That in recognition of the services rendered to the corporation by______________, and in consideration of his future services, there shall be paid to his wife, if he is survived by his wife, otherwise in equal shares to his children who survive them, per stirpes, the sum of $5000.00 within thirty (30) days after his death, provided that he was an employee of the corporation at the time of his death. The foregoing shall not be revoked or modified without his written consent.

Even if such a plan is not adopted, the $5000 tax free benefit is still available when the death benefit under a qualified retirement plan is distributed to the employee's beneficiary in a lump sum, *or in the form of an annuity.*[38] This is true even if the employee had a nonforfeitable right to the assets credited to his account in the retirement plan.

GROUP TERM INSURANCE

A professional corporation provides a unique opportunity to offer its employees inexpensive insurance coverage by adopting a group term insurance plan. The advantages of such a plan are as follows:

1. The premiums paid by the corporation for group term insurance are deductible.[39]
2. The cost of the first $50,000 of insurance is not included in the employee's gross income.[40]
3. Insurance may be obtained for employees who might otherwise be uninsurable.
4. Even though the cost of the value of insurance protection in excess of $50,000 is taxable to the employee, this "cost" is considerably less than if the employee purchased the same coverage personally and is considerably below the price of the insurance paid by the corporation.[41]
5. If state law permits, the employee may assign his "incidents of ownership" in the insurance to another, in which event the proceeds can not be included in computing his federal estate tax.[42]
6. Group term insurance is not available to a partner in a partnership or a sole practitioner.[43]

What Is Group Term Insurance

To obtain the benefits enumerated above, the corporation must adopt a "plan of group insurance" for its employees.[44] The corporation may draft its own plan setting forth the terms and provisions in a "separate written document" or the plan may be incorporated in the insurance company's master policy.[45] Benefits under the plan may be provided from individual term policies or from a master policy provided by the insurance company.[46] If the corporation expects to fund the plan with individual policies, then it will have to adopt its own plan.

Group term life insurance does not apply to travel insurance or accident and health insurance (including amounts payable under a double indemnity clause or rider) and to amount of insurance in excess of the maximum which can be provided by a master policy under applicable state law.[47]

WATCH THIS

The cost of term insurance varies greatly from company to company, and the corporation should make a comparison of premium rates before it adopts a plan. Furthermore, in many cases, it is often less expensive to fund a plan of group term insurance with individual policies rather than to adopt an insurance company's master policy. In addition, there are other advantages to using individual term policies, which are as follows:[48]

1. guaranteed premiums.
2. guaranteed renewability.
3. superior premium and dividend structure.
4. convertibility at attained age or original age.
5. right to continue should the employer drop or change plans.

A corporation may adopt a plan of group insurance regardless of the number of employees it may have. However, the Treasury regulations have established different criteria for plans adopted by corporations consisting of fewer than 10 full-time employees and for the corporation consisting of more than 10 full-time employees. The rules established are illustrated in the following charts.

PLAN OF GROUP INSURANCE

10 Or More Employees[49]

1. Coverage:

The plan must make life insurance available to a group of lives upon some method which precludes individual selection. An eligible employee may waive his right to participate.

a. Coverage may be based upon age, marital status, or membership in union.

b. A plan available only to shareholder employees will not qualify.[51]

2. Benefits:

The amount of insurance protection provided under the plan must be based upon some formula which precludes individual selection of such amounts.

Benefits must be based upon factors such as salary, years of service or position, or a combination of these factors.

3. Insurability

Evidence of insurability may be required, including the use of medical examination.[52]

Less Than 10 Employees[50]

1. Coverage:

The plan must cover all full-time employees with more than six months of service with the corporation.

Employees whose customary employment is for not more than 20 hours in any one week or five months per year are considered part time and do not have to be included in a plan.

Plan will qualify even though an eligible employee has elected not to participate.

2. Benefits:

Amount of protection may be computed by one of two alternative methods.

1. As a uniform percentage of salary, or;

2. On the basis of coverage brackets under which no bracket exceeds 2½ times the next lower bracket and the lowest bracket is at least ten percent of the highest bracket.

3. Insurability

Eveidence of insurability is only attainable from a medical questionnaire, and medical examinations are not permitted.

4. Employees age 65 or Over

The corporation does not have to cover employees who continue to work after they attain age 65. If they are covered, coverage must be on same basis as other employees under age 65, or the corporation may provide a separate schedule of coverage brackets for the over 65 group.

Examples of Coverage Brackets for Corporation with Less than 10 Employees

1.	Professional employees - officers	$50,000
	Professional employees - non-officers	25,000
	Secretaries	10,000
	Receptionists - Clerks	5,000
2.	Employees whose salary exceeds $20,000	$50,000
	Employees earning $15,000-20,000	25,000
	Employees earning $10,000 but less than $15,000	10,000
	Employees earning up to $10,000	5,000

Cost of Insurance in Excess of $50,000

As stated previously, if an employee receives insurance protection in excess of $50,000, the value of such excess protection is taxable to the employee. This taxable amount is computed by using the "Uniform Premium Table"[53] which is reprinted below.

UNIFORM PREMIUMS FOR $1000 OF GROUP-TERM LIFE INSURANCE PROTECTION

5-year age bracket	Cost per $100 of protection for one-month period
Under 30	8 cents
30 to 34	10 cents
35 to 39	14 cents
40 to 44	23 cents
45 to 49	40 cents
50 to 54	68 cents
55 to 59	$1.10
60 to 64	$1.63

This table determines the cost of each $1000 of group term insurance on the employee's life for each one month period.

Example

A 43 year old[54] professional has $100,000 of group term coverage. The amount he will include in his income is computed as follows. 50 (number of $1000 of insurance in excess of 50,000) x .23 (cost per $1000 for one-month period) x 12 (number of months) = $138.00

The $138 is then added to the professional's gross income for tax purposes, and if he is in the 50% tax bracket, the additional tax is $69.00.

Should the Corporation Adopt a Group Plan - Observation

Whether or not a corporation should adopt a group term insurance plan is generally based on the cost of providing such a program. If a corporation consists of one or two professional employees who are young and three or four older non-professional employees, then the tax savings obtained by purchasing their insurance is offset by the high cost of maintaining term insurance for the other employees. Therefore, the overall cost of maintaining the program must be computed, not only for the present year but for future years as well.

Unless the cost is prohibitive, group term insurance is an attractive fringe benefit, since it will provide inexpensive insurance coverage for the corporation's employees. However, the professional should be cautioned against using term insurance to satisfy his entire insurance needs. Most professionals will have a need for life insurance for liquidity purposes at the time of their death, and since the term insurance coverage will cease when the employee retires, the professional will have no insurance unless he has maintained his personal insurance program or has insurance as an asset in his pension or profit sharing plan which has been transferred to him at retirement. Although the plan may provide that the term insurance may be converted by the employee when his employment terminates, the cost of so doing may be exorbitant if conversion is exercised when the employee is in his sixties.

It is the author's opinion that term insurance should be coordinated with the professional's personal insurance and the insurance purchased through the retirement plan for his benefit. Such coordination will produce a well-rounded insurance program for the professional.

The following is sample language for a group term insurance plan for a corporation consisting of fewer than ten employees.

Group Term Insurance Plan - Less than 10 Employees

Effective, , 19__, XYZ, P.C. (hereinafter referred to as the employer) shall provide a plan of Employee Group Term Life insurance for all eligible employees, as specified herein.

1. It is the intent of this plan to quality as a "plan of group insurance" under §79 of the Internal Revenue Code and the regulations pertaining thereto.
2. *Benefits* - Use either paragraph a or b.

a. Each eligible employee will be entitled to insurance protection based upon his job classification as of the effective date of this plan.

Job Classification	*Insurance Protection*
a.	
b.	
c.	
d.	

b. The amount of term life insurance to be purchased for each employee shall be equal to ____% of his annual salary rounded off to the nearest $1000, as of the effective date of this plan.

3. As of the effective date, all full-time employees who have six months of service with the employer shall be eligible to participate in the plan. Any employee becoming a full-time employee or who completes six months of service shall immediately become eligible to participate in this plan.
4. This plan shall be funded with individual term insurance policies purchased and paid for by the employer and owned by the individual employees who have been insured.
5. Each eligible full-time employee shall have the right to elect not to participate in this plan. Any employee who shall elect not to participate or who shall be found to be uninsurable for the issuance of the life insurance to be provided by this plan shall be excluded.
6. In the event a covered employee shall terminate his employment, the Employer shall have no further obligation under this agreement.
7. The employer retains the right to amend or terminate this plan of insurance by giving notice to each participating employee prior to any anniversary date.
8. All of the provisions of the individual policies which comprise this plan of group insurance shall be considered a part of this plan document.

FOOTNOTES

[1]Regs.§1.162-10(a).

[2]Payments received by an employee are not included in his income if they do not exceed his expenses for medical care as defined by §213(e); payments will be included in the employee's income to the extent such payments are used in computing a medical expense deduction under §213 in a previous taxable year. The exclusion applies only to amounts which are paid specifically to reimburse the employee for medical expenses which are not used in computing the medical expense deduction under §213.

[3]IRC §213(a)(1).

[4]IRC §213(b).

[5]IRC §213(a).

[6]This list only represents some of the most common medical expenses and is not intended to represent an exhaustive list of such expenses.

[7]Legislative history indicates quite clearly that discrimination is permissible under medical reimbursement plans. As originally passed by the House, Section 105 contained nondiscrimination provisions applicable to qualified plans (H. Rept. No. 1337, 83rd Congress, Second Session, p. 15) The Senate Finance Committee deleted these nondiscrimination provisions and the Senate version was adopted (Conf. Rept. No. 2543, 83rd Congress, Second Session, pp. 24-25). In addition, the Senate Finance Committee Report on Section 106, which provided an exclusion from the employee's gross income for employer contributions to a medical plan, contemplated discriminatory treatment. (S. Rept. No. 1622, 83rd Congress, Second Session, pp. 15-16).

[8]Regs. 1.105-5(a).

[9]Ibid.

[10]A.B. Larkin 48 T.C. 629, 1967 Smithback T.C. Memo 1969-136, S. Levine 50 T.C. 422, (1968) Charlie-Sturgroeill Motors T.C. Memo 1973-281 and American Foundry 59 T.C. 231 (1972) where the court held that the payments made through the medical reimbursement plan would be considered as additional compensation to the employee and thus deductible to the corporation.

[11]Note 8.

[12]John C. Lang 41 T.C. 352(1963) - In a subsequent Revenue Ruling (Rev. Rul. 71-403 IRB 1971-36), the Treasury indicated that payments received by employees under a medical reimbursement plan would be excluded from their income even though they were unable to work at the time of the adoption of the plan.

[13]A.B. Larkin, E.B. Smith, A.R. Seidel (See Charts-this chapter, commencing on Pg. 107).

[14]American Foundry Note 10; Bogene, Inc. TC Memo 1968-147.

[15]The court stated that the fact that the benefits actually paid to the non-shareholder employee were small is not a factor in determining whether there is a plan for employees. "The provisions of Section 105 were not directly dependent upon benefits actually paid, but relate rather to a prior existing plan to pay."

[16]Note 8.

[17]Although the Treasury regulations state that a plan is not required to be in writing, a written plan provides the best evidence as to the existence of a plan. Otherwise, the plan's existence must be shown by the corporation's custom or practice to reimburse employees for their medical expenses. This might prove quite difficult in a new professional corporation which has not had the time to develop corporate policy or custom.

[18]Reference should not be made to shareholders.

[19]Benefits will be considered definite of they are limited to a specified dollar amount, such as $5000 per year; up to a certain percentage of compensation, or all the medical expenses of the employee.

[20]IRC §106.

[21]Note1.

[22]Rev. Rul. 66-262, 1966-2 CB 105 However, any benefits received by the corporation under the insurance policy will be tax free to the corporation.

[23]IRC §106.

[24]Rev. Rul. 58-90, 1958-1 CB 88.

[25]§105(d) This section further provides that if the amount of said pay received by the employee during the first 30 days of disability is less then 75% of his compensation, then the employee may exclude up to $75 per week after the first seven days of disability. If the employee was hospitalized during the first seven days, then there is no waiting period. If the said pay exceeds 75% of the employees's regular pay, then no portion of the proceeds will be excludable from his income.

[26]IRC 104(a)(3).

[27]Regs. §1.105-4(a) (2) (i).

[28]Regs. §1.105-1(d).

[29]It has been suggested that the professional purchase and pay the premiums on the disability income protection insurance policy, and that the corporation reimburse him after the close of the corporation's taxable year for such premiums paid, if the professional has not become disabled. In this manner, if the professional becomes disabled, the proceeds will be tax free since he paid for the premiums personally. If he is not disabled, then the corporation will deduct the cost of the premium when it reimburses the professional, and the professional has paid nothing for the insurance protection for the previous year. The author is of the opinion that such a plan will not achieve the desired objective. The plan is an obvious circumvention of the IRC. The professional is adopting a "wait and see" attitude before he determines whether to be reimbursed or not, depending upon which choice will provide the most advantageous tax benefits to him. If the corporaiton has only a small number of shareholders, the discretion of the Board of Directors of whether or not to allow said benefits is really meaningless because of the control the

affected professional has over the Board of Directors. Although a stronger argument might be made in cases where the professional is not a shareholder or a director, it is unlikely that the Internal Revenue Service will permit such a plan. It is even possible that the Internal Revenue Service might take the position that the premiums paid by the corporation are not deductible and if the professional becomes disabled, that the proceeds are only partially excludable from his gross income since the premiums were, in fact, intended to the paid for by the corporation. See "an alternative possibility in Sec. 105-106 plans" Robert W. Osler, The Health Insurance Underwriter, October 1973.

[30]See chapter 5 "Drafting the Employment Contract" Period of Disability, page 73, The Use of Disability Income Protection Insurance, page, 74.

[31]Rev. Rul. 61-146 1961-2 CB 25 provides that the corporation can reimburse an employee for premiums paid on his own policies. Therefore, it will be better to assume the cost of the employee's disability insurance policy which was taken out at a lower premium rate than purchase a new policy for the same coverage at a higher premium.

[32]IRC §101(b).

[33]IRC §101(b) (3).

[34]IRC 404(a) (5) Rev.Rul. 55-212 1955-1 CB 299.

[35]IRC§101(b) (2) (B); See Regs. §1.101-2(d) (1) for what constitutes a nonforfeitable right.

[36]Regs. §1.101-2(d) (2) Example 6.

[37]Regs. §1.01(2) (d) (1).

[38]IRC § 101(b) (2) (B) (i) and (D), Regs. §1.72-16(c) (3) examples 1 and 2.

[39]Rev. Rul. 56-400, 1956-2 CB 116.

[40]IRC §79(a) (1).

[41]Regs. §1.79-3(d); IRC §79(b) provides these exceptions to the rule that the cost of coverage in excess of $50,000 will be taxed to the employee, which are as follows:

1. If the employee has terminated his employment with the corporation and has obtained his retirement age or has become disabled permanently.

2. The employee has named a charitable organization as beneficiary under the policy.

3. The corporation has been named as beneficiary under the policy. In this instance, the corporation will not be able to deduct the cost of the insurance premiums.

[42]Rev. Rul 72-307 IRB 1972-25,9.

[43]Regs. §1.79-1(b) (2).

[44]Regs. §1.79-1(b) (1) (iii) (b).

[45]Ibid.

[46]Regs. §1.79-1(b) (1) (i).

[47]Ibid.

[48]Hinckley "Group Life Insurance for Small Professional Corporations" CLU Journal, January 1974, p. 23.

[49]Regs. §1.79-1(b) (I) (iii).

[50]Regs. §1.79-1(b) (1) (iii) (d).

[51]This raises the issue of whether a corporation consisting of only shareholder employees can adopt a group term insurance program for their benefit under the "Smithback" rationale as discussed in this chapter under Medical Reimbursement Plan. It is the author's impression that a classification of "shareholders" would not qualify when other employees are excluded, but the plan would qualify when coverage is available to all employees and shareholder employees happen to be the only employees.

[52]Rev. Rul. 71-576, IRB 1971-51, 8.

[53]Regs. §1.79-3(d).

[54]Regs. §1.79-3(d) (1) provides that the age of the employee is this attained age on the last day of his taxable year.

8

SELECTING THE RETIREMENT PLAN

"What type of retirement program should a professional corporation adopt?" This is the most important question facing the practitioner in advising his professional clients who incorporate. There are many varieties of plans that may be selected, and the practitioner must have a thorough understanding of the characteristics, advantages and disadvantages of each before he can begin to select the most appropriate retirement program. There are no set rules which can be established in selecting the "right plan," and one plan which maximizes the professional's objectives in one corporation may not in another. The Pension Reform Act further complicates matters since it has substantially altered some of the established rules pertaining to qualified plans. This chapter will examine in detail the various plans — defined benefit, money purchase, target benefit and profit sharing — available to a professional corporation and how they are affected by the Pension Reform Act.[1]

PENSION PLANS

General Characteristics

A pension plan is a plan established by and maintained by an employer primarily to provide for the payment of definitely determinable benefits to his employees or their beneficiaries over a period of years, usually for life, after retirement. A plan designed to provide benefits upon retirement, or over a period of years after retirement, is considered a pension plan if the employer contributions can be determined actuarily on the basis of definitely determinable benefits, or, if contributions are fixed. Benefits and contributions to provide such benefits are not dependent upon profits.

Benefits are not considered definitely determinable if funds arising from forfeitures in termination of services, or other reason, may be used provide increased benefits for the remaining participants. Forfeitures must be used to reduce subsequent employer contributions.[2]

A qualified pension plan may provide for disability retirement benefits and incidental death benefits, but cannot provide for lay-off, sickness, accident, hospitalization benefits except for retired particpants to the extent permitted under Section 401(b) of the Internal Revenue Code.[3]

There are three kinds of pension plans available to a professional corporation — defined benefit, money-purchase and target benefit — all of which will be discussed in detail.

Minimum Funding Requirements

The Pension Reform Act has established minimum funding requirements which establish the minimum annual contribution which must be made to the plan.[4] The purpose of these new rules is to assure that plans will have sufficient assets to pay the promised benefits.

As a general rule, in regard to professional corporations, the required minimum contribution will equal the maximum deductible contribution.

However, if the required contribution is not made to the plan, i.e., the minimum funding standard is not met for any plan year, then a tax will be imposed upon the corporation on the deficiency (referred to as ''accumulated funding deficiency in the Pension Reform Act). The tax is imposed on two levels, as follows:

1. An initial tax is imposed on the employer in an amount equal to five percent of the accumulated funding deficiency. The tax is mandatory and is imposed irrespective of the fact that the underfunding was accidental.[5]

2. If the deficiency is not made up by the employer within 90 days after the Internal Revenue Service makes a notice of the deficiency with respect to the five percent tax, then a tax equal to 100% of the accumulated funding deficiency will be imposed.[6] The Secretary of Treasury may waive the 100% penalty tax at his discretion.[7]

DEFINED BENEFIT PENSION PLAN

General Characteristics

A defined benefit pension plan is a plan which guarantees a stated retirement benefit to be received by each participant at his retirement. The retirement benefit may be expressed as a percentage of an employee's compensation, which is called a fixed benefit plan, or in a manner that reflects both the employee's salary and years of service or participation in the plan which is called a ''unit benefit plan.'' Since almost all professional corporations will adopt a retirement plan on or near its inception, a unit benefit plan would be based upon years of participation in the plan.

Example:

1. *Fixed Benefit*

A participant will receive 60% of his salary at retirement for life. Thus, a participant whose average compensation is $50,000 will receive $30,000 a year for the rest of his life.

2. *Unit Benefit*

A participant will receive 3% of his salary for each year that he is a participant in the plan. Thus, a participant age 49 whose average compensation is $50,000 per year and who retires at age 65 will receive a retirement benefit of $24,000 for the rest of his life. (50,000 x .03 x 16 - $24,000)

The Corporation then contributes the amount which is actuarially required to be contributed each year to accumulate the funds necessary to provide the guaranteed benefit to each participant. Factors which determine the annual contribution are the age and sex of the participant, the participant's compensation, the number of years of participation in the plan prior to attaining the normal retirement date and an assumed rate of interest to be earned by the pension fund.

What is the Maximum Benefit that Can Be Provided Under a Defined Benefit Plan

Prior to pension reform there was no statutory provision which limited contributions to a defined benefit pension plan to a fixed percentage of payroll, provided that the benefits received by the participants bore a uniform relationship to the total compensation, or the basic or regular rate of compensation of each participant,[8] and the retirement benefit did not exceed the highest average salary of the participant for any reasonable period of time while a participant in the plan.[9] The amount which could then be deducted by the corporation was that amount which would be required to fund the stated benefits, if reasonable and generally accepted actuarial methods and assumptions were used for computing this contribution. Therefore, a professional corporation was able to provide retirement benefits for its participants equal to 100% of the average compensation.

The Pension Reform Act has now limited the annual benefit which can be provided to a participant under a non-contributory plan in the form of a straight life annuity without ancillary benefits ("normal benefit") to the lesser of (a) $75,000 or (b) 100% of the participant's average compensation for his three highest consecutive years of employment with the employer while a participant under the plan.[10] The 100% limitation is a clarification of present law. However, if the retirement benefit which is based upon 100% of compensation exceeds $75,000, then the annual retirement benefit must be restricted to $75,000. Congress, when it imposed this limitation felt "... that it is desirable to impose some dollar limitation on the size of a pension which may be paid out of tax-sheltered dollars, and the $75,000 limitation which is imposed under the Bill is generous enough to afford a reasonable standard of living."[11] However, to prevent the erosion of the value of the employee's pension due to inflation, the Pension Reform Act provides that the $75,000 maximum benefit may be increased annually to reflect the cost of living increases.[12]

WATCH THIS

In order to take advantage of the maximum benefit, a particpant must be an employee for at least ten years. If an employee has less than ten years of service, then the maximum benefit which he would otherwise be entitled to must be reduced by multiplying said benefit by a fraction, the numerator of which is the number of years of service with the employer and the denominator of which is ten.[13] This prevents a situation where an individual might receive an extremely high pension even though he had only a few years of active service under the plan.

Example

If an employee who had three years of service had an average high three years of salary of $50,000 (and no other adjustments were required) his maximum benefit could not exceed 3/10 of $50,000 or $15,000 per annum.

Exception to maximum benefit rules

The plan may provide for an annual benefit of up to $10,000 notwithstanding the 100% limitation or the required adjustment for certain ancillary benefits to an employee who has not participated in a qualified defined contribution plan.[14] However, if the participant has less than ten years of service with the employer, this benefit must be reduced as discussed above.[15]

Adjustment for benefits other than the "normal benefit"

If the annual benefit under the plan is payable in a form other than in the form of a straight life annuity without ancillary benefits (normal benefit), the said benefit must be adjusted to be equivalent to the normal benefit, pursuant to regulations to be issued by the Secretary of Treasury. Generally, for purposes of adjustments, there is no required reduction in the retirement benefit for pre-retirement ancillary benefits, such as medical, death and disability benefits, but there would have to be an adjustment for post-retirement ancillary benefits, such as term certain annuities, post-retirement death benefits, or a guaranteed payment for a period of years.[16] In addition, the joint and survivor feature of a qualified joint and survivor annuity is not taken into account when making the adjustments, unless the survivor benefit is greater than the joint benefit.[17]

Adjustment for employee mandatory contribution

In case of a contributory plan, upward adjustments in the benefit schedule will be permitted, pursuant to regulations to be issued by the Secretary of Treasury, to reflect the fact that part of the annuity had been purchased with the employee's own after-tax dollars.[18]

Early retirement benefits

Benefits paid in the event of early retirement will not have to be scaled down from the 100% of salary level on an actuarial basis. However, the $75,000 limitation must be scaled down in the event of early retirement prior to age 55, but not below $10,000.[19]

Effective date

These new rules regarding maximum benefits are effective for plan years commencing after December 31, 1975.[20]

Grandfather clause

However, participants in a defined benefit plan which was effective on or before October 2, 1973 will not have to reduce their pension benefits if the following conditions are met:[21]

1. The annual retirement benefit does not exceed 100% of the participant's compensation on October 2, 1973.
2. The annual retirement benefit is no greater than the benefit which would have been payable at retirement if all the terms and conditions of the plan in effect on October 2, 1973 had remained unchanged until the participant's retirement.
3. The participant's compensation taken into account under plan for any period after October 2, 1973 had not exceeded his annual compensation on that date.

Determining the Maximum Deduction for Contributions to Defined Benefit Pension Plans

The maximum deduction the corporation can take in any one year for contributions to a defined benefit pension plan is determined by using two alternative tests. The corporation is permitted to use whichever method is most advantageous.

"Level Method" - An actuary determines what amount will be needed at the normal retirement date of the participants to fund their stated benefits. The cost of these benefits is then contributed in level amounts over the remaining working period of the participants.[22]

WATCH THIS

This type of funding method permits large contributions to be made to participants who are within a few years from retirement. However, if more than fifty percent of such remaining unfunded cost is attributable to any three individuals, the contributions made by the corporation for the benefit of such individuals must be contributed over a period of at least five taxable years.[23]

Thus, in such a situation, the professional will be required to participate in the plan for at least five years and any contribution made by the corporation which exceeds the "more than 50 percent" funding limitation will not be deductible.

"Normal Cost Method" - A corporation can deduct each year an amount equal to the normal cost of the plan plus an amount necessary to amortize the outstanding unfunded past service cost over a ten-year period.[24]

"Normal Cost" for any year is the level amount actuarially determined which would be required as a contribution by the corporation in such year to maintain the plan if it had been in effect from the beginning of each participant's employment, and if such cost for prior years had been paid.

"Past Service" represents the amount which would have accumulated had the normal cost actually been contributed from the date of the inception of the plan.

Prior to the Pension Reform Act, the corporation was only required to contribute an amount equal to the plan's normal cost plus the interest on its past service cost. This requirement prevented the past service liability from growing any larger, but did not reduce the principal amount of the past service liability. The Pension Reform Act, under the normal cost method, now requires that the past services plus other liabilities, such as expenses, losses, etc. be amortized over a specified period of time.[25]

OBSERVATION

The normal cost method is not really applicable to a defined benefit plan which is adopted by a professional corporation, since the corporation will usually adopt the plan in the initial year of incorporating and thus, there will be no past service for which credit can be given for pension benefits. In almost all cases the level method will be used.

Excess contribution

If the corporation contributes an amount in excess of the maximum amount deductible under the minimum funding requirements, the excess will not be currently deductible. However, the excess may be carried over to subsequent years within the maximum deduction limits.[26]

Defined benefit plans provide biggest tax breaks for senior professionals

Very often a practitioner will hear, when discussing professional corporations with a professional client, "I am too old to incorporate, it is better for younger professionals." This is not the case. Incorporation gives the biggest tax break to senior professionals. The reason is as follows: A defined benefit pension plan is based upon a stated guarantee to be received by each participant at his retirement. Since the older professional has less time available to accumulate the funds necessary to provide the stated benefit, larger annual contributions will be required to fund his benefit than for the younger professionals who have a longer period of participation in the plan before attaining the normal retirement age. Some older professionals will be able to reduce their taxable income up to fifty percent or more in order to accumulate the funds necessary to provide their stated pension.

Example

How defined benefit plan provides larger contributions to older participants

Employee	*Age*	*Salary*	*Benefit*	*Annual contribution required to provide benefit*	*Monthly Pension*	*Amount needed to provide benefit*
Professional	55	$50,000	60% of compensation	$26,310.	$2,500	$357,375.
Professional	45	50,000	60% of compensation	9,716	2,500	357,375.
Professional	35	50,000	60% of compensation	4,677	2,500	357,375.

Assumptions Used

5.5%
Annuity
Purchase Price

6.997 Male	1,429.10/10	Life Annuity
6.196 Female	1,613.90/10	

WATCH THIS

In a corporation which has some professional employees whose ages equal or exceed those of the professional employees, the corporation may find itself in a position of contributing a greater percentage of the nonprofessional employee's salary to the pension plan than the professional's.

Minimum Funding Requirements

The minimum funding requirements of a defined benefit plan are quite complex[27] and generally will be determined by a qualified actuary, and thereofre, will not be discussed in this book. Generally, in a professional corporation, the minimum funding requirements will equal the maximum deductible contribution to which the corporation will be entitled in a particular tax year.

OBSERVATION

As mentioned earlier, the penalties for not meeting the minimum funding requirements may impose a financial hardship upon a corporation. Therefore, great care must be given to this potential pitfall before a corporation obligates itself to contribute large sums of money to fund stated benefits which it might not be able to make as a result of reduced corporate earnings.

Other Characteristics of Defined Benefit Plans

Permits adjustments in contributions to fund benefits

Pension benefits that are based upon the average "highest three consecutive years" of compensation will require larger contributions to be made to the plan as the participant's income continues to rise in order to provide the necessary funds to fund the stated benefit. Thus, a defined benefit pension plan, covering professionals in their thirties and forties, may result in larger contributions being made for their benefit during their participation in the plan than a money-purchase pension plan or profit sharing plan whose contributions are based upon the participant's compensation for each respective plan year.

Over-funding-results in reduction of corporate contributions to plan

In determining the amount which a corporation must contribute each year to a defined benefit plan to provide the funds necessary to provide the required benefit, the actuary assumes that said annual contribution will earn an assumed rate of interest each year. If the trust investment performance exceeds the assumed rate of interest, then there will be more funds available than are required to provide the guaranteed benefit. When this occurs, the plan is considered overfunded. In such an event the corporation is required to reduce its contribution to the plan for the following year by the amount of the excess.[28] Excess earnings cannot be used to increase the pension benefits of the participants.

WATCH THIS

If the corporation continues to contribute to the pension plan an amount which is not reduced by the excess earnings, the corporation will not be able to deduct the portion which represents this excess since such additional contribution would not be considered an ordinary and necessary business expense.

> This situation may be likened to rent paid in taxable year in excess of the amount required under the lease. The excess is a prepayment for subsequent years and is not deductible in the taxable year. Similarly, if there are enough funds under the plan to provide the benefits which have accrued through the taxable year, additional contributions are not expenses for such year or any prior year.[29]

Underfunding-requires increased contributions to the plan

If a defined benefit pension plan has an assumed interest rate of 5% and the investment experience is less than the assumed rate, then the plan has become underfunded. In this event, the corporation must not only contribute the amount required to meet the minimum funding requirements under the plan but must contribute an additional amount equal to the losses sustained in the plan as a result of the poor investment experience. In addition, failure to keep the plan funded will result in a tax being imposed upon the deficiency, as previously discussed.

Death benefits in a defined benefit plan

Pre-retirement death benefits are permitted in a defined benefit pension plan provided they are "incidental" to the primary purpose of the plan, which is to provide retirement benefits to its participants. An "incidental" death benefit may be defined to be (1) the greater of (a) 100 times the monthly anticipated retirement benefit, or (b) the reserve under the life insurance contract (approximately equal to the cash value) and the auxiliary fund,[30] (2) the face amount of the insurance policy and the amount credited to the participant's auxiliary fund, provided that less than 50% of the participant's account is used to purchase insurance.[31] The second definition is the most favorable, since there will never be a forfeiture of a participant's account in the event of his death before retirement.[32]

Retirement benefit is limited in event of premature termination of plan[33]

If a defined benefit pension plan is terminated within ten years of its inception, the benefits of the 25 highest-paid employees at the time the plan was established and whose anticipated annual retirement benefit exceeds $1,500, must be restricted to the greater of

(1) $20,000; or

(2) The product resulting by multiplying the number of years since the establishment of the plan, or amendment by the lesser of

(a) Twenty percent of the participant's annual compensation; or

(b) $10,000[34]

Example

Plan covering two employees, one of whom is the key shareholder employee, and the other is a common law employee, has been in effect for eight years. The annual compensation of the shareholder employee involved is $30,000, and $85,000 has been contributed on his behalf in accordance with the funding method under the plan. The restricted portion will then be $37,000. ($85,000 - 20% x $30,000 x 8)

This provision has the potential to cause a serious loss to the professional in the event of the plan's premature termination, and the effects of this section must be carefully explained by the practitioner to the professional before a defined benefit plan is adopted.

DEFINED BENEFIT PENSION PLAN - SUMMARY

Advantages	*Disadvantages*
1. Favors older participants.	1. Overfunding-good investment experience results in reduction of corporate contribution.
2. Permits adjustment in contributions to fund benefits.	2. Underfunding- poor investment experience requires larger contributions than originally contemplated.
3. Provides guaranteed benefit to all participants at retirement.	3. Does not favor younger participants

4. Limitation of retirement benefit in the event of premature termination.
5. Actuarial services required on an annual basis.
6. Unable to have segregated investment accounts.
7. Penalties imposed if minimum funding requirements are not met.

MONEY-PURCHASE PENSION PLAN

General Characteristics

A money-purchase pension plan (also referred to as "class year plan," "individual account plan," and "defined contribution plan" by the Pension Reform Act[35])is a plan whereby the employer obligates itself to contribute annually a certain uniform percentage of each participant's compensation.

Example

> The employer shall make contributions on behalf of each participant equivalent to 20% of his compensation.

Since the contribution is based upon a fixed percentage of compensation, the actual amount which will be required to be contributed annually will depend upon the compensation received by each participant for each year; and unless the plan is amended, there can be no variance from the stated contribution rate and the contribution must be made each year by the corporation even though profits may be low.[36]

The Employer does not guarantee that a predetermined retirement benefit will be paid to each participant upon his retirement. The earnings and losses incurred by the money-purchase pension plan will be used to increase or decrease the benefits to be received by the participant at retirement. Therefore, the corporation will not be required to increase contributions in the event of poor investment experience or decrease contributions in the event of good investment experiences. Thus, the retirement benefit actually received by each participant is directly determined by the investment experience of the fund.

Corporate Contributions to Money-Purchase Pension Plan

What percent of a participant's salary can be contributed to the money-purchase plan

Prior to the Pension Reform Act, the "rule of thumb" adopted by the Internal Revenue Service was that any corporate contribution to a money-purchase pension plan would be considered reasonable, and thus deductible, irrespective of what percent of the participant's compensation the contribution represented, provided that the expected retirement benefit would not exceed 100% of the participant's highest average salary covering any reasonable period of employment with the employer.[37] The expected retirement benefit was computed by multiplying the participant's annual contribution by a compound interest factor which represented an annual expected rate of return, i.e. 5½%, and the number of years before the participant's normal retirement date. Thus, many practitioners were able to qualify plans requiring corporate contributions equal to 50%, 60% and even 70% of a participant's compensation.

Unfortunately, the Pension Reform Act did not adopt this rule of thumb, and has established permitted deductible limits for contributions to a money-purchase plan. Under present law, corporate contributions and other "annual additions" may not exceed the lesser of

(a) 25,000 or

(b) 25% of the participant's compensation.[38]

"Annual additions" include the sum of

(a) the employer's contribution

(b) the lesser of (1) one-half of all the employee's contribution or

(2) the employee's contributions in excess of 6% of his compensation; and

(c) any forfeitures which are added to the employee's account. Forfeitures would not be considered an "addition" in a money-purchase pension plan since they are used to reduce corporate contributions under the plan.[39]

OBSERVATION

A provision in a pension plan permitting voluntary contributions was an effective way for a professional to make additional contributions to the plan. Even though these contributions were made from after tax dollars, the earnings thereon were tax free. Unfortunately, the Pension Reform Act will have the effect of discouraging the use of voluntary contributions since in some cases the voluntary contributions will require the corporation to reduce its contribution to the plan.

Example

Employee makes a voluntary contribution to a money-purchase plan equal to 9% of his compensation. The employer will only be permitted to deduct an amount equal to 22% of his compensation. That is, 3% is considered an "annual addition" (9% - 6%) and since the permitted deductible contribution cannot exceed 25%, the corporate contibution may not exceed 22%.

However, if the employee's voluntary contribution in the above example was only equal to 6% of his compensation, the corporation will be permitted to deduct an amount equal to 25% of the participant's compensation, since only the amount in excess of 6% is considered an annual addition.[40]

OBSERVATION

Although the Pension Reform Act will limit the permitted deductible contribution to a money-purchase plan two a smaller percentage of a participant's compensation than was previously allowed, there is one favorable result. That is, in some cases, because of a professional's age, the maximum deductible contribution which could be made to the plan for his benefit would be an amount equal to 25%-30% of his compensation. In such cases, if the investment experience exceeded the assumed rate of interest used in computing the maximum percent of compensation which could be made to the plan, then the plan would become overfunded, just as in the case of a defined benefit pension plan, and the corporate contributions would have to be reduced in subsequent years. However, the overfunding problem would now seem to be eliminated under the statutory limits established by the Pension Reform Act. Thus, it may now be possible for some professionals to derive even greater retirement benefits now than what they would have been able to acquire prior to the Pension Reform Act.

Cost of Living Increases

Adjustments to the $25,000 limit may be made as a result of increases in the cost of living. The adjustment will be made pursuant to regulations promulgated by the Secretary of the Treasury providing procedures similar to those used to adjust the primary insurance amounts under Section 215(i)(2)(a) of the Social Security Act.[41]

Excess contributions

Excess contributions may be carried over to subsequent years and deducted within the maximum deductible limits.[42]

Other Characteristics of Money-Purchase Plans

Death benefit in money-purchase plan

A death benefit in a money-purchase pension plan may be defined as the entire amount credited to the participant's account, which includes life insurance and the auxiliary fund.[43]

No limitations of benefits in event plan is terminated within ten years

Since contribution to a money-purchase pension plan is based upon a uniform percentage of all participants' compensation, no participant may obtain a disproportionate benefit because of his age or the method of funding. As a result, the limitation of benefits placed upon the "25 highest paid employees" under Regs. 1.401-4(c) (2) does not apply to money-purchase pension plans.[44]

Large contributions may be required for non-professional participants

Since contributions are based upon a uniform percentage of the participant's compensation, a money-purchase pension plan with a contribution formula of 25% of compensation must make this contribution subject to the integration rules for all participants, non-professional as well as professional. Thus, if the proposed non-integrated plan requires a contribution of 25% of compensation, and the corporation employs two nurses earning $7800 and $10.400 respectively, a total pension contribution of $4,550 will be required to be made for these benefits.[45] Many corporations consisting of one shareholder will find a contribution of this size prohibitive. The only solutions to this dilemma are to: (1) If the non-professional participants are considerably younger than the professional participant, adopt a defined benefit or target benefit plan, or (2) reduce the contribution formula.

Minimum funding requirements

A money-purchase will meet the minimum funding requirements of the Pension Reform Act if it contributes annually that amount required to be contributed under the plan's formula.[46]

OBSERVATION

Unless it is certain that a particular corporation should have little difficulty in making the required contributions to the plan, it might be better to have the corporation adopt both a money-purchase pension plan and a profit sharing plan. In this manner, the required contribution to the pension plan will be reduced and thus, the problem of meeting the minimum funding requirements is also reduced, since those requirements do not apply to profit sharing plans.[47] For example, instead of adopting a money-purchase plan with a contribution formula of 25% of compensation, the corporation could adopt a money-purchase plan with a 10% contribution formula and a profit sharing plan, which would permit another 15% of compensation to be contributed. Although the cost of adopting two plans will increase the annual administration costs, this increase may be far less than the penalties imposed by the minimum funding requirements of the Internal Revenue Code on "accumulated funding deficiencies."

MONEY-PURCHASE PLAN SUMMARY

Advantages	*Disadvantages*
1. Benefits increased as a result of good investment experience.	1. Investment experience below assumed rate of interest will result in reduced benefit. No increased contribution as a result of poor investment experience.
2. No limitation of benefits in event of premature termination.	2. Contribution may be smaller than what may be permitted under a defined benefit plan.

3. Favors younger participant - benefit increases with good investment performance.
4. Actuary not required.
5. Contributions not required to be increased as a result of poor investment performance.
6. Segregated investment accounts permitted.
7. Contributions not required to be reduced in the event of good investment performance.

3. Contributions for non-professional employees may be greater than if defined benefit or target benefit plan was adopted.
4. Penalties will be imposed if minimum funding requirements are not met.

TARGET BENEFIT PENSION PLANS

The target benefit pension plan, which is often referred to as assumed benefit or variable benefit pension plan, is a unique concept which combines the most attractive features of the defined benefit plan and the money-purchase plan. The target benefit plan is based upon an "assumed" or "target" retirement benefit to be received by each participant upon his normal retirement date. For example, the plan may provide for an assumed or target benefit of sixty percent of a participant's compensation at retirement. The actual amount required to be contributed to the plan annually is determined in the same manner as the defined benefit plan. However, the actual retirement benefit to be received by each participant under the target benefit plan is defined as the benefit which can be provided with the funds accumulated in the pension account at his normal retirement date. Thus, as in the money-purchase plan, the actual retirement benefit is directly related to the investment experience of the pension fund. Therefore, unlike the defined benefit plan, if the investment experience of the trust exceeds the anticipated rate of return, the corporation will not be required to reduce its contribution to the plan nor will it have to increase its contribution if investment experience is less than what was anticipated.

Corporate Contributions to Target Benefit Plan

What percent of a participant's salary can be contributed to the target benefit plan

Prior to the Pension Reform Act, there was no statutory provision which limited contributions to a target benefit pension plan, provided the retirement benefit did not exceed the highest average salary of the participant for any reasonable period of time while a participant in the plan,[48] computed upon reasonable and generally accepted actuarial assumptions. Thus, a target benefit plan could provide for an assumed or target benefit for each participant equivalent to 100% of his compensation averaged over a reasonable period of time.

However, target benefit plans are considered to be defined contribution plans, i.e., money-purchase pension plans, for contribution purposes,[49] and as a result, a corporation cannot now deduct in respect to a participant, an amount which exceeds the lesser of

a. $25,000 or
b. 25% of the participant's compensation.

Adjustments in the $25,000 amount may be made annually to reflect cost of living increases.

Excess contributions

Excess contributions may be carried over to subsequent years and deducted within the maximum deductible limits.[50]

Other Characteristics of Target Benefit Plans

Death benefits in target benefit plan

The death benefit in a target benefit plan may consist of the face amount of the life insurance policy, if any, on the life of the participant plus the total amount credited to his account in the auxiliary fund.[51]

Retirement benefits limited in event of premature termination of plan

As in the defined benefit plan, the benefits received by the highest 25 employees will be restricted in the event the plan is terminated within ten years of its adoption under Regs. 1.401-4(c) (2).

Minimum Funding Requirements

The minimum funding requirements of the Pension Reform Act are applicable to target benefit pension plans. For these purposes, the target benefit pension plan is treated as a money-purchase pension plan,[52] and thus, a corporation will satisfy the funding requirements if it contributes annually the annual required amount under the plan's formula.

Effectiveness of Target Benefit Plan After Pension Reform

Prior to the Pension Reform Act and the issuances of Revenue Ruling 74-307 which permitted defined benefit plans to adopt the same death benefit definition as money purchase and target benefit plan, a target benefit plan provided the practitioner with the best of both worlds; i.e., the plan could use the same contribution formula as used by a defined benefit plan while still being able to retain most of the advantages of a money-purchase pension plan.[53] Thus, in appropriate cases, many professionals were able to contribute a large percentage of their salary without being required to contribute the same percentage for their non-professional employees while avoiding the limitation of death benefit problem and the overfunding and underfunding problems.

However, with the issuance of Revenue Ruling 74-307 and the reduction of the permitted deductible contribution to the lesser of $25,000 or 25% of a professional's compensation by the Pension Reform Act, the effectiveness and usefulness of the plan has been greatly diminished. The target benefit plan cannot now be used as a substitute for a defined benefit plan, and if an older professional wishes to maximize his contribution to a retirement plan then a defined benefit plan is going to have to be adopted. In this author's opinion, the only time a target benefit plan should be considered is when a professional only wishes to contribute 25% of his compensation to a retirement plan and his employees are significantly younger than he. In such a case, the percentage of compensation that would be contributed for the non-professional employees will be substantially less than the 25% of salary being contributed for the professional.

WATCH THIS

The contribution savings must be weighed against the potential limitation of retirement benefits if the plan is terminated within ten years of its adoption.

If there is no significant age difference between the professional and non-professonal employees, this author can see no reason why a target benefit plan should be adopted rather than a money-purchase plan or a combination of money-purchase plan and profit sharing plan.

TARGET BENEFIT PENSION PLAN SUMMARY

Advantages	*Disadvantages*
1. Benefits increase as a result of good investment experience.	1. Reduced benefit in event of poor investment experience.
2. No limitation of death benefit.	2. Actuary may be required.

3. Favors younger participants — benefits increased with good investment performance.
4. Contributions not required to be increased in event of poor investment performance.
5. Segregated investment accounts permitted.
6. Contributions not required to be reduced in the event of good investment performance.

3. Restricted benefit in event plan terminated within ten years.
4. Penalties will be imposed if minimum funding requirements are not met.
5. Contribution may be smaller than what would be permitted in a defined benefit plan.

PROFIT SHARING PLANS

General Characteristics

A profit sharing plan is a plan which is established and maintained by an employer to provide for the participation in his profits by his employees or their beneficiaries.[54]

The plan must provide that contributions come from and be dependent upon the profits of the corporation.[55] Contributions are not required to be made from current profits only, but may be made from accumulated earned surplus, as determined by generally acceptable accounting principles, without regard to whether the corporation has current or accumulated earnings and profits for federal income tax purposes.[56]

WATCH THIS

If a professional corporation has losses as a result of, for example, substantial depreciation deductions, the corporation may still contribute to the profit sharing plan even though it may not have profits for corporate income tax purposes.

> A qualified profit sharing plan is a plan established and maintained by an employer to provide for the participation in his profits by his employees or their beneficiaries (cite omitted). The term ''profits'' for this purpose is not limited to taxable profits or to earnings and profits from which taxable distributions are paid to shareholders.[57]

Allocation of Contributions

A profit sharing plan must provide a definite predetermined formula for allocating the profits which are contributed to the plan. The most common acceptable formula is one which allocates the contributions to each participant, in proportion, his basic compensation represents to the total compensation of all participants.[58] It is possible to allocate contributions by some other method, such as years of service or by some other factors, provided the method used will not discriminate in favor of the prohibited group. If the formula adopted by the plan results in the professional employees receiving proportionately larger contributions than the nonprofessional employees, the plan is discriminatory and will not qualify.[59]

Contribution Formula Not Required

There is no requirement that a profit sharing plan provide for a definite formula for determining the amount of profits that the corporation must contribute each year.[60] Thus, subject to the requirement that contributions be recurring and substantial, the professional corporation may vary its contributions to the plan based upon the profits available and the needs of the corporation to retain profits for possible expansion or purchase of equipment. A profit sharing plan containing a definite contribution formula may remove it by amendment without having to resubmit the plan to the Internal Revenue Service for approval.[61]

Distributions During Employment

Although most professionals who are participating in a profit sharing plan will desire to accumulate the plan contributions allocated to their account until their retirement, the plan may provide for "... distributing the funds accumulated under the plan after a fixed number of years, the attainment of a stated age, or upon the prior occurrence of some event such as layoff, illness, disability, retirement, death, or severance of employment."[62] The IRS has ruled that "a fixed number of years" shall mean not less than two years, but if some event, as previously enumerated, occurs during the two year period, a distribution may still be made.[63] Thus, a professional who is concerned that he is "freezing" large sums of money in a retirement plan, until his retirement, can take great comfort to learn that funds in a profit sharing plan may be distributed to him in the event of his financial hardship or financial emergency as well as for the other events enumerated above.[64]

Forfeitures

Forfeitures are not required to be used to reduce subsequent year contributions, which is required in pension plans, but can be reallocated among the remaining participants. Since the accounts of the remaining participants will be increased, the plan must provide for a method of reallocating such forfeitures in a manner which does not favor the professional employees.[65] Usually the plan will reallocate forfeitures in the same manner as the contributions are allocated. It is possible to reallocate forfeitures in proportion to the account balances of the participants. But since the professional employees will have the largest accounts, a disproportionate amount of the forfeitures may be allocated to them resulting in discrimination in favor of the prohibited group. Even though this method may be acceptable, you will not obtain a ruling qualifying the plan, except on a year-to-year basis.[66]

The plan may provide that forfeitures will be used to reduce the corporation's contributions that would otherwise be made under the plan,[67] but at no time may forfeitures revert back to the Corporation.[68]

Health Insurance

A profit sharing plan may provide for the purchase of incidental health and/or accident insurance.[69] If funds used to purchase health and/or accident insurance have not been accumulated for at least two years, the cost of such insurance will be considered incidental if, in the aggregate, it does not exceed 25% of the funds allocated to a participant's account.[70]

If both ordinary life insurance and health and accident insurance are purchased with funds not accumulated for at least two years, the amount expended for the accident and/or health insurance plus one half of the amount expended for the ordinary life insurance premiums may not, in the aggregate, exceed 25 per cent of the funds allocated to a participant's account.

These limitations will not apply to funds which have been accumulated for two years or more.[71]

Determining Maximum Deductions

A corporation's deductible contribution to a profit sharing plan is limited to 15% of all compensation paid to the participants during the plan year.[72]

Example — *Maximum Amount Deduction*

Employee	*Salary*	*Maximum Deduction*
Professional	$85,000	
Nurse	$ 8,000	
Secretary	$ 7,000	
TOTAL	$100,000	$15,000

Contribution carry-over

If the corporation contributes an amount in excess of $15,000, it may deduct the excess contribution in the following year or years as part of the 15% annual deductible contribution. That is, the carryover and the contribution made for the current taxable year cannot exceed 15% of all participants' compensation.[73]

Example: Contribution Carry-over

Year	*Total Compensation*	*Maximum Deduction*	*Actual Contribution*	*Carry-over*
1974	$100,000	$15,000	$18,000	$3,000
1975	100,000	15,000	14,000	2,000
1976	100,000	15,000	13,000	0

WATCH THIS

Avoid language in the profit sharing plan to the effect that the corporation may not contribute an amount to the plan which exceeds the allowable deduction for the taxable year in which the contribution was made. Language of this kind is prevalent in profit sharing plans, is not required, and the corporation will lose its right to the contribution carry-over. Thus, good drafting would dictate that there be no limitation placed upon corporate contributions if maximum flexibility is to be achieved.

Credit carry-over

A corporation for any one year may decide not to contribute the total amount which it is entitled to deduct for that year. The difference between the amount the corporation could have contributed and deducted and what it actually contributed may be contributed and deducted in the succeeding year or years. This is called a credit carry-over. Prior to the Pension Reform Act, a corporation could contribute and deduct in one taxable year an amount equal to 30% of compensation, i.e., the credit carry-over from the previous year(s), (not to exceed 15% of compensation) plus the current permitted deductible contribution (15%). The Pension Reform Act has now reduced the 30% amount to 25% of compensation.[74]

Example: Credit Carryover

	Total Compensation	*Maximum Deduction*	*Actual Cash Contribution*	*Actual Contribution- % of total compensation*	*Credit Carryover*
1974	100,000	15,000	5,000	5%	10,000
1975	100,000	25,000	20,000	20%	5,000
1976	100,000	20,000	20,000	20%	0

OBSERVATION

The credit carryover provides maximum flexibility for the young professional who desires to contribute more to a retirement plan than is permitted under the Keogh Plan, but because of personal income needs, is unsure as to the exact percent of his salary he will be able to contribute to a retirement plan on an annual basis. This individual will be able to contribute, subject to the "recurring and substantial contribution rules" an amount which he feels he can afford based upon his current personal situation. As his earnings increase, he may then contribute any unused contributions which he was entitled to make in the previous years. As a result, the professional is able to contribute a larger percent of his salary in years when his income is higher and is now able to afford such large contributions, and smaller contributions in the beginning years of his practice. Thus, a young professional may take advantage of the benefits of a corporate retirement program and the other fringe benefits available to him under the corporation, without committing himself to a fixed contribution to the retirement plan.

Other Characteristics of Profit Sharing Plans

No overfunding problem

Since contributions are dependent upon profits and upon the discretion of the corporation in determining the amount of profits it wishes to contribute to the plan, benefits cannot be actuarily determined as in a pension plan.[75] As a result, earnings on the corporate contributions may inure to the benefit of the participants without the possibility of the plan becoming overfunded.

Death benefit in profit sharing plan

The death benefit in a profit sharing plan may be defined as the entire amount credited to the participant's account - which includes the face amount of his life insurance policy, if any, and his auxiliary fund.

No limitation of benefit in the event the plan is terminated within ten years

Restriction of benefits, under Regs. 1.401-4(c) (2) applicable to defined benefit pension plans and target benefit pension plans do not apply to profit sharing plans since the allocation formula of corporation contributions is designed to preclude the prohibited discrimination.[76]

Minimum funding requirements

The minimum funding of the Pension Reform Act does not apply to profit sharing plans.[77]

PROFIT SHARING PLAN SUMMARY

Advantages	*Disadvantages*
1. No fixed contribution.	1. Does not benefit older participants - senior professionals would be able to contribute a larger percentage of their compensation under a Pension Plan than permitted under a profit sharing plan.
2. Benefits younger professionals - may vary contributions to meet personal income needs and contributions dependent upon the earnings of the corporation.	2. Benefits not guaranteed.

Advantages

3. Unused contributions may be carried over to subsequent years.
4. Forfeitures may be reallocated among remaining participants provided no discrimination results.
5. Withdrawals of Employer contribution prior to retirement permitted.
6. No restriction of benefits in event plan terminated within ten years.
7. Actuary not required.

PENSION AND PROFIT SHARING PLAN COMBINATION

Permitted Contribution

As a general rule, if a corporation contributes to both a pension and profit sharing plan and an employee of such corporation participates in both plans, the maximum deductible contribution is an amount equal to twenty-five percent (25%) of the participant's compensation, paid or accrued during the taxable year.[78] Before the twenty-five percent limitation is applied, the contributions to both the pension plan and profit sharing plan must be within the applicable limits for deductibility.[79] That is, if a corporation contributes 7% of compensation to a pension plan, it will not be entitled to deduct the contribution equal to 18% of compensation to the profit sharing plan, since the maximum deductible contribution to a profit sharing plan, when no carry-over contribution is involved, is 15% of compensation. This rule applies even though in the aggregate both contributions equal 25% of compensation.

When to Use Combination

A professional who incorporates is not always able to determine the exact amount he will be able to contribute annually to a retirement program because of the uncertainty of the corporation's earning capacity and of his own personal income needs. As a result, he wishes to avoid adopting a program whereby the corporation is obligated to contribute a fixed percentage of income to the plan each year. In such a situation, a pension and profit sharing plan combination will often provide the solution. The professional can adopt a money-purchase pension plan obligating the corporation to contribute 10% of compensation. The profit sharing plan would then permit him to contribute up to another 15% of compensation. If he felt the earning capacity of the corporation was sufficient for a particular year and his own personal needs were met, the corporation could contribute the full 15% of compensation to the profit sharing plan. If the earnings of the corporation were not sufficient, or because of his financial position, he elects to take more of the profit as additional salary, the corporation may elect to contribute 5% or 10% of compensation to the profit sharing plan. The unused contribution can then be carried over to subsequent years. Furthermore, if the professional does not desire to contribute an amount in excess of 25% of his compensation to a retirement plan, then the adoption of both a pension and profit sharing plan will reduce the minimum funding requirements, since a profit sharing plan is not subject to the minimum funding requirements.

Retirement Plan Summary Checklist

Characteristic	*Defined Benefit*	*Money Purchase*	*Target Benefit*	*Profit Sharing*
1. Contribution fixed	Yes — subject to investment performance.	Yes — percent of compensation is fixed.	Yes — must contribute fixed amount to achieve assumed benefit.	No — depends upon profits and amount of profits corporation elects to contribute.
2. Limitations on deduction	No — provided annual benefit does not exceed 100% of compensation or $75,000, whichever is less.	Yes — 25% of compensation or $25,000, whichever is less.	Yes — 25% of compensation or $25,000, whichever is less.	Yes — 15% of compensation.
3. Earnings above assumed rate used to increase benefits	No	Yes	Yes	Yes
4. Earnings below assumed rate of return require increased contributions	Yes	No	No	No
5. Loans permitted	Yes	Yes	Yes	Yes
6. Withdrawals prior to retirement for hardship or other stated reasons other than for death, retirement, disability or termination of employment.	No	No	No	Yes
7. Forfeitures	Used to reduce subsequent year's contribution.	Used to reduce subsequent year's contribution.	Used to reduce subsequent year's contribution.	May be allocated among remaining participants provided discrimination does not result.
8. Death benefits.	100% of account credited to participant.	100% of account credited to participant	100% of account credited to participant.	100% of account credited to participant.
9. Restriction of benefits in event of termination within 10 years of plan's adoption.		No	Yes	No
10. Minimum funding requirements applicable.	Yes	Yes	Yes	No

FOOTNOTES

[1]There are other qualified plans besides those discussed in this book, such as annuity pension plans, stock bonus plans, bond purchase plans, and thrift and savings plans. Because of their limited use or applicability to professional corporations, they will not be discussed.

[2]Regs. §1.401-1(b) (1) (i).

[3]Ibid.

[4]IRC §412.

[5]IRC §4971(a).

[6]IRC §4971(b).

[7]ERISA S 3002(b).

[8]Rev. Rul. 71-225, IRB 1971-24.

[9]Rev. Rul. 72-3, IRB 1972-2.

[10]IRC 415(b) (1).

[11]Congressional Reports-House Explanation, Prentice-Hall, Handbook on Pension Reform Law, September 6, 1974, Bulletin No. 8, 924, P. 710.

[12]IRC §415(d).

[13]IRC §415(b) (5).

[14]IRC §415(b) (4).

[15]See Note 12.

[16]IRC §415(b) (2) (B).

[17]Ibid.

[18]Ibid.;

[19]IRC §415(b) (2) (C).

[20]ERISA §2004(d) (1).

[21]ERISA §2004(d) (2).

[22]IRC §404(a) (1) (A) (ii).

[23]Ibid.

[24]IRC §404(a) (1) (A) (iii).

[25]IRC §412(b) (2).

[26]IRC §404(a) (1) (D).

[27]IRC §412(b).

[28]Rev. Rul. 59-153, 1959-1, CB 89.

[29]I. Goodman, "Maximum Employer Deductions Under Pension and Profit Sharing Plan," January 20, 1966, Prentice-Hall Pension Library, 19,0335; See also Rev. Rul. 57-89, IRB 1957-10; Rev. Rul. 59-153, 1959-1; CB 89,; Rev. Rul. 64-159, IRB 1964-21.

[30]Rev. Rul. 68-453, IRB 1968-34.

[31]Rev. Rul. 74-307 IRB 1974-26.

[32]See chapter 11 "Handling Investments and Life Insurance in the Qualified Plan," Section entitled, "Insurance in the Retirement Plan." p. 197.

[33]For full discussion, see chapter 9, "Qualifying Retirement Plan," Section entitled, "Premature Termination — defined benefit and target benefit plans" p. 163.

[34]Reg. §1.401-4(c) (2) (iii).

[35]IRC §411(d) (4).

[36]Rev. Rul. 73-206, IRB 1973-18; Rev. Rul. 72-556 IRB 1972-47.

[37]Rev. Rul. 72-3, IRB 1972-2; "Pension Trust Audit Guidelines" IR Manual 45(10)5-1 (12-4-72), §512.

[38]IRC §415(c) (1).

[39]IRC §415(c) (2).

[40]For full discussion, see chapter 10 "Retirement Plan Drafting Techniques," Section entitled "The Effect of Pension Reform on Voluntary Contributions." p. 181

[41]IRC §415(d).

[42]See Note 26.

[43]Rev. Rul. 74-307 IRB 1974-26, p. 11.

[44]Rev. Rul. 69-415, IRB 1969-31.

[45]If the plan was integrated using a 7% differential, the contribution required for the two non-professional employees would be $3,278.00.

[46]Congressional Reports, Prentice-Hall, Handbook on Pension Reform Law, September 6, 1974, Bulletin No. 9, 893, p. 659.

[47]IRC §412(h) (1).

[48]Rev. Rul. 72-3, IRB 1972-2.

[49]Congressional Reports, CCH, Pension Reform Act of 1974, September 4, 1974, 5082, pg. 373.

[50]See Note 26.

[51]Rev. Rul. 74-307 IRB 1974-26, p. 11

[52]See Note 46.

[53]The only disadvantage is that a target benefit plan is required to restrict benefits in the event of the plan's premature termination under Regs. 1.401-4(c) (2).

[54]Reg. §1.401-1(b) (1) (ii).
[55]Rev. Rul. 70-182, IRB 1970-16.
[56]Rev. Rul. 66-174, IRB 1966-26.
[57]I. Goodman, "Recent Tax Ruling on Profit Sharing Plans," November 21, 1966.
[58]See Note 54.
[59]I. Goodman, "Some Do's and Don'ts in Operating Tax Qualified Pension and Profit Sharing Plans," October 23, 1962; Rev. Rul. 71-26, IRB 1971-3.
[60]Rev . Rul. 56-366, CB 1956-2, 976.
[61]Rev. Proc. 72-9, IRB 1972-1, §3.0111.
[62]See Note 51.
[63]Rev. Rul. 54-231, 1954-1 CB 150; Rev. Rul. 71-295, IRB 1971-28.
[64]Rev. Rul. 69-421, IRB, 1969-32, Part 5(m); Rev. Rul. 71-224, IRB 1971-20; See chapter 10, "Retirement Plan Drafting Techniques," Section entitled "Withdrawals," p. 177.
[65]Reg. §1.401-4(a) (1) (iii); Rev. Rul. 71-4, IRB 1971-1; IR Manual Pension Trust Audit Guidelines 45(10) 5-1 (12-4-72), §412.41 and 412.43.
[66]Rev. Rul. 71-4, Ibid
[67]Rev. Rul. 71-313, IRB 1971-29.
[68]Rev. Rul. 71-149, IRB 1971-12.
[69]See Note 54.
[70]Rev. Rul. 61-164, 1961-2 CB 58.
[71]Ibid.
[72]IRC §404(a) (3) (A); Reg. §1.404(a)-9(c).
[73]Ibid.; Rev. Rul. 73-608 IRB 1973-53, 15.
[74]IRC §404(a) (3) (A).
[75]I. Goodman, "Insurance Contracts under Employee Benefit Plans," March 30, 1965.
[76]I. Goodman, "New Guides for the Qualification of Pension and Profit Sharing Plans," February 18, 1966.
[77]IRC §412(h) (1).
[78]IRC §404(a) (7).
[79]Parker Pen Co. v. O'Day (CA 7 - 1956) 234 F2d 607.

9

QUALIFYING THE RETIREMENT PLAN

"Qualification" means the success or failure of the professional corporation's retirement program. The key to qualification is that the plan not be drafted in such a manner that it operates in favor of the professional employees. If a retirement plan is determined by the Internal Revenue Service not to be qualified, then all of the tax advantages and objectives of the program will be lost. The following is an eight-point checklist for the requirements of a qualified plan. It is the purpose of this chapter to discuss these points in detail and to show their applicability under various circumstances.

CHECKLIST FOR A QUALIFIED RETIREMENT PLAN

1. Plan must be in writing setting forth all of the provisions essential for qualification.
2. Plan must be in effect before end of corporation's taxable year.
3. Plan must be communicated to all employees.
4. Coverage tests must be met.
5. Contribution or benefits must not discriminate in favor of the professional employees.
6. Plan must not discriminate in operation.
7. Plan must be permanent.
8. Trust must not permit diversion of funds for the benefit of Employer.

DEFINITE WRITTEN PROGRAM

In most professional corporations a retirement program will consist of a plan and a trust.[1] The plan, among other things, will set forth the requirements for eligibility, the benefits under the plan, and the rights of the participants in the funds allocated to their account in the event of their death, disability, retirement or termination of employment for any reason. The trust is created to receive and invest, pursuant to the powers confirmed upon the trustees, the contributions made to the plan by the corporation.

A qualified retirement plan must be in writing setting forth all of the provisions essential for qualification.[2] If a trust is involved it, too, must be in writing and executed before the end of the taxable year in which contributions were made to the plan.[3] The Internal Revenue Service will not recognize oral trusts even if recognized under the law of the jurisdiction in which created.[4]

PLAN AND TRUST MUST BE IN EFFECT

Not only must the plan and trust be in writing, but they must be in effect before the end of the taxable year for which the contributions made to the plan by the corporation are to be deducted.[5]

A plan is considered to be in effect when all requirements for qualification have been met. The trust must be organized and created in the United States and maintained at all times as a domestic trust,[6] and is considered to be in effect when it is recognized as such under the law presiding in the jurisdiction to which the trust is subject, and which contains language to the effect that the funds cannot be used for any purpose other than for the exclusive benefit of the employees or their beneficiaries.[7] Thus, the practitioner should avoid waiting for the last minute to adopt a retirement plan and trust and should make sure they are both executed before the close of the taxable year.

Although this appears to be a small point, serious problems may arise if the plan and trust are submitted to the Internal Revenue Service for qualification just prior to the close of the corporation's taxable year. Prior to the Pension Reform Act, if an amendment or amendments were required to be made to qualify the plan, the amendments were made two and one-half months after the close of the corporation's taxable year, the corporation would not be entitled to deduct its contribution to the plan, because the plan was not in effect, to wit, qualified, within the permitted period of time. The Pension Reform Act has somewhat liberalized this rule by providing that a corporation will be allowed to make retroactive changes correcting a defect in a new plan (or to cure an amendment to an existing plan) if such changes are made within the time for filing the employer's tax return for the year in which the plan was put into effect (or in which the amendment was adopted)[8]. In addition, the Secretary of the Treasury may grant even a longer period of time to the corporation to correct any defect, if he so determines.[9] Nevertheless, the corporation should submit both the plan and trust to the Internal Revenue Service leaving a sufficient amount of time to make the appropriate amendments, if required. Undue delay may cause the corporation to lose its deduction for any contribution made to the plan, if the corporation cannot cure the defect prior to the filing of its income tax return and the Secretary of the Treasury does not grant additional time to make these necessary amendments.

PLAN MUST BE FUNDED

A qualified trust is not recognized as such until it has become funded. A corporation on the accrual basis of accounting is able to deduct its contribution to the retirement plan if the contributions were made no later than the time prescribed by law for filing the tax return for such taxable year.[10] However, most professional corporations are on the cash basis of accounting and prior to the Pension Reform Act, they were required to make their contributions before the last day of the taxable year. As a consequence, a great burden was placed on these corporations to make the required contribution when the information needed to make such a contribution was often incomplete at that time.

The Pension Reform Act now provides that a corporation which is on the cash basis of accounting will be treated in the same manner as accrual-basis taxpayers.[11] Thus, the anxiety many practitioners had as a result of not being able to accurately determine the compensation for each employee as of the close of the corporation's taxable year upon which contributions were based, has now been removed.

WATCH THIS

The ability to make deductible contributions after the close of the corporation's taxable year but no later than the time required to file the return will not apply to a corporation which has adopted a discretionary profit sharing plan, if the corporation was not obligated to contribute to the plan prior to the close of its taxable year. In such an event, a liability has not accrued and the corporation will not be entitled to a deduction even if the contribution is made prior to filing its tax return.[12]

A corporation incurs a liability for contributions to its profit sharing plan having no definite contribution formula in the year it executes a resolution providing for the amount to be contributed and notifies the employees orally or in writing.[13]

THE PLAN MUST BE COMMUNICATED—PENSION REFORM ACT REQUIREMENTS

It is not uncommon for a professional corporation to adopt a retirement plan and the only employees aware of its existence or its terms are the professional employees. A retirement plan must be communicated to *all employees* if its is to be qualified.[14] Even if the plan is qualified in all other respects, until the plan or its provisions are communicated to the employees, the Corporation will not be entitled to deduct the contributions it made to the plan.[15]

Prior to the Pension Reform Act, the Internal Revenue Service held the position that the plan could be communicated to each employee by furnishing each employee with a copy of the plan or by providing a summary of the plan's essential features.[16]

Disclosure to Participants After Pension Reform

The Pension Reform Act has eliminated the furnishing of the plan itself as a method of communication and now provides that each participant or beneficiary must receive a summary plan description which is:[17]

1. written in a manner calculated to be understood by the average plan participant or beneficiary, and
2. which is sufficiently accurate and comprehensive to reasonably apprise such participants and beneficiaries of their rights and obligations under the plan.

In addition, a summary of all material modifications must also be given to plan participants.[18] Although the Pension Reform Act does not require that each participant receive a copy of the plan, or other related material, the plan and such other related material must be available for examination by any participant or beneficiary at the principal office of the plan administrator.[19]

Time Period for Furnishing Required Information

1. Summary plan descriptions are to be furnished to participants within the latter of 120 days after the plan is established or 90 days after an individual becomes a participant.[20]
2. Descriptions of material changes in the plan must be given to participants within 210 days after the end of any plan year in which a material change occurs.[21]
3. The summary plan description must be filed with the Secretary of Labor at the same time such summary is required to be given to participants and beneficiaries.[22]
4. All material modifications and changes must be filed with the Secretary of Labor within 60 days after such modification or change.[23]
5. Every five years after the adoption of the plan, an updated summary of plan description must be given to each participant or beneficiary. If there have been no amendments during this period, then the five-year update need not be given.[24]

6. Every ten years after the adoption of the plan, an updated summary plan description shall be given to each participant or beneficiary.[25]

COVERAGE REQUIREMENTS

A qualified plan must be established and maintained for the exclusive benefit of employees or their beneficiaries. Although it is not required that the plan benefit all employees, it must benefit employees in general and the plan cannot provide benefits exclusively for the officers, stockholders or other highly-paid employees of the corporation to the exclusion of the lower-paid employees.[26]

One-Man Professional Corporation

The Internal Revenue Service has ruled that a retirement plan may be qualified even though it covers only one employee who is the sole shareholder, provided that the plan was not designed or operated as a means of siphoning profits to the shareholder, or is designed in such a way that only the prohibited group will be eligible to participate.[27] The Internal Revenue Service appears to have had professional corporations in mind when it issued this ruling stating "the principle is equally applicable to a pension plan established by an employer dealing exclusively in the services of its sole employee who is also a shareholder."

Relatives May Be Covered

A professional who incorporates and adopts a qualified retirement plan may permit his relatives to participate in the plan provided they are bona-fide employees of the corporation.[28] In fact, it would appear, subject to this coverage requirement, that they must participate if the plan is to qualify.[29] Both of these rulings applied to Keogh Plans but their conclusion can equally be applied to professional corporations.

Who is An Employee

Employee vs. independent contractor

If a person is not considered an employee, but an independent contractor, the corporation is not required to include that person in applying the coverage tests. Therefore, the question "who is an employee" is of prime concern. Failure to make an accurate determination may result in the disqualification of the retirement plan.

Generally, a person will be considered an employee if the employer exercises control over the method and procedures to be followed by the employed individual.[30] Nurses, secretaries, receptionists and hygienists and other similar individuals are obviously under such control of the corporation and should be considered employees.

However, it may become very difficult to determine whether a professional is an employee when he renders services to a corporation but is not an officer or stockholder and has no managerial authority. It may also be difficult to determine when a pathologist, radiologist or some other hospital-based specialist is the employee of the corporation, whose president and shareholder is the director of said department.

Since the practice of medicine requires the exercise of almost unlimited discretion by the physician with respect to the precise manner of its performance, the corporation will not be able to supervise the specific details of the work to be performed. Therefore, supervision is not the primary test that is used in determining an employer-employee relationship.

> The primary test, in ascertaining the status of a physician or other professional person ... is the presence of elements of control as indicated by such factors as (1) the degree to which such individual has become integrated into the operating organization of the employer; (2) the substantial nature, regularity and continuity of his work for the employer; (3) the

authority vested in or reserved by the employer to require compliance with his general standards and policies, and (4) the degree to which the individual under consideration has been accorded the rights and privileges of other clearly recognized employees.[31]

The "leased employee"

To avoid the costs of having to contribute to its common law employees, some professional corporations have taken unusual steps to transfer these employees to another company while still obtaining their services. The objective is that the non-professional employees are not employees of the new company and therefore, are not eligible to be covered under the retirement plan of the professional corporation. This might occur in one or two of the following ways:

1. The corporation transfers the employees to an unrelated company which then leases the same employees back to the corporation. The employees perform the same services but the payroll records, social security payments and salary checks are made by the unrelated company.
2. The professional corporation establishes a new corporation, to which it then transfers all its common law employees. The professional corporation then leases these employees in the same manner as in the above arrangement.

The Internal Revenue Service has specifically ruled that the first arrangement will not be recognized and that the transferred employees must be recognized for retirement plan purposes. "A contractual arrangement will not be determinative of the employer/employee relationship when the realities of the situation contradict the terms of the contract ... The only change, from the viewpoint of the employees, was the source of the paychecks. The contract in no way changed the realities of the situation."[32] Although the ruling applied to a partnership which adopted a Keogh Plan, its rationale should be equally applicable to a professional corporation.

The rationale of the above cited ruling would seem to apply to the second situation as well. In any event, the Pension Reform Act specifically addressed itself to the second situation, and provides that employees of controlled corporations (within the meaning of Internal Revenue Code §1563(a) are to be treated as if they were employees of the same corporation.[33]

Therefore, the situations described above will not be successful in avoiding the coverage and anti-discrimination provisions by operating through separate corporations.

COVERAGE TESTS

Prior to Pension Reform Act

A retirement plan will be considered for the exclusive benefit of employees if a sufficient number of employees are covered. Prior to the Pension Reform Act, the Internal Revenue Code provided three tests as to what would constitute adequate coverage for purposes of plan qualification. The tests were in the alternative, and if any one of the three tests were met, then the coverage requirements were satisfied. These tests were as follows:

1. If 70% of all full-time and permanent employees are covered, then the plan will meet the coverage requirements.
2. If 80% or more of the eligible employees participate, then the coverage requirements will be met provided 70% or more of the employees are eligible.
3. If the percentage requirements are not met, the employer may set up a classification for eligibility provided such classification is found by the commissioner not to be discriminatory in favor of employees who are officers, shareholders, or highly salaried.

Examples

Test 1

Professional corporation has 10 employees. If 7 are covered in plan, coverage is sufficient. When multiplying 70% by the number of employees, you must round off to the next highest number to determine employees who must be covered. Thus, if a corporation employs 6 employees, 5 employees must be covered even though 70% times 6 = 4.2.

Test 2

Professional corporation has 12 employees. If 70% or 8 (70% x 12 = 8 employees) are eligible to participate, then 7 must actually participate. (80% x 8 = 6.4 = 7 employees). This test becomes applicable when employees must contribute to the plan if they are to be covered. 80% of the 70% whom are eligible must in fact contribute, otherwise the coverage test will not be met.

OBSERVATION

Although many corporations would like to have their employees share in the contributions to the plan, there is always the danger that a sufficient number of employees will not elect to contribute to the plan. If the mandatory contributions are found to be burdensome, then the plan will not qualify. In a professional corporation covering a small number of employees, it is best to avoid contributory plans. Furthermore, mandatory contributions will reduce the corporate contribution to a defined contribution plan as provided in Internal Revenue Code §415 (c) (1).

Test 3

A corporation may set up any classification of employees it wants covered under its retirement plan. For example, the corporation may only want to cover physicians and nurses, and exclude all secretaries and receptionists, or the plan may cover only salaried employees, and exclude those who are paid on an hourly basis. If as a result of such coverage classification, the percentage tests are not met, the plan may still qualify, if the Internal Revenue Service determines that the classification does not favor employees who are officers, shareholders or other contained in the prohibited group. The Internal Revenue Service in making its finding, compares the excluded employees with those covered to determine whether the highly-compensated employees are favored to the detriment of those lower compensated. Hence, there must be sufficient participation by the lower paid employees to demonstrate that in practice the plan does not discriminate in favor of the high-paid employees.[34]

OBSERVATION

In applying the "non-discriminatory classification" test, employees who are employed on a part-time basis may not be disregarded.[35]

The "non-discriminatory classification" will have limited application in most professional corporations because of the small number of employees, but it can be used to exclude professional employees who do not want to participate in the plan.[36]

The coverage tests are objective and plan will qualify if the required number of employees are covered.[37] Thus, non-professional employees may be excluded to the extent that only professional employees are covered provided the required percent is covered. For example, if a corporation consists of four employees, three professional and the other non-professional, it would appear that if the non-professional is excluded, the plan will still meet the coverage test because the covered professionals represent 75% of the employees.

After Pension Reform Act

The Pension Reform Act has continued the 70%/80%[38] and non-discriminatory tests, but has now established "minimum participation standards" which must be met if the plan is to be qualified. These minimum standards are as follows:

1. An employee cannot be excluded from participation if he is at least 25 years old and has completed at least one year of service.[39] Thus, if an employee is age 26 when he commences his employment, the plan may require one year of service before he is eligible to participate. Alternatively, an employee who is employed at the age of 21 may be required to attain age 25 before participating even though he will have completed four years of service.

2. If the plan provides for full and immediate vesting for all participants, the plan may require employees to be age 25 with three years of service in order to participate.[40]

3. The plan cannot exclude a participant from participating if he has attained a specified age unless the plan is a defined benefit or target benefit plan, in which case, an employee may be excluded from participating if he is within five years of attaining the normal retirement age under the plan when he was first employed.[41]

WATCH THIS

Employees who are excluded from participating in a defined benefit or target benefit pension plan because they are within five years of attaining the normal retirement age under the plan when they are employed, must be included when computing the "percentage test."[42]

Furthermore, if such employees are to be excluded because their age is within five years of the normal retirement date, then the normal retirement date cannot be defined as "the later of age 65 or the tenth anniversary of the time a participant commenced participation in the plan," since no participant will ever be within five years of the normal retirement date. Thus, if such exclusion is to be utilized the normal retirement date must be defined as age 65.

OBSERVATION

The Act specifically states that a plan cannot require as "condition of participation" that an employee attain a minimum age greater than 25 and complete a service requirement in excess of one year. Therefore, if exclusion from participation is based upon a job classification or some other criteria, such exclusion will not affect the qualification of the plan if the percentage or non-discriminatory tests are met, even though the employee or group of employees excluded have attained the age of 25 and have completed one year of service.

Permitted Exclusion

Prior to the Pension Reform Act

In computing the percentage test, the following individuals were not considered employees and could have been automatically excluded from participating in the plan:

1. A person who has not been employed by the corporation for the minimum period of time by the plan not exceeding five years.
2. A person whose customary employment is for not more than 20 hours in any one week; and
3. A person whose customary employment is for not more than 5 months in any calendar year.

After Pension Reform Act

The new pension act has reduced the five-year service requirement to one year and has redefined the part-time and seasonal provisions. Under the Act, an employee may still be excluded if his employment is seasonal or part-time. However, "part-time" or "seasonal" employment is no longer determined by whether the employee works for more than 5 months a year or 20 hours a week, but whether the employee works for not less than 1,000 hours for a twelve-month period.[43]

Therefore, under the Pension Reform Act, the following employees may be excluded in determining whether the percentage tests have been met:

1. Employees who have not attained the age of 25.
2. Employees who have not completed one year of service, and
3. Employees who do not work more than 1,000 hours for a 12-month period of time.

Year of Service Requirement-Past Service with Proprietorship or Partnerhsip

Most corporations will adopt a retirement plan simultaneously with its incorporation or very soon thereafter. Consequently, there cannot be a one-year service requirement with the corporation since the corporation has not been in existence for one year. As a result, the professionals may try to apply the one-year service requirement to the period of employment while a sole proprietor or partnership.

The Internal Revenue Service position is that a sole proprietor or partner is not considered an employee and cannot obtain credit for past service as such prior to becoming an employee of the corporation.[44] Employment with a sole proprietorship or partnership may be credited to common law employees (which does not include in its definition self-employed individuals or partners),[45] and if the new corporation is employing inidividuals who were employed by the sole proprietorship or partnership and who meet the services requirement, they will be the only participants in the plan. If the new corporation has no employees who meet the required period of employment, then the plan will have no participants and will not qualify under section 410(a) of the Internal Revenue Code.[46] However, two cases[47] have held that past service with a sole proporietor or partnership could be credited to such proprietorship or partner in the new corporation. However, these cases were never acquiesced to by the Internal Revenue Service, and it is unlikely that the Internal Revenue Service will change its current position.

Therefore, if the new corporation desires to have a service requirement, it should adopt its retirement program toward the end of its tax year. In such an event, it would be possible to have a service requirement equal to the period of time from the inception of the corporation to the adoption of the retirement plan.

However, submitting the retirement plan too close to the close of the corporation's taxable year may not allow sufficient amount of time to make the required amendments, if any, within the period of time permitted. This will result in the corporation being prohibited from deducting its contribution to the plan.

Time of Participation

Many plans in defining eligibility provide that "Each present and future employee shall be eligible to participate on the effective date or anniversary date of the plan after fulfilling the requirements for eligibility." The effect of such language is that in many cases, future employees will have a longer waiting period than the original employees who were eligible to participate when the plan was originally adopted.

Example

A pension plan's anniversary date is July 1 of each year and the plan has a 12-month service requirement. If a nurse is employed on August 1, 1974 and said language is adopted, she will not be eligible to participate until July 1, 1976. However, if she was eligible immediately upon completing 12 months of service, she would be eligible on August 1, 1975. Alternatively, if the nurse was hired on June 1, 1974, she will be eligible to participate on July 1, 1975, which is the first anniversary date after her employment.

Thus, a corporation by hiring a new employee at the "proper time" could exclude that person from participating in the plan for a period of time in excess of the time required of the original participants, which results in a longer service requirement than required by the plan.

The Pension Reform Act specifically addressed itself to the potential problem and provides that an employee who satisfies the "minimum participation standards" must be eligible to participate, unless otherwise excluded upon some other criteria, no later than the earlier of

1. The first day of the first plan year beginning after the anniversary date of his employment, or
2. Six months after the date on which he satisfies said requirements.[48]

Therefore, in the above example, the nurse who was employed on August 1, 1974 must be eligible to participate on February 1, 1976; and if she was employed on June 1, 1974, she would be eligible to participate on July 1, 1975.

Professionals Who Share Employees

It is not uncommon that two or more professionals who have independent practices share the expenses of maintaining an office, including secretarial employees. When one professional decides to incorporate, the question arises whether the shared employee, who may work less than 1000 hours for a 12-month period for the particular individual, must be considered an employee for purposes of retirement in his retirement plan. The Internal Revenue Service has concluded in two revenue rulings that shared employees must be considered as full-time employees of the incorporating professional for retirement plan purposes.[49] The facts of the two cited rulings were that the shared employees worked various hours for each professional, depending upon the professional's workload, and the Internal Revenue Service held that such variation would not permit that employees be considered part-time. A different conclusion might have been reached if each secretary or nurse had a specified number of hours that she was to work for each professional in the office.

Different Eligibility Requirements For Present and Future Employees

The corporation may wish to have different eligibility requirements for present employees and future employees. This will be permitted if the employees who are members of the prohibited group can meet the requirements for the future employees.[50] Thus, if a corporation adopts a plan in which all present employees are eligible to participate at the plan's effective date, but future employees must be employed for a period of 12 months before being eligible to participate, the plan will be qualified if the officers, shareholders or other highly-compensated employees meet the 12-month service requirements at the plan's effective date.[51]

The problem may arise in another manner. A professional incorporates and then adopts a retirement plan which provides that all employees who work more than 1,000 hours in a 12-month period will be eligible to participate. No service requirement or other requirements for eligibility are provided. One year after the adoption of the plan, the corporation amends the plan to provide for a one-year service requirement for all future employees. The Internal Revenue Service has considered such an amendment and has ruled that either the percentage test or the "non-discriminatory test" must be met if the plan is going to continue to be qualified. Thus, if such an amendment results in less than 70% of employees as classified above from participating in the plan and the amendment benefits the prohibited group, this plan will not qualify.[52]

Mandatory Contributions

A plan may be designed whereby eligible participants are required to make mandatory contributions to the plan before they can participate. However, if "the contributions required of the employee participant are so burdensome as to make the plan acceptable only to the highly-paid employees, the classification will be considered discriminatory in favor of such highly-paid employees."[53]

Thus, if the Internal Revenue Service determines that only the highly-paid employee will be able to participate in the plan, then the plan will not qualify. The Internal Revenue Service has ruled that generally a mandatory contribution of six percent (6%) or less may not be considered burdensome.[54]

However, this is a general rule and even mandatory contributions of six percent (6%) or even less may be found discriminatory if the lower paid employees do not elect to participate.[55]

WATCH THIS

In view of the fact that employee contributions will reduce the amount that the corporation will be able to contribute to the retirement plan under Internal Revenue Code §415(c) (1), it is seriously questionable whether mandatory contributions will serve any useful purpose in a professional corporation.[56]

CONTRIBUTIONS AND BENEFITS

Contributions or benefits in a qualified plan must not discriminate in favor of the officers, shareholders or other members of the prohibited group.[57] It is important to note that the requirements as to non-discrimination are prescribed in the alternative. The prohibited discrimination must not exist either in contributions *or* in benefits. It is not required that both contributions and benefits be non-discriminatory.

Defined Benefit and Target Benefit Pension Plans

Contributions to a defined benefit and target benefit pension plan may vary among the participants provided the retirement benefits to be received by each participant are uniform. Thus, if the retirement benefits are equal to forty percent of each participant's compensation at retirement, the plan will not be discriminatory even though there is a wide variance in the rate of contributions made for the benefit of the older participants and in the rate of those for the younger participants.[58]

WATCH THIS

There is no limit on the contributions or benefits that may be provided for officers or shareholders, provided the plan is not discriminatory and the benefits bear a uniform relationship to compensation.[59]

Money Purchase and Profit Sharing Plans

A plan will not be considered discriminatory merely because contributions bear a uniform relationship to the total compensation, or basic or regular rate of compensation of the covered employees.[60] Thus, if in a money purchase pension plan, the same percent of each participant's compensation, subject to the integration rules, is required to be contributed, and if under a profit sharing plan the contributions are allocated among participants in proportion to the compensation or in some other non-discriminatory manner, there is no discrimination even though larger contributions are made for the benefit of the higher paid employees.

Contributions Based Upon Years of Service or Other Factors May Cause Discrimination

Money purchase pension plans and profit sharing plans may give credit for past service or for years of participation in the plan, or for other factors, provided the formula by which contributions are determined does not discriminate in favor of the professional employees.[61] Thus, if a money purchase pension plan provides that contributions will be based upon years of participation in the plan and there is a high turn-over in nonprofessional participants, then it is obvious the corporation will be making larger contributions for the benefit of professional employees than for the others, and the plan will be disqualified.[62]

Example

> A plan provides that the employer will contribute at least four percent (4%) of each participant's compensation to the plan for his first year of participation plus one percent (1%) of compensation for each additional year of participation. The maximum contribution permitted is fifteen percent (15%) of a participant's compensation for any one year. If, as a result of a high turnover of lower paid participants, the corporation contributes fifteen percent (15%) for the benefit of the prohibited group, and a much lower percent for the other employees, the plan will not qualify.[63]

A profit sharing plan whose allocation formula is based upon the training and experience of the participants will not qualify where larger allocations are made for the benefit of the prohibited group.[64]

As a general rule, contributions based upon years of service are not applicable to a professional corporation because the retirement plan is usually adopted in the same year of incorporation. However, where years of service may be applied, it should be done with great caution. Since the professional employees will usually have the longest service with the corporation, it may be impossible to avoid discrimination. In fact, the Internal Revenue Service has taken the position that discrimination is so likely to occur in profit sharing plans where years of service is used to determine the allocations of employer's contributions, it will not issue a qualifying letter and the plan will be examined each year.[65]

DISCRIMINATION IN OPERATION

"The law is concerned not only with the form of the plan, but also with its effect in operation."[66] Thus, even though a plan when submitted to the Internal Revenue Service for qualification meets the requirements for qualification, the plan may subsequently be disqualified if it appears that the plan in actual operation is resulting in discrimination in favor of the prohibited group.

Discrimination in operation most commonly occurs in two situations:

1. If there is a high turnover of employees and the vesting schedule is of such a duration that only the prohibited group can expect to receive benefits under the plan, and
2. If the employer engages in employment practices which prevent plan participants from receiving their benefits.

The problem of discrimination in operation arising from prolonged vesting schedules and employment practices is subsequently discussed in more detail.

VESTING

Prior to Pension Reform Act

Prior to the Pension Reform Act, full vesting was not required by the Internal Revenue Code except in the following circumstances:

1. When a participant attained his normal retirement date in a pension plan;[67]
2. When a participant attained the stated age or other specified event in a profit sharing plan;[68]
3. In the event that the plan was terminated or upon its complete discontinuance.[69]

As a result, vesting schedules ranged from complete and immediate, through different forms of graduated vesting to no vesting until the attainment of the normal retirement date or stated age or event.

However, although there was a wide range of vesting methods available, a corporation could not select a vesting schedule which would result in only the prohibited group receiving their benefits. Therefore, if upon submitting the plan to the Internal Revenue Service for approval, it was determined that the prohibited discrimination would probably result, the plan would not be qualified, unless the plan was amended to provide for fully-vested rights after a reasonable period of time.[70] Furthermore, even if the plan was initially qualified, if there was a high turnover in employees and the vesting schedule was of such a duration that only the professional employees would benefit from the corporate contribution allocated to their accounts, the plan would be considered discriminatory in operation and would lose its qualification.[71]

Therefore, the problem confronting the practitioner was to devise a vesting schedule which would reasonably be expected to provide benefits for all participants and not just the professionals. However, devising a vesting schedule which would not produce the discriminatory results was made quite difficult since no definite guidelines were available and the determination of whether a vesting schedule was discriminatory was made on a case-by-case basis.[72]

Thus, a vesting schedule which would be satisfactory in one case might be found to be discriminatory against the lower echelon employees in another. For example, if an employer was fortunate to have a low turnover in employees, his vesting schedule would not be discriminatory in operation even though vesting was prolonged, since all employees would be receiving benefits. However, if an employer had a high turnover of employees, his vesting schedule might be found to be discriminatory if the terminated employees received none or only a small portion of their retirement account.[73]

Fortunately, the Pension Reform Act has established minimum vesting requirements, and as a result, much of the indefiniteness in the area has been removed.

After Pension Reform Act

The Pension Reform Act provides that a retirement plan must meet certain minimum vesting requirements if the plan is to be qualified. As a result, the case-by-case approach of determining whether a particular vesting schedule will meet the requirements for qualification has been substantially eliminated.

The minimum vesting requirements which must be met if the plan is to be qualified are as follows:

1. An employee must be 100% vested in his normal retirement benefit when he attains the normal retirement age.[74] This is a restatement of the present law.
2. The employee must be 100% vested to all accrued benefits arising from his own contributions.[75] Most plans contain this provision now and will have no particular effect upon the professional corporations, and
3. In respect to employer contributions, the plan, other than a money purchase, stock bonus or profit sharing plan, (called class year plans) must meet one of three alternative vesting schedules.[76]
    1. Ten-year vesting
    2. Five- to Fifteen-Year vesting
    3. Rule of 45

These vesting schedules and other new rules regarding vesting requirements are hereinafter discussed in more detail.

MINIMUM VESTING REQUIREMENTS

Ten-Year Vesting - Under this rule, an employee with at least ten years of service must be 100% vested in his accrued benefit derived from employer contributions.

OBSERVATION

It appears that there is no requirement as to how much the employee should be vested in any one particular year, provided he is 100% vested after ten. Thus, it is possible to have no vesting of benefits during the first nine years of service, and 100% upon the completion of the tenth.

Five-to Fifteen-Year Vesting - Under this rule, an employee must be vested in at least 25% of his accrued benefit derived from employer contributions after completing five years of service and must vest to an additional 5% of such benefit for each of the next five years of service, and 10% for each of the next five years.

Example

Years of Service:	Nonforfeitable percentage
5	25
6	30
7	35
8	40
9	45
10	50
11	60
12	70
13	80
14	90
15 or more	100

Again, it appears that there is no requirement for any vesting prior to the completion of five years of service.

Rule of 45 - Under this rule, an employee with five or more years of covered service must be at least 50% vested when the sum of his age and years of covered service total 45. For each additional year of coverage service, the employee must vest an additional 10% per year.

OBSERVATION

This method provides greater protection for the older employee who may not accrue sufficient retirement benefits if he terminates his employment prior to retirement.

If years of service equal or exceed	*and sum of age and service equals or exceeds*	*then the nonforfeitable percentage is*
5	45	50
6	47	60
7	49	70
8	51	80
9	53	90
10	55	100

However, if an employee has at least ten years of service, he must be at least 50% vested regardless of his age and he must vest at least an additional 10% for each additional year of service thereafter.

EXCEPTIONS TO MINIMUM VESTING REQUIREMENTS

Class Year Plans

A class year plan (money purchase, stock bonus and profit sharing plan) will satisfy the minimum vesting requirements without being required to adopt one of the above alternative vesting methods, if the plan provides for 100% vesting of benefits derived from employer contributions within five years after the end of the plan year in which they were made.[77]

Variations

The Secretary of Labor may allow a different vesting method to plans in effect prior to January 1, 1974, only if he finds that:[78]

1. The application of the minimum vesting rules would increase the cost of the plan to such an extent that there would be a substantial danger that the plan will be terminated or substantial reduction in plan benefits;
2. The application of the minimum vesting rules or discontinuance of the plan would be adverse to the interest of the plan participants as a whole; and
3. That the hardship described in items 1 and 2 above cannot be sufficiently reduced by granting a funding variance.

OBSERVATION

As a practical matter the provision for a variance to the minimum vesting rules will have little application to the professional corporation since it has, in most cases, already met these minimum requirements, and the hardship contemplated by this section has in mind plans consisting of many participants, and plans consisting on an average of only two to ten employees.

Discrimination in Operation

Generally, if the plan adopts one of the alternative vesting methods discussed above, the plan will qualify under §401(c) of the Internal Revenue Code unless:[79]

1. There has been a pattern of abuse under the plan tending to discriminate in favor of employees in the prohibited group, or
2. There has been, or there is reason to believe there will be, an accrual of benefits or forfeitures tending to discriminate in favor of employees in the prohibited group.

Therefore, the non-discrimination rules which were used by the Internal Revenue Service prior to the enactment of the Pension Reform Act are still applicable. If the Internal Revenue Service determines when initially considering a plan for qualification, that the minimum vesting alternatives provided by the Pension Reform Act will not be sufficient to prevent the prohibited discrimination, then the Service may require the plan to adopt a quicker vesting schedule. However, the Congressional Committee on Pension Reform has instructed the Internal Revenue Service " . . . not to require a vesting schedule more stringent than forty percent vesting after four years of employment with five percent additional vesting for each of the next two years, and ten percent additional vesting for each of the following five years."[80]

Thus, the Congressional Committee has established a maximum vesting schedule which will have the effect of avoiding the case-by-case approach and void different vesting schedules which were required by the various pension districts in fact situations of a similar nature. Furthermore, it will be highly unlikely that the Internal Revenue Service will be able to disqualify a plan for being discriminatory in operation in respect to vesting of benefits if the maximum vesting schedule is adopted. Thus, the practitioner now has more certainty that a plan will not be disqualified as a result of a high turnover of employees than ever before (unless, of course, the employees are fired before their accrued benefits vest).[81] In addition, many practitioners will find that this maximum vesting schedule is more liberal than what they have previously been able to qualify under. Unfortunately, the Congressional Committee stated that "...it generally is not intended that any plan ...which is presently under a more rapid vesting schedule should be permitted to cut back its vesting schedule ..."[82] Thus, an existing retirement plan which requires more rapid vesting than that required under the maximum vesting schedule cannot be amended to the new maximum requirements.

HOW TO COMPUTE "YEARS OF SERVICE" FOR VESTING PURPOSES

Generally, once an employee becomes eligible to participate in a retirement plan, all his years of service with the employer are taken into account for purposes of determining his place on the vesting schedule. However, there are exceptions to this general rule, which are as follows:

1. Years of service before the employee attained the age of 22 may be ignored. However, if the "Rule of 45" is adopted, service before age 22 may be ignored only if the employee was not a participant in the plan during the years before age 22.[83]
2. The plan may ignore periods for which the employee declined to make mandatory contributions.[84]
3. The plan may ignore periods for which the employer did not maintain the plan or a predecessor plan.[85]
4. If the employee has had a "break in service," his service performed prior to the break may be ignored to the extent provided by the "break in service rules."[86]
5. Services performed prior to January 1, 1971 may be ignored, unless the employee has at least three years of service after December 31, 1970.[87]
6. Service as a seasonal or part-time employee (less than 1,000 hours of service per year) may be ignored.[88]

Example

Nurse A was hired by ABC, Professional Corporation, when she was 21. The plan provides for participation in the plan at age 25, and the plan has adopted the vesting schedule of 10% for each year of service. When Nurse A is eligible to participate, she will be 40% vested after completing her first year of participation in the plan. The year prior to her attaining age 22 may be ignored.

PERMITTED FORFEITURES OF VESTED BENEFITS

An employee's vested interest in benefits arising from his own contributions may never be forfeited. However, a plan may provide that an employee's vested rights in benefits attributable to employer contributions may be forfeited in the following circumstances:

1. In the event of the employee's death before retirement, unless a joint and surviving annuity is to be provided.[89]
2. Benefits may be suspended in the event a retired employee is re-employed by the same employer under whose plan the benefits are being paid.[90]
3. In the event an employee who is less than 50% vested in his benefits withdraws all or part of his mandatory contributions to the plan. However, in each case, the plan must provide that forfeited

benefits will be fully restored if the employee repays the withdrawn contribution with interest of 5% per annum. If the employee is more than 50% vested, no forfeiture is permitted.[91]

Record-Keeping Requirements

The employer must keep records of each employee's vested percentage and his years of service. In addition, each plan participant has the right to request the employer to inform him of his vesting and accrued benefit status. An employee, however, shall not be entitled to make such a request more than once during any 12-month period.[92]

CHANGES IN THE VESTING SCHEDULES

If at any time the vesting schedule is amended, the vesting percentage for each participant in his accrued benefit accumulated to the date when the plan amendment is adopted cannot be reduced as a result of the amendment. [93] In addition, as further protection for long-service employees with at least five years of service may elect to remain under the pre-amendment vesting schedule with respect to all of his benefits accrued both before and after the plan amendment.[94]

EFFECT OF VESTING ON PROFESSIONALS WHO TERMINATE EMPLOYMENT

It must be remembered that the vesting schedule which is adopted applies to all participants including the professional participants. Therefore, in a corporation consisting of two or more professionals, if a professional employee terminates his employment prior to becoming 100% vested in the contributions allocated to his account, he will forfeit a portion of his account, which will be used either to reduce subsequent year contributions required to be made to the plan by the corporation, or may be reallocated among the many participants if a profit sharing plan was adopted. A professional will often reduce his income upon incorporating to provide the funds necessary to fund a retirement plan, and upon termination of his employment he may find a portion or all of his deferred income, in effect, inuring to the benefit of his professional colleagues. There is no way that this result can be avoided. The plan cannot distribute any more than that portion of his account which is vested in him as of the date of his termination of employment without disqualifying the plan.[95] The professionals certainly should not enter into any agreements providing that any resulting forfeiture will be paid to the terminating participant by the corporation. Such an agreement will certainly disqualify the plan, since all employees are not being treated equally.

Therefore, the practitioner should be certain that this most undesirable result is perfectly understood by the professionals when adopting a vesting schedule for the plan. In such cases, it is often better to provide a more rapid vesting schedule.

Avoid Employment Practices Which Will Preclude Participation In The Plan By The Non-Professional Employees

A professional corporation should avoid employment practices that will preclude participation in the plan by the non-professional employees or prevent them from receiving the benefits under the plan. Thus, if the plan requires a continuous 12-month service requirement before the employee is eligible to participate or if the plan requires an employee to attain the age of 25 before being eligible to participate, the corporation should not terminate an employee's employment just prior to becoming eligible to participate. If this is done on a regular basis, the plan will be held to be discriminatory in operation. In addition, the corporation should certainly avoid terminating the participant's employment with the corporation just prior to becoming vested in a portion of the retirement account. If this practice is followed on a regular basis, the corporation will be hard pressed to explain that this was not done to preclude vesting in benefits in the retirement plan by the non-professional employees.

It must be emphasized that a qualified retirement plan is for the benefit of all employees, and any practices adopted by the corporation which preclude or limit participation in the plan or benefits thereunder by the non-professional employees will cause the plan to discriminate in favor of the prohibited group and the plan will be disqualified.

ACCRUED BENEFITS

The Pension Reform Act refers to the term "accrued benefits" throughout the Act and especially in the vesting provisions. The "accrued benefit" is the "what" of vesting, that is, a participant's non-forfeitable percentage in the plan's vesting schedule is applied against his accrued benefit in order to determine "what" is vested. For example, assume that a participant is 40% vested and his accrued benefit is computed to be $20,000. In this instance, the participant would have a non-forfeitable right to $8,000 (.40 x S20,000). Prior to the Pension Reform Act, there was no requirement to have the accrued benefit defined in the plan. The term "accrued benefit" refers to retirement benefits. It does not apply to ancillary benefits, such as medical or disability benefits, early retirement benefits, death benefits or the value of Social Security supplements or other benefits under the plan which are not continued for any participant after he has attained the normal retirement age.[96]

Defined Contribution Plans

In the case of a money-purchase, target benefit or profit sharing plan, the participant's accrued benefit is the balance of his individual account. Therefore, if $40,000 has been allocated to a participant's account, then his accrued benefit will be $40,000 against which the applicable vesting percentage will be multiplied.

Defined Benefit Plans

In the case of a defined benefit plan, the accrued benefit is determined by the plan, subject to certain requirements. In general, the accrued benefit is defined in terms of the benefit payable at the normal retirement age. The normal retirement age may not be later than age 65 or the tenth anniversary of the time the participant commenced participation, whichever last occurs.

The Pension Reform Act provides three basic methods of determining an employee's accrued benefit in a defined benefit plan. The calculations are quite complex and generally will be computed by an actuary. For this reason, the three alternative methods are briefly discussed.[97]

The Three Percent Test

Under this alternative each participant must accrue for each year of participation at least three percent of the benefit which is payable under the plan to a participant who begins participation at the earliest possible entry age and serves continuously until age 65, or the normal retirement age under the plan, whichever is earlier.[98]

The 133 1/3 Percent Test

Under this method, the retirement benefit is calculated as though the employee has continued to accrual rate for the previous year. For example, if the accrual rate in one year was one percent, then the accrual rate for the following year could not exceed 1 1/3 percent.[99]

The Pro Rata Rate

Under this method, the retirement benefit is calculated as though the employee had continued to earn the same rate of compensation until his normal retirement age. This amount is then multiplied by a fraction, the numerator of which is the employee's total active participation in up to the date of the computation, and the denominator of which is the total number of years of active participation he would have if he continued his employment until the normal retirement age.[100]

PLAN MUST BE PERMANENT

A plan which is intended to qualify under Section 401(a) of the Internal Revenue Code must be established on a permanent and continuing basis.[101] There are two basic reasons for this requirement: (1) It will restrict corporations from establishing plans during a period of high profits only to discontinue the plan in a few years as profits decline and (2) it will prevent discrimination in favor of the professional employee by prohibiting the termination of the plan after their benefits have been provided before the benefits of the other participants have been similarly funded.[102] The termination or curtailment of a pension or profit sharing plan may affect the qualification of the plan. This does not mean that once a professional corporation adopts a retirement plan it must continue it forever regardless of its ability to do so. The corporation may reserve the right to modify or terminate the plan and to discontinue contributions thereunder without affecting its qualified status provided a valid reason exists for exercising such rights and if the plan is otherwise qualified under Section 401(a) of the Internal Revenue Code.[103]

When a corporation first submits its retirement plan to the Internal Revenue Service for qualification, it is presumed that the plan is being established in good faith and will be continued permanently unless there is clear evidence to the contrary. "Therefore, in most cases the issue of intended permanence is resolved in the favor of the taxpayer at the time of the adoption of the plan."[104] However, if in a few years, the corporation terminates the plan and there has been no unforseeable development in its business which makes it impossible to continue the plan, then the original presumption of permanence is replaced with the presumption that the corporation did not intend the plan as the permanent program from the beginning. In the absence of evidence rebutting this presumption, such a plan will be disqualified retroactively as not being a permanent plan for the exclusive benefit of employees in general.[105]

The presumption that the plan was not intended to be a permanent program may be overcome by showing that the abandonment was due to business necessity that could not reasonably have been forseen when the plan was adopted. The term "business necessity" has reference to adverse business conditions, not within the control of the corporation, under which it is not possible to continue the plan.[106] There are no established rules which determine when a plan has been terminated for a valid reason. A reason that may be satisfactory in one case may not be necessarily controlling in another. The facts in each case must govern. It appears, however, that the corporation's bankruptcy, insolvency, the sale of its business in an arm's length transaction, and financial inability to continue the plan will generally be considered a valid reason, provided the surrounding facts and circumstances are sufficient to establish the plan was not adopted in anticipation of a short existence, after providing for the benefits for the prohibited group.

When a Plan is Terminated

The answer to this question is not as obvious as one would first think. A plan is obviously terminated when the corporation discontinues all business operations.[107] However, a plan may terminate when the plan is amended to provide reduced benefits to the participants or by making the eligibility requirements less liberal.[108] Such an event is referred to as a curtailment and the plan is considered partially terminated.

Although almost all professionals who incorporate will not have any difficulty complying with the rules of permanency, it must be emphasized that the practitioner must make the professional realize that when he incorporates and adopts a retirement plan, he is adopting a plan that must be operated as a permanent program and that he is not able to vary the contributions to the plan from year to year, as he elects, unless a profit sharing plan is adopted, and even in a profit sharing plan the contributions are subject to a "substantial and recurring" rule.

Effect of Termination

The Internal Revenue Service has set forth two rules as to the effect of terminating a qualified plan. The first rule is that upon the termination of a qualified plan all participants' rights in their accounts must become 100% vested, regardless of their vested interest prior to termination.[109] Thus, if an employee has been a participant in a plan for two years and is 20% vested at that time, and the plan is then terminated, that participant becomes 100% vested in his account. If a partial termination is found, then the requirement for vesting applies only to the part of the plan which is terminated.

The second rule provides that if a fixed benefit or target benefit pension plan is terminated within ten years of its adoption, the benefits attributable to the highest twenty-five employees whose anticipated annual pension exceeds $1,500 will be restricted pursuant to Section 1.401.4(c) (2) of the Internal Revenue Code.

Premature Termination—Defined Benefit and Target Benefit Pension Plan

A defined benefit and target benefit pension plan permits a corporation to contribute large sums of money for the benefit of older participants in order to have the necessary funds available to provide the stated or assumed benefits at retirement. This is permitted even though the corporation will make significantly smaller contributions for the younger participants on the theory that all participants will receive the same uniform benefit when they attain the normal retirement age. If, however, the older participants are professional employees and the plan is terminated soon after their benefits have been fully funded where those for others have not, or benefits for the lower paid employees have not been funded at least to the same extent as for the highest paid, discrimination arises in favor of the professional employees.

As previously pointed out, if the plan is determined by the Internal Revenue Service to have been terminated without a valid business reason, the plan from its inception will be held not to have been a bona fide program for the exclusive benefit of employees in general and the corporation will not be entitled to deduct the contributions made to the plan. Nevertheless, the professional employee will still receive his full pension whereas the lower paid employee will receive a smaller distribution which will furnish her with only a negligible benefit compared to what she would have received if the plan continued until she attained her retirement age. In order to protect the lower paid employees from this result, a qualified defined benefit and target benefit pension plan are required to contain a restriction on the funds which may be used to provide benefits for the higher paid employees, in the event of the early termination of the plan. This is commonly referred to as the "termination rule." This rule has been specifically retained by the Pension Reform Act.[110] The termination rule provides that if the defined benefit or target benefit pension plan is terminated within ten years of its inception, the benefits of the 25 highest paid employees at the time the plan was established and whose anticipated annual retirement benefit exceeds $1,500, must be restricted to the greater of:

1. $20,000; or
2. The product resulting by multiplying the number of years since the establishment of the plan, or amendment, and its termination, by the lesser of
   a. Twenty percent of the participant's annual compensation; or
   b. $10,000[111]

Example

Plan covering two employees, one of whom is the key shareholder employee and the other is a common law employee, has been in effect for eight years. The annual compensation of the shareholder employee involved is $30,000, and $85,000 has been contributed on his behalf in accordance with the funding method under the plan. The restricted portion will then be $37,000. ($85,000 - 20% x $30,000 x 8)

In the above example, the restricted portion for the professional employee is used to fund the benefit of the non-professional employee in full. Any remaining balance may then be used for the benefit of said professional employee.[112] Observe, however, that this problem does not arise if the annual contribution for the benefit of the professional is $10,000 or less. You only become involved with the problem if the annual contribution exceeds this amount.

In addition to restricting employee benefits in the event of early termination, the termination rule also applies if the benefits of an employee among the highest twenty-five employees becomes payable within ten years after the plan is established, or the benefits of such employee become payable after the plan has been in effect for ten years, but its current costs for the first ten years have not been fully funded.[113]

In the event benefits become payable within the ten-year period of time, the multiplication factor is determined by the number of years since the adoption of the plan and the date the benefits become payable. In case the plan has been in effect for ten years but its full current costs have not been met, then the multiplication factor is determined by the number of years since the adoption of the plan and the date of the failure to meet the full current costs.[114]

Thus, in the above example, if the plan was not terminated, the restricted portion would be released as soon as the plan has been in effect for ten years and the full current costs have been met.

Corporation's deductions are not affected by these restrictions; they are allowable within the applicable limits.[115]

These restrictions also apply to corporate contributions which are used to provide death benefits to the extent that such contributions are used to pay for the cost of benefits on behalf of employees who die after retirement income commences. They *are not* applicable to the cost of any death benefit with respect to an employee who dies prior to commencement of retirement benefits, or to the actual benefits payable to an employee who dies after retirement, provided the plan is in effect and the full current costs have been met.[116]

If the plan is amended to increase benefits to be provided by the corporation, the restrictions under the plan before the amendment remain applicable to all benefits. Further, the restrictions are also extended to the increased portion and continue in effect for a new ten-year period of time as though a new plan was established on the date of the amendment.[117]

Exceptions to Termination Rule

The restricted portion, however, may be exceeded for the purposes of making current retirement income benefit payments to retired employees under the following circumstances:

1. Employer contributions on behalf of an employee subject to the restrictions are applied to provide level amounts of an annuity in the basic form of benefit under the plan at retirement or an optional form, provided this is not greater than the benefits provided under the basic form of annuity provided under the plan. However, this exception will apply only if the full current costs of the plan are met.[118]

2. A lump sum distribution may be made to a highly-paid employee provided an agreement, adequately secured, guarantees the repayment of any part of the distribution that is restricted. Thus, the employee must put up collateral whereby if the plan is terminated, the restricted portion will be refunded to the pension plan. Any plan which provides for a lump sum payout, without adequate security will not be qualified.[119] Collateral equal to 125% of the restricted portion has been held to be adequate security,[120] but the assignment of rights to retirement benefits under a separate non-qualified plan of the corporation was held not to be adequate security.[121]

OBSERVATION

The consequences of terminating a defined benefit or target benefit pension plan may have disastrous results for the professional individual and without doubt, is the most serious disadvantage in adopting such plans. It makes no difference for what reason the plan is terminated. The rule applies whether the plan was terminated for the inability of the corporation to continue the plan, or as a result of the disability of the key professional which results in the cessation of corporate business.[122] Termination may result in large sums of money which were originally allocated to the professional's retirement account being used to fund the full pension benefits of his 30-year-old nurse or 25-year-old secretary, and whatever remains of the restricted portion after funding the benefits of his other employees may then be used to fund the professional's pension benefit. This certainly is not the desired result. In addition, the same result may occur when a professional sells his corporation to another and the new shareholder then terminates the plan within the ten-year period. Thus, great caution must be taken before adopting a defined benefit or target benefit pension plan.

Premature Termination - Money Purchase Pension Plan and Profit Sharing Plan

The rules restricting benefits in the event of early termination do not apply to money purchase pension plans since all employees are treated alike with respect to corporate contributions and the increments thereon. The contributions, however, must bear a uniform relationship to each employee's total compensation and no employee may obtain a disproportionate benefit because of his age or method of funding.[123]

In addition, the termination rule does not apply to profit sharing plans, since acceptable allocation formulas under such plans are designed to preclude the prohibited discrimination.[124]

EFFECT OF CORPORATION NOT BEING ABLE TO MAKE REQUIRED CONTRIBUTIONS TO RETIREMENT PLAN

Complete Discontinuance of Contribution-Effect of Pension Reform Act

Contributions to a retirement plan were considered discontinued if all contributions ceased or even if the corporation made contributions if such contributions were not substantial enough to reflect the intent on the part of the corporation to continue to maintain the plan.[125]

Prior to the Pension Reform Act, if a corporation discontinued its required contribution to the retirement plan, the plan was considered terminated and the participant's interest in his account vested.[126] This rule has not been continued by the Pension Reform Act to plans subject to the minimum funding requirements of the Pension Reform Act,[127] since the penalties placed on corporations who do not make their required contributions are considered to have solved this problem.

Substantial and Recurring Contributions Requirement in Profit Sharing Plans

The rule requiring 100% vesting in the event of complete discontinuance of contribution is still applicable to a profit sharing since profit sharing plans are not subject to the minimum funding standards of the Pension Reform Act.[128] In the case of a profit sharing plan, there must be recurring and substantial contribution out of profits for employees. If contributions are not recurring and substantial, then contributions will be deemed to be discontinued and participants will become 100% vested in their accounts. "It is not necessary that the employer contributes the same amount or contributes in accordance with the same ratio every year. However, merely making a single or occasional contribution out of profits for employees does not establish a plan of profit sharing."[129]

The courts have rejected this position and have held that the making of even one contribution to a plan might not disqualify a profit sharing plan.[130] However, it is unlikely that the Internal Revenue Service will alter its position, and if profits are present, a corporation should contribute to the profit sharing plan to avoid having the suspension of contributions classified as a discontinuance of the plan.[131]

OBSERVATION

The requirement that contributions to a profit sharing plan be recurring and substantial should not present problems to a professional corporation. The corporation will certainly contribute as much as it is able to afford to the plan. This was the objective when the professional incorporated. In addition, the requirement that is established is that the corporation's recurring and substantial contributions must come from profits. Thus, if there are no profits or profits are low for any one year, then the contributions can be reduced for that year.[132] Problems may arise, if there are substantial profits each year and the corporation elects not to make any or very small contributions to the plan.

MISCELLANEOUS PROBLEMS

Effect If Corporation Reduces The Benefits Payable Under A Retirement Plan

When benefits or employer contributions are reduced, or the eligibility or vested requirements are made less liberal, then the plan has been curtailed.[133] Thus, if a plan is amended whereby the required contributions to the plan are reduced, for example, reducing a money-purchase pension plan contribution from 20% of compensation to 10% of compensation causes a curtailment of part of the plan, or reducing the benefits to be received at retirement will cause a curtailment of the plan. A curtailment is considered a partial termination of the plan. Hence, criteria applicable to termination, i.e., valid business reason and absence of prohibited discrimination, are similarly applicable to curtailments.[134] If a partial termination is found, then the requirements for vesting apply only to the part of the plan which is terminated.

Other examples of events causing curtailments are as follows:

1. An amendment converting a non-contributory plan into one requiring employee contributions and providing the same benefits which were previously paid for exclusively by the Employer.[135]
2. An amendment increasing the required period of service before vested rights are acquired.[136]
3. A reduction in a significant number of employees participating in the plan.[137]

As in a termination case, the mere fact that a plan has been curtailed does not necessarily result in adverse tax consequences. The Internal Revenue Service is only concerned that the curtailment does not result in the prohibited discrimination. Thus, for example, a curtailment which limits the benefits for the prohibited group is not discriminatory.[138]

What Happens If A Professional Corporation Changes One Type Of Retirement Plan For Another

The change from one plan to another may result in a reduction of benefits to the participants. For example, if you change a fixed benefit pension plan to a money purchase plan and the benefits under the money purchase plan are not equal to the benefits being provided under the fixed benefit plan, you have a curtailment and the applicable rules apply.[139] In addition, if you change a profit sharing plan to a pension plan or vice versa, then the profit sharing plan, or the pension plan, if applicable, is considered terminated, and the benefits which are conveyed to the new plan are vested in the participants.

PLAN TERMINATION INSURANCE — PENSION BENEFIT GUARANTY CORPORATION

Title IV of the Pension Reform Act provides for the creation of a plan termination insurance program which is to be administered by the newly-established Pension Benefit Guaranty Corporation. The underlying philosophy of the program is that it will guarantee retirement benefits up to a certain maximum limit (ERISA §4022) in the event plan assets are not sufficient. In order to fund the program, each plan is charged a certain premium rate which is based upon the number of participants in the plan (ERISA §4006). The rate is generally one dollar per participant.

However, these provisions will have little applicability to almost all professional corporations since the following plans are specifically excluded from coverage (ERISA §4021(b)).

1. Money-purchase pension plans.
2. Profit sharing plans.
3. Defined benefit pension plans of professional corporations which do not cover more than 25 participants.

Thus, the plan termination insurance program will affect only those professional corporations which have adopted a defined benefit plan which covers more than 25 participants.

DIVERSION OF TRUST FUNDS FOR BENEFIT OF EMPLOYER PROHIBITED

The trust must provide that it is impossible for any part of the trust corpus or income to be used for, or diverted to, purposes other than for the exclusive benefit of such employees or their beneficiaries.[140]

Exceptions

Erroneous actuarial computation

A defined benefit pension plan permits the corporation to reserve the right to recover at the termination of the trust any balance then remaining after the satisfaction of all fixed and contingent obligations. Erroneous actuarial computation may arise as a result of mathematical errors on the part of the actuary. They may also arise because of a variance between the assumptions and actual experience. For example, the earnings of the fund may be greater than expected or the anticipated turnover may be greater than expected.[141]

WATCH THIS

The key phrase to be aware of is "after the satisfaction of all fixed and *contingent* obligations."[142] The impact of this phrase is as follows: If a corporation is terminated, all obligations must be funded before reversion is permitted. Thus, the corporation must fund in full the benefits of all employees regardless of their age at the time the plan was terminated even though they might subsequently terminate their employment with the corporation. After this is done, any remaining balance may then revert back to the corporation.

There can be no reversion of any kind in a qualified profit sharing plan or money purchase plan since such plans do not provide benefits which are based on actuarial assumptions or computations.[143]

Contributions conditioned upon qualification

A new plan may provide for the return of corporate contributions in the event the plan is found not to qualify by the Internal Revenue Service under Section 401(a) of the Internal Revenue Code. Thus, if a professional corporation makes contributions to a plan before the plan is qualified and the plan is subsequently held not to qualify, then such contributions may be refunded to the corporation.[144]

Contributions made by mistake

Contributions which are made by the corporation by a mistake of fact may be returned to the corporation within one year after the payment of the contribution.[145]

Contribution conditioned upon deductibility

If a contribution is conditioned upon being deductible under §404 of the Internal Revenue Code, then any part or all of the contribution which is disallowed as a deduction may be returned to the corporation within one year after the disallowance of the deduction.[146]

OTHER REQUIREMENTS FOR QUALIFICATION

The following are additonal provisions which are now required to be provided in a retirement plan by the Pension Reform Act if such plan is to be qualified under §401 of the Internal Revenue Code.

Most of these additonal requirements were provided to solve or eliminate problems which are really not applicable to most professional corporations. Therefore, as a practical matter, these provisions which must be provided will be more of a matter of form rather than a real change in the nature or operation of the plan.

1. Joint and Survivor Annuity Requirement

When a plan provides for a retirement benefit in the form of an annuity and the participant has been married for a one-year period ending on the annuity starting date, the plan must provide for a joint and survivor annuity.[147] The survivor annuity must not be less than half the amount payable to the participant during the joint lives of the participant and his spouse. A participant, however, shall have the right not to receive his benefits in the form of a joint and surviving annuity.[148]

2. Mergers and Consolidations

A qualified trust must provide that in the event of any merger or consolidation of a plan, or any transfer of assets or liabilities of a plan, to any other plan, each participant's post-merger retirement benefits will be equal to or greater than the pre-merger termination benefits.[149]

3. Non-alienation Provisions

A qualified trust must provide that a participant's benefits under the plan can not be assigned or alienated.[150] Bona fide loans to participants are not considered as an assignment or alienation if the fiduciary requirements are not violated.[151]

4. Payment of Benefits

A qualified trust must provide that unless the participant otherwise elects, payment of benefits must begin no later than the sixtieth day after the close of the plan year in which the latest of the following events occurs:[152]

1. the participant attains age 65
2. ten years have elapsed from the time the participant commenced participation in the plan, or
3. the participant terminates his service with the employer.

Furthermore, if the plan permits an employee who has not separated from service to receive a subsidized early retirement benefit if he meets certain age and service requirements, the plan must provide that an employee who fulfills the service requirement but separates from service before he meets the age requirement, will receive benefit payments on an actuarially reduced basis when he meets the age requirement.[153]

5. Effect of Social Security Increases on Retirement Benefits

A qualified trust must provide that the plan will not reduce plan benefits that are already in pay status as a result of increases in Social Secrurity benefits.[154]

6. Withdrawal of Employer Contributions

A qualified trust must provide that a participant who is 50% or more vested in the employer contributions to the plan will not forfeit any portion of his accrued benefits attributable to said employer contribution because of the withdrawal of all or a portion of his mandatory contributions which were made to the plan.[155]

FOOTNOTES

[1]Some qualified plans do not require trusts. This chapter will assume that all plans are trusted. For a discussion of non-trusteed plans, see chapter 11 "Handling Investments and Life Insurance in the Qualified Plan," section entitled "The Insured Plan," page 189.

[2]Reg. Section 1.401-1(a) (2); ERISA Section 402(a) (1).

[3]Rev. Rul. 69-231, IRB 1969-19.

[4]Ibid.

[5]IRC §401(b).

[6]Reg. §1.401-1(a) (3) (i).

[7]IRC §401(a) (2).

[8]See Note 5.

[9]Ibid.

[10]IRC §404(a) (6).

[11]See Note 10

[12]Reg. §1.404(a)-1(c); Rev. Rul. 63-117, IRB 1963-25.

[13]Rev. Rul. 71-38, IRB 1971-3.

[14]Rev. Rul. 72-509, IRB 1972-43.

[15]Ibid.

[16]"Guides for Qualification of Pension, Profit Sharing and Stock Bonus Plans," Internal Revenue Service Publication 778 (2-72) Part 2(i).

[17]ERISA §102(a) (1).

[18]Ibid.

[19]ERISA §104(b) (2).

[20]ERISA §104(b) (1) (A) + (B).

[21]ERISA §104(b) (1) (B).

[22]ERISA §104(a) (1) (C).

[23]ERISA §104(a) (1) (D).

[24]See Note 21.

[25]Ibid.

[26]IRC §401(a) (4); Regs. §1.401-4(a) (1) (i).

[27]Rev. Rul. 72-4, IRB 1972-2; Rev. Rul. 55-81, 1955-1 CB 392.

[28]Rev. Rul. 69-144, IRB 1969-13.

[29]Rev. Rul. 68-436, IRB 1968-33.

[30]Illinois Tri-Seal Products, Inc., 353 F2d 216 (1965); A. Levine "Current Factors that distinguish between "employee" and "independent contractor" J. Tax September, 1972, p. 188.

[31]Rev. Rul. 66-274, IRB 1966-37.

[32]Rev. Rul. 68-303, IRB 1968-24.

[33]ERISA §210(c); IRC §414(b)

[34]I. Goodman "Nondiscriminatory Pension and Profit Sharing Plans" November 14, 1968.

[35]Rev. Rul. 73-283 IRB 1973-27;

[36]See Chapter 10 "Retirement Plan Drafting Techniques," Section entitled "How to Exclude Professional Employees from Participating," p. 175.

[37]I. Goodman "Nondiscriminatory Pension and Profit Sharing Plans," November 14, 1968; I. Goodman "Assured Retirement Benefits," March 11, 1968, Questions and Answers, Question #27; I. Goodman, "Tax Treatment of Employees Under Pension and Profit Sharing Plan," April 24, 1965, Questions and Answers, Question #12; I. Goodman "Coverage Under Pension and Profit Sharing Plans," March 24, 1966, Questions and Answers, Question No. 3.

[38]IRC §410(b) (1).

[39]IRC §410(a) (1) (A).

[40]IRC §410(a) (1) (B).

[41]IRC §410(a) (2).

[42]IRC §410(b) (1) (A).

[43]IRC §410(a) (3) (A).

[44]Rev. Rul. 69-36, IRB 1969-5; "Pension Trust Audit Guidelines," IR Manual 45(10)5-1 (12-4-72) Section 313.5(1) (a).

[45]Ibid.

[46]Rev. Rul. 70-316 IRB 1970-25.

[47]Sherman Construction Company v. U.S. 358 F.Supp. 446(1973); Farley Funeral Home, Inc. v. Commissioner 62 T.C. 150 (1974).

[48]IRC 410(a) (4).

[49]Rev. Rul. 67-101 IRB 1967-14; Rev. Rul. 73-447 IRB 1973-44 p. 9.

[50]Rev. Rul. 70-75 IRB 1970-7; "Guides for Qualification of Pension, Profit Sharing and Stock Bonus Plans" IRS Publicaiton 778(2-72) Part 4(e).

[51]Ibid.

[52]Rev. Rul. 70-659 IRB 1970-52.

[53]Reg. Section 1.401-3(d).

[54]Rev. Rul. 69-421 IRB 1969-32, Part 4(g).

[55]I. Goodman, "Coverage Under Pension and Profit Sharing Plans," March 24, 1966, Questions and Answers, Question No. 6; "Pension Trust Audit Guidelines" IR MANUAL 45(10)5-1 (12-4-72) Section 312.3(1)(f).

[56]See chapter 8 "Selecting the Retirement Plan," Section entitled "Corporate Contributions to Money-Purchase Pension Plan," p. 132.

[57]IRC §401(a)(4).

[58]I. Goodman "Permanency as a Requisite for Tax Qualified Pension and Profit Sharing Plans," November 15, 1960; IRC Section 401(a) (5).

[59]Rev. Rul. 71-255, IRB 1971-24; Rev. Rul. 74-142 IRB 1974-13, p. 11.

[60]IRC §401(a)(5).

[61]Rev. Rul. 59-67, 1959-1 CB 87; Rev. Rul. 68-652 IRB 1968-52; Rev. Rul. 68-653, IRB 1968-52; Rev. Rul. 68-592, IRB 1968-46.

[62]Rev. Rul. 72-303, IRB 1972-25.

[63]Ibid.

[64]Auner v. U.S., 440 F2d 516, Seventh Circuit, 1971; Rev. Rul. 69-158 IRB 1969-14.

[65]Rev. Proc. 72-9 IRB 1972-1 Section 3.0111(c).

[66]Regs. §1.401-1(b)(3).

[67]Rev. Rul. 69-421 IRB 1969-32 Part 5(c) (2).

[68]Ibid.

[69]Ibid., Part 6 (a) + (d).

[70]Ibid., Part 5(c)(1).

[71]Rev. Rul. 68-302, IRB 1968-24; Rev. Rul. 71-150, IRB 1971-12; Rev. Rul. 71-151, IRB 1971-12; Rev. Rul. 71-263, IRB 1971-25.

[72]Ibid.

[73]Rev. Rul. 73-299, IRB 1973-30.

[74]IRC §411(a).

[75]IRC §411(a) (1).

[76]IRC §411(a) (2).

[77]IRC §411(d) (4).

[78]ERISA §1012(c).

[79]IRC §411(d) (1).

[80]Prentice-Hall Handbook on Pension Reform, Sept. 6, 1974, Report Bulletin No. 8, ¶892.

[81]IRC §411(d) (1) (A).

[82]See Note 80.

[83]IRC §411(a) (4) (A).

[84]IRC §411(a) (4) (B).

[85]IRC §411(a) (4) (C).

[86]IRC §411(a) (4)(D).

[87]IRC §411(a) (4) (E).

[88]IRC §411(a) (4) (F).

[89]IRC §411(a) (3) (A).

[90]IRC §411(a) (3) (B).

[91]IRC §411(a) (3) (D).

[92]ERISA §105(a) and (b).

[93]IRC §411(a) (10) (A).

[94]IRC §411(a) (10) (B).

[95]Rev. Rul. 71-501, IRB 1971-46

[96]Congressional Reports, Prentice-Hall Handbook on Pension Reform Law, September 6, 1974, Report Bulletin No. 8, ¶828.

[97]Plans that provide for voluntary contributions or require mandatory contributions as a condition of participation have additional requirements regarding determining accrued benefits arising from such employee contributions. See Chapter 10 "Retirement Plan Draftng Techniques," Section entitled "Accounting for Voluntary Contributions," p. 180.

[98]IRC §411(b) (1) (A).

[99]IRC §411(b) (1) (B).

[100]IRC §411(b) (1) (C)

[101]Regs. Section 1.401-1(b) (2).

[102]I. Goodman "Permanency as a Requisite of Tax Qualified Pension and Profit Sharing Plans," November 15, 1960.

[103]Reg. §1.401-1(b)(2); Rev. Rul. 69-24 IRB 1969-4.

[104]Rev. Rul. 69-25 IRB 1969-4.

[105]Ibid.

[106]Ibid.

[107]Reg. §1.401-6(b)(1).

[108]Rev. Rul. 69-24, IRB 1969-4.

[109]IRC §411(d) (3); Regs. § 1.401-6(a)(1).

[110]IRC §411(d) (3).

[111]Regs. § 1.401-4(c) (2) (iii).

[112]I. Goodman "Developing Pension and Profit Sharing Requisites," October 8.,1971, Questions and Answers, Questions Nos. 16 and 17; Rev. Rul. 65-294, IRB 1965-50.
[113]Reg. Section 1.401-4(c) (2) (ii).
[114]Note 111.
[115]I. Goodman "Assured Retirement Benefits," March11, 1968.
[116]Reg.§1.401-4(c) (2) (vi) (a); ibid.
[117]Rev. Rul. 67-114 IRB 1967-16; Regs. §1.401-4(c) (5).
[118]Regs. §1.401-4(c) (4).
[119]Rev. Rul. 72-577, IRB 1972-49.
[120]Rev. Rul. 61-10, 1961-1CB 143.
[121]Rev. Rul. 73-3 IRB 1973-1.
[122]I. Goodman "Developing Pension and Profit Sharing Requisites," October 8, 1971, Questions and Answers, Questions Nos. 16 and 17.
[123]Rev. Rul. 69-415 IRB 1969-31.
[124]Rev. Rul. 69-421 IRB 1969-32 Part 6(c).
[125]Reg. §1.401-6(c).
[126]"Guides for Qualification of Pension, Profit Sharing and Stock Bonus Plans," IRS Publicaiton 778 (2-72) Part 6(d).
[127]IRC §411(d) (3) (B).
[128]IRC §412(h) (1).
[129]Reg §1.401-1(b) (2).
[130]Lincoln Electrical Co. Employees' Profit Sharing Trust 190 F2d 326 (1951); See also Sherwood Swan and Co., Ltd., Employees' Benefit Fund v. Commissioner 42 TC 291, aff'd (CA 9, 1965) 65-2USTC ¶9742
[131]Rev. Rul. 66-251, IRB 1966-35; Rev. Rul. 71-94, IRB 1971-7.
[132]Rev. Rul. 74-419 IRB 1974-35, p. 7.
[133]Rev. Rul. 69-24 IRB 1969-4.
[134]I. Goodman "Developing Pension and Profit Sharing Requisites," October 8, 1971.
[135]I. Goodman "Permanency as a Requisite of Tax Qualified Pension and Profit Sharing Plans," November 15, 1960.
[136]Ibid.
[137]Rev. Rul. 72-510 IRB 1972-43; Rev. Rul 73-284 IRB 1973-27, p. 10.
[138]Rev. Rul. 69-24 IRB 1969-4.
[139]I. Goodman "Master and Prototype Pension and Profit Sharing Plans in Operation" June 19, 1970, Questions & Answers, Question No. 22.
[140]IRC § 401(a) (2); ERISA §403(c) (1).
[141]Reg. §1.401-2(b) (1), (2); I. Goodman "The Role of the Actuary in Processing Pension and Profit Sharing Cases before the Internal Revenue Service, " October 7, 1958.
[142]Regs. §1.401-2(b) (2).
[143]"Guides for Qualification of Pension, Profit Sharing and Stock Bonus Plans" IRC Publication 778 (2-72) Part 3(e).
[144]ERISA §403(c) (2) (B).
[145]ERISA §403(c) (2) (A).
[146]ERISA §403(c) (2) (C).
[147]IRC §401(a) (11).
[148]IRC §401(a) (11) (F).
[149]IRC §401(a) (12).
[150]IRC §401(a) (13).
[151]Ibid.
[152]IRC §401(a) (14).
[153]Ibid.
[154]IRC §401(a) (15).
[155]IRC §401(a) (19).

10

RETIREMENT PLAN DRAFTING TECHNIQUES

The primary objective of a professional who incorporates his practice is the ability to adopt a qualified retirement plan through which he may "now do with his pre-tax dollars what he was doing with his after-tax dollars." That is, the professional may now conduct his investment and life insurance program with tax deductible dollars.

However, the success of the retirement program will usually be determined by factors other than the professional's retirement benefit. The plan must provide maximum flexibility. For instance, the professionals participating in the plan may have different investment objectives, different retirement goals, and different personal income requirements. In some cases, some professionals may wish not to participate in a retirement plan. In addition, the professionals may be concerned that they will have a need for the funds that they are contributing to the retirement plan prior to their retirement. Careful draftsmanship will solve these different needs and concerns. Furthermore, careful draftsmanship may also result in the professionals being able to save additional tax dollars.

The purpose of this chapter is to discuss in detail drafting techniques which will provide the practitioner's professional client with the maximum flexibility and security which the law allows. The following are some of the subjects which will be discussed:

1. How a cash-option profit sharing plan will permit the participants to vary their contributions to the plan.
2. How to exclude professional employees from participating in the retirement program.
3. How the provision for employee loans and withdrawals of corporate contributions will enable participants to use trust assets for current income needs.
4. How voluntary employee contributions can be used to increase an employee's retirement fund.

5. How integrating the retirement plan with Social Secutrity will reduce the amount required to be contributed to the non-professional employees.
6. How to permit the participants to invest their respective accounts as they deem appropriate.
7. Whether or not to adopt a prototype retirement plan or to prepare an individually designed plan.

HOW PARTICIPANTS MAY VARY CONTRIBUTIONS TO THE RETIREMENT PLAN — CASH OPTION PROFIT SHARING PLANS

It is not uncommon to find that two or more professionals who incorporate have different retirement objectives and current personal requirements. A senior professional who has most of his personal obligations behind him, may wish to maximize the contributions to the pension and profit sharing plan, whereas the younger professional who has a greater need for income to meet his current obligations, is not yet ready to maximize his contributions to a retirement program. This difference in retirement objectives may cause serious problems between the two equal shareholder-professionals when they sit down to decide how much the corporation should contribute to the profit sharing plan near the end of the corporation's taxable year.

The solution to this problem may be found by adopting a cash-option profit sharing plan.[1] A cash-option profit sharing plan permits each participant to irrevocably elect prior to the close of the corporation's taxable year to receive his share or a portion thereof, of the corporate contribution which, in the absence of an election, would otherwise be allocated to his account in the plan, in cash. Thus, the younger professional will have the election to withdraw his entire profit sharing contribution as additional salary.

One serious problem that arises with an unlimited right to withdraw one's profit sharing contribution is that employees who elect to take their share in cash will not be considered in determining the coverage tests, and, as a result, if a sufficient number of employees elect to take their contribution in cash, the coverage tests may not be met and therefore the plan will not be qualified.[2] This is especially true if most of the lower paid employees elect to take their contribution in cash since only the members of the prohibited group will then be participating in the plan. The Internal Revenue Service is not concerned with the number of professional employees who elect the option.

As a result, since qualification of the plan depends upon the coverage tests being satisfied and since it cannot be determined if the coverage tests will be met until the end of a taxable year of the corporation, the Internal Revenue Service does not issue qualifying letters on such plans, and the plan must qualify on a year-to-year basis.[3]

However, this problem may be solved by providing for a limited cash option provision. The Internal Revenue Service has issued a ruling stating that a cash option plan will not be considered discriminatory in regard to coverage if more than one-half of the participants are among the lowest two-thirds of all eligible participants.[4] In that same ruling, the Service took the position that a weighted calculation can be used in determining whether the qualification test is met. "For example, if a plan provided that employees could elect either to receive all of their shares of the company's contribution in cash or one-half of their shares in cash, those employees who elected to receive one-half of their shares in cash will be given half-weight in determining whether the coverage requirements have been met."[5]

Thus, it would appear that if the cash option provision is drafted to provide for automatic deferral of 51% of the corporation contribution to the plan for each participant and permits each participant to elect to withdraw up to 49% of the remaining contribution in cash, the plan should qualify (example, p.174).

The second problem to avoid is constructive receipt to the participants of the amount which they could have elected to take in cash but chose rather to contribute to the profit sharing plan. This problem can be avoided by providing that each participant is required to make an irrevocable election prior to the close of the corporation's taxable year whether or not he wishes to exercise the cash option

Example:

	Employee	Compensation	Paid In Cash	Paid to Trust	Participants
Top 1/3	(1	15,000	0	1)	2
	(2	12,000	0	1)	
	(3	8,000	½	½)	
Bottom	(4	7,000	½	½)	
2/3	(5	6,000	½	½)	2
	(6	5,000	½	½)	

provision.[7] In addition, the portion which could have been elected in cash by the participant but was chosen to be deferred should be classified as a corporate contribution to the plan, and not as a contribution to the plan by the employee. In the latter case, the portion which is contributed will be considered constructively received by the employee and taxable to him.[8]

Thus, with careful draftsmanship, it is possible to vary contributions among the participants.

Sample Language to Use

Cash-Option

A participant may irrecovably elect in writing within thirty days of the close of the plan's taxable year, to receive as a cash payment up to 49% of the Employer's contribution, which would otherwise be allocated to the Trust Fund on his behalf, had he not made such an election. Cash-option payments shall be made by the Trustees as soon as practicable after the close of the plan year. Unless specifically directed by a participant to make a cash distribution pursuant to this section, the Employer shall allocate the entire contribution to the profit sharing account of each participant.

OBSERVATION—CASH OPTION PLANS AFTER PENSION REFORM

Whether or not cash option profit sharing plans can still be effectively utilized has been seriously questioned since the passage of the Pension Reform Act.

Prior to December 6, 1972, the position of the Internal Revenue Service was that the amount which a participant could have withdrawn in cash but instead was contributed to a cash option profit sharing plan would not be considered the employee's contribution, and therefore, such contributions were not included in the participant's income. On December 6, 1972, the Service issued proposed regulations[9] which reversed their prior positon.

The Pension Reform Act prevents the Service from adopting these proposed regulations and further prohibits the Internal Revenue Service from issuing further regulations on the subject before January 1, 1977.[10] This is intended to give Congress time to resolve the issues of salary reduction and cash-option profit sharing plans. If Congress has not acted, then the Internal Revenue Service may issue new regulations, but such regulations shall not be retroactive prior to January 1, 1977.[11]

Until new regulations are adopted, all cash option plans that are in existence on or before June 27, 1974 will be treated under the law as it was applied prior to January 1, 1972, i.e., contributions will not be considered employee contributions.[12] However, contributions to cash-option plans which came into existence after June 27, 1974 will now be treated as employee contributions and therefore, taxable to the participant.[13]

Thus, it would appear that the ability of a professional corporation take advantage of a profit sharing plan with a cash-option provision has been curtailed. However, it is the author's opinion that the Act does not pertain to plans as discussed in the previous section. The Act specifically provides that "...a contribution...shall be treated as a contribution made by an employee if the contribution is made under an arrangement under which the contribution will be made only if the employee elects to receive a reduction in his compensation or to forego an increase in his compensation.''[14] Therefore, plans covered by the Pension Reform Act require an affirmative act on the part of the participant, i.e., the participant must elect to contribute to the plan. If such an election is not made, then the participant will automatically receive the contribution which would have been allocated to his account in cash. On the other hand, the cash option plan discussed by this author requires a different form of election, i.e., the particpant must elect to withdraw a portion or all of his contribution. If such an election is not made, then his allocated contribution will be automatically contributed to the plan.

This issue will probably be clarified in future regulations. In the interim, it is this author's opinion that cash option plans should be submitted to the Internal Revenue Service requesting a ruling as to the effect of said cash option provision.

HOW TO EXCLUDE PROFESSIONAL EMPLOYEES FROM PARTICIPATING

In corporations consisting of several professional employees, it sometimes occurs that one or more of them do not wish to participate in the retirement program for one reason or another. Often it is because of their need for current income to meet present obligations. Alternatively, a corporation may wish to exclude a new professional employee from participating in the plan since the contributions that would be required to be made to the plan for his benefit would be prohibitive. In such cases, the new professional is often excluded until he becomes a shareholder in the corporation and can then share the burden of his own contributions.

When a corporation consists of professional and non-professional employees, the qualification of the plan will usually not be affected by excluding a professional employee from the plan since the plan is not discriminating against the lower paid employees. This will be true even though less than 70% of the employees are eligible to participate. However, there are many corporations whose only employee is the professional employee and if an additional professional is employed, the qualification of the plan may be affected if he is excluded. Since the percentage tests under Section 410(b) (1) (A) [formerly IRC S401(a) (3) (A)] of the Internal Revenue Code cannot be met, then the Commissioner of the Internal Revenue Service must determine that such exclusion does not discriminate in favor of the prohibited group by using the ''nondiscriminatory'' test under Section 410(b) (1) (B) [formerly IRC S401 (a) (3) (B)]. However, the classification of who is a lower paid employee depends upon the facts in the particular case. Thus, an employee who earns $20,000 in one corporation may be the highest paid employee and in another corporation he may be the lowest. Therefore, the pathologist or radiologist who employs an assistant and who desires to exclude him from participating in the plan may find that this will not be permitted since the new assistant is considered a member of the lower paid group even though he is earning $40,000 or $50,000 a year, since his exclusion will result in the prohibited discrimination. In addition, even the voluntary exclusion of the associate from the plan will not change the result, if the remaining participants are members of the prohibited group.[15]

One possible solution to this problem, which this author has used successfully, is to make the new assistant an officer of the corporation, and then have the assistant voluntarily withdraw from participating in the plan. Since a member of the prohibited group is not participating, the ''nondiscriminatory'' test under Section 410 (b) (1) (B) is satisfied.

Alternative Solutions

The professional who wishes to exclude himself from the plan because of his personal income needs may be benefited by the adoption of a cash option profit sharing plan, or if the retirement program consists of both a pension and profit sharing plan, he may elect to participate in only one plan. On the other hand, another solution may be to limit the contributions to a salary which will not exceed a certain figure. That is, if a plan limits contributions to compensation not in excess of $50,000 and the professional receives $60,000, then he will be able to draw an extra $10,000 upon which no contribution will be made. However, the other professionals may not want such a limit to be placed on their contributions. In such an event, compensation may be defined so as not to include bonuses. Then the professional who prefers to contribute less to the retirement program may do so by having his compensation consist of a base salary and bonuses.

WATCH THIS

When professionals incorporate, they usually reduce their income in order to create the surplus necessary to fund the retirement program for themselves as well as for the other participating non-professional employees. If one or more professionals elects not to participate in the retirement program and receives the salary that he received prior to incorporation, the burden of contributing for the non-professional employees is placed upon the remaining professionals who are participating in the plan. This can place a serious financial hardship upon the professionals and it is possible that this extra cost may outweigh the advantages of incorporating. One possible solution is to have the professional who elects not to participate still share his pro rata contribution that he would have made for the benefit of the non-professional employees if he participated. Generally, in a larger group the exclusion of one or more professionals does not create serious problems. However, if it appears that some professionals do not wish to participate in the retirement plan and are incorporating only for the purpose of not "splitting up" the group, the practitioner must determine the additional cost to the participating professionals and they should be clearly advised of this burden they are assuming.

LOANS

Very often a professional who incorporates expresses a concern that he is "locking in" a sizable amount of money in a retirement program until his retirement or stated age or event, if a profit sharing plan is adopted, and that he will not be able to use this money in the event of a financial emergency prior to such time. This concern can be partially alleviated by providing for loan privileges in the retirement program. The Internal Revenue Service has ruled that provision may be made for granting loans to participants provided the loans are granted in a uniform and nondiscriminatory manner.[16] In fact, it is possible to borrow a sum which exceeds one's vested interest in the plan.[17]

The practitioner must make his professional clients aware that a legitimate loan must be established which must be repaid. A loan cannot be used to distribute funds prior to the permitted time. If there is a tacit understanding that collection is not intended, then a distribution has occurred which will disqualify the plan if a pension plan is involved, or if a profit sharing plan is involved, if the distribution has occurred prior to the stated event.[18] In addition, a pension plan will not be qualified if it permits loans that have not been repaid to be subtracted from a participant's account.[19] The loan must be adequately secured, bear a reasonable rate of interest and provide for repayment within a specified period of time.[20]

Examples of Adequate Security:[21]

1. A security bond issued by a recognized company doing a surety bond business under applicable state law.
2. An assignment of an insurance contract having a cash surrender value sufficient to cover the loan, interest and possible cost of collection.
3. A first mortgage on real property in an amount not in excess of fifty percent of its assessed value for local tax purposes.
4. Securities listed in a recognized exchange of an aggregate value equal to twice the amount of the loan.
5. An accommodation endorser financially capable of meeting the indebtedness.

Reasonable Rate of Interest

Interest would be considered reasonable if it were at least comparable to the rate charged by a bank or other lending institution in the same community on a similar loan.[22]

Specified Period of Time

The requirement that a loan be repaid within a specified period of time would appear to be met if the loan was required to be repaid within the same period of time which would be required by a bank or other lending institution in the community. However, some pension district offices require that loans be repaid within a two-year period of time.[23]

LOANS AFTER PENSION REFORM

The Pension Reform Act has generally not affected the requirements as set forth above, and loans will not be considered a prohibited transaction under Internal Revenue Code if made by the plan to an officer, 10% shareholder of the corporation, or highly compensated employee who is also a participant in the plan,[24] if the following conditions are met:

1. The loan is available to all participants on a reasonably equivalent basis.
2. Loans are not granted in amounts to the prohibited group greater than what is available to other employees.
3. The loans are made in accordance with specific provisions set forth in the plan.
4. The loan bears a reasonable rate of interest.
5. The loan is adequately secured.

WATCH THIS

Practitioners should watch for and avoid the "revolving door" result. That is, a professional should not be allowed to borrow the amount which has been allocated to his account immediately or shortly after it has been contributed to the plan by the corporation. Such a practice certainly appears to be a means of siphoning off profits for the benefit of the prohibited group, and the professional will find it difficult to persuade the Internal Revenue Service that the plan should not be considered discriminatory in operation. Loans should be an escape clause in the event of an unexpected emergency, they should not be used on a regular basis.

WITHDRAWALS

Hardship Distribution Permitted

A profit sharing plan may provide that each participant shall have the right to withdraw the contributions made to the plan by the corporation which have been allocated to his account in the event of "hardship."[25] The term "hardship" must be defined, the definition must be uniformly applied to all participants and the amount which may be distributed to the participant may not exceed his vested interest in the plan.[26]

A distribution in the event of hardship may not be made from corporate contributions within 24 months after being contributed.[27] However, the plan may provide that if the participant has 60 months of participation he may withdraw all corporate contributions including those which have been made within the last 24 months.[28]

WATCH THIS

No provision for "hardship" distribution is permitted in a pension plan,[29] or in an integrated profit sharing plan.[30].

Defining Hardship

In one revenue ruling, the Internal Revenue Service held that hardship may be defined as "circumstances of sufficient severity that a participant is confronted by present or impending financial ruin or his family is clearly endangered by present or impending want or privation."[31] This language is so restrictive that the objective of providing for "hardship" distribution is extremely limited. Language of this kind would surely be of no real use to most professionals. However, it appears that the definition may be far more liberal than the language provided above. In a later revenue ruling, the Internal Revenue Service referred to hardship as "financial need" or financial necessity,"[32] and the author continually defines hardship which has consistently been approved by the Internal Revenue Service to be an event of personal emergency, or financial necessity, such as sickness, college expenses for children, medical or hospital bills, the purchase of a home, casualty loss or an unexpected or unusual expense.

OBSERVATION

The money that is withdrawn under the hardship provision of the plan is taxable to the participant in the year withdrawn. However, the desirability of such language is clearly obvious. Not only can the contributions to the profit sharing plan be used to provide retirement benefits for the professional, but can also be used to meet his current income needs. Thus, a young professional may accumulate funds in a profit sharing plan tax free to help pay for the college expenses of his children if no other funds are available.

Avoiding Constructive Receipt

One serious problem which is raised when providing for distributions in the event of hardship is the problem of constructive receipt. That is, if the participant has a right to the income allocated to his account, then he will be taxed on such amount even though it is not in fact distributed to him. One such example of this problem is where a participant is permitted to withdraw $500 for reason of financial need and in fact only withdraws $300. The participant will be taxed on the full $500.[33]

If withdrawal of corporate contributions is made dependent upon the approval of the administrative committee and only in the case of proven financial necessity, the participant will not be held to be in constructive receipt of the contributions allocated to his account.[34] However, if a professional corporation consists of only a few professionals who in fact are the administrative committee or if the corporation consists of only one professional, it can be argued that since said professionals have the power to make distributions to themselves, they should be held to be in constructive receipt of the corporate contributions. Although distributions can only be made in the event of "hardship" and although a distribution should be made within the confines of its definition, the practitioner should provide for other "substantial restrictions" upon withdrawals to the professionals other than approval by the trustee or committee which may be or include the affected professional.

Therefore, when a professional corporation is involved, a penalty should be imposed upon the participant who makes a withdrawal for hardship. A penalty which requires the discontinuance of participation in the plan by the affected participant is considered a "substantial restriction" and will usually prevent constructive receipt.[35] A suspension of participation for a period of six months has been held substantial where the contributions were made on a periodic basis to the plan.[36] If contributions are made to the plan only at the close of the corporation's taxable year, a suspension of six months would be no penalty at all. In such cases, the plan should provide that the participant be prohibited from participating in that yearly contribution.[37] What constitutes a "substantial restriction or penalty" depends upon the facts in the particular case.[38]

CHECKLIST FOR AVOIDING CONSTRUCTIVE RECEIPT

1. Provide that distribution can be made only for financial necessity or personal emergency, providing illustrations of what will be considered such a necessity or emergency.

2. Provide that no more than the amount actually needed to meet such emergency can be distributed to the participant.
3. Provide that the affected participant will not be permitted to participate in future contributions to the plan for a stated period of time which should be as follows:
   a. If contributions are made out of accumulated earnings and profits on a periodic basis, then a minimum period of six months should be inserted.
   b. If contributions are made once a year, then participation should be suspended for a period of one year.

OBSERVATION

Some practitioners feel that withdrawal provisions should not be inserted in one-man professional corporations or even in corporations consisting of several professionals because of the constructive receipt problem. This author feels that this is being overcautious and is not necessary. If guidelines are established providing for what constitutes hardship and if a substantial penalty is imposed upon the affected professional, then the constructive receipt problem is met.

WATCH THIS

The right of withdrawal of participant's interests, in spite of restrictions imposed as discussed above, may cause the plan to become operated primarily for the benefit of the prohibited group, if withdrawals are made in disproportionately greater amounts by the non-professional employees.[39]

Sample Language

In the event of personal emergency or financial necessity, a Participant who has completed 24 months of participation in the plan may request from the Employer permission to withdraw the amount to the credit of his profit sharing account which has become vested, or any portion thereof. A participant who has completed 60 months of participation may withdraw corporate contributions allocated to his account which have been made within the last 24 months. The Employer in its discretion may direct the Trustees to permit such participant to make such a withdrawal if in its discretion it finds a financial emergency or necessity exists. The amount permitted to be withdrawn shall be no greater than that needed to meet the emergency or financial necessity of the Participant. In making its determination, the Employer shall adopt and follow uniform and non-discriminatory rules and its determination shall be final and binding.

A participant who withdraws any or all of his account pursuant to this section shall be penalized as follows:

1. If the corporation contributes to the plan in a periodic manner out of accumulated earnings and profits, then the participant shall not be allowed to participate for a period of six months.

2. If the corporation customarily contributes to the plan only at the end of the Employer's fiscal year, then the participant shall not be allowed to participate in the Employer's contribution for that year.

The above penalties will apply to only professional employees.

VOLUNTARY EMPLOYEE CONTRIBUTIONS

Using Voluntary Contributions to Increase Retirement Benefits and to Meet Future Income Needs

A pension and profit sharing plan may provide that a participant may make voluntary contributions, within the prescribed limits, to the retirement plan. Although the contributions are made from income that has already been taxed to the participant and there is no personal deduction for such voluntary contribution, the earnings on the contribution are not taxed to the participant and thus, provide an additional method of accumulating money for retirement, tax free. For example, if a professional is in the 50% tax bracket and receives $500 interest on a $10,000 savings account, he will keep only $250 after taxes. If the same $10,000 were voluntarily contributed to the retirement plan, the $500 interest would be completely tax free.

A participant may contribute an amount no greater than ten percent of his aggregate basic compensation for all the years since he has become a participant under the plan.[40] Thus, if a professional's annual base salary is $50,000, he may make a voluntary contribution to the plan in the sum of up to $5,000. If he elects not to make a voluntary contribution in one year, he may voluntarily contribute $10,000 in the following year, providing his base salary remains the same.

If a corporation has adopted both a pension and profit sharing plan, voluntary contributions may only be made to one plan. If both plans allowed voluntary contributions in an amount up to 10% of the participant's compensation, a participant would in effect, be able to voluntarily contribute 20% of his salary, which is not permitted.[41]

A qualified retirement plan must specifically provide that an employee's rights in his accrued benefit derived from his own contribution are nonforfeitable.[42]

Voluntary contributions may be made in cash or in kind. If made in kind, the contribution is valued at fair market value and gain is recognized to the extent the fair market value of the property exceeds the participant's basis. No loss is recognized.[43]

Withdrawing Voluntary Contributions

A participant who makes voluntary contributions to the plan may withdraw not only his contributions but may also withdraw any accumulated interest thereon provided such withdrawals do not affect the member's participation in the plan, the employer's past and future contributions on his behalf, and the basic benefits provided by the employer's contributions and any required employee contributions.[44] However, if a participant is to have the right to withdraw at any time his voluntary contribution including interest thereon, the problem of constructive receipt must be avoided. That is, if the interest can be withdrawn at any time without restriction, then the participant will be deemed to have received the interest earned even though it has not been withdrawn and will be currently taxed on such interest. Thus, a restriction or penalty should be placed upon the participant who makes a withdrawal to avoid the constructive receipt problem. One such penalty which will avoid this problem is to provide that a participant who makes a withdrawal of his voluntary account will not be permitted to make another voluntary contribution for a period of one year.

ACCOUNTING FOR VOLUNTARY CONTRIBUTIONS

Separate Accounting

A defined benefit plan must provide for separate accounting for the portion of each employee's accrued benefit derived from his voluntary contributions.[45] In the case of a defined contribution plan, i.e., money purchase, target benefit, and profit sharing plan, the plan must require a separate accounting for each employee's accrued benefit.[46]

WATCH THIS

The portion of an accrued benefit derived from voluntary employee contributions to a defined benefit plan is treated as an employee's accrued benefit from a defined contribution plan.[47] Thus, the method of allocating employee voluntary contributions to both a defined benefit and a defined contribution plan will be the same. It should be noted that this rule does not apply to mandatory contributions to a defined benefit plan.[48]

Allocations

In the case of a defined contribution plan and a defined benefit plan which permit voluntary contributions, the accrued benefit derived from employee contributions is the balance of the employee's account, consisting only of his contributions and the income, expenses, gains and losses attributable thereto.[49]

If separate accounts are not maintained for employee voluntary contributions, the amount allocated to the accrued benefit derived employee contributions is that percentage of the entire account which his contribution (less withdrawals) is to the total amount of the employee's and employer's contributions (less withdrawals).[50]

In the case of a defined benefit plan which requires mandatory contributions as a condition of participation, then a different set of rules for computing the allocation between the employee and the employer contributions is involved.[51]

THE EFFECT OF PENSION REFORM ON VOLUNTARY CONTRIBUTIONS

The Pension Reform Act has reduced the attractiveness of voluntary contributions to a money-purchase or target benefit plan by providing that the corporation's contributions to the plan must be reduced by the lesser of:

1. One-half of all employee contributions to the plan; or
2. The employee's contributions in excess of 6% of his compensation.

Thus, although the law permits voluntary contributions of up to 10% of the participant's aggregate compensation, if the professional did contribute 10% of his annual salary, then his corporate contribution will be reduced by 4% of compensation. Furthermore, if the participant contributes an amount which equals 10% of his aggregate compensation for the number of years he has been participating in the plan, then the corporate contribution will be reduced even further. This is obviously not the desired result, since the objective is to maximize the corporate contribution to the plan. Therefore, if the use of voluntary contributions is to be maximized, then the participant should make such contributions yearly and in an amount no greater than 6% of his compensation for that plan year.

In addition, the attractiveness of voluntary contributions to defined benefit plans is also reduced. If a defined benefit plan permits voluntary contributions, then contributions to the voluntary account will probably be considered a separate defined contribution plan and subject to the limitation of contributions to a corporation which maintains both a defined benefit and defined contribution plan under Internal Revenue Code §415(e).[52]

INTEGRATING THE RETIREMENT PLAN WITH SOCIAL SECURITY

The topic of integrating a retirement plan with social security is one of the most complex areas of qualified retirement plans, especially when integrating a defined benefit pension plan. In plans in which sophisticated integration techniques are used, it is almost always necessary to employ the services of an actuary. Therefore, the following discussion will not be detailed since this will be of little practical use to most practitioners, but will provide the basic concepts of integration which will make the practitioner aware of its purposes and how its use can reduce the corporate contributions to the retirement plan.

GENERAL

At the present time all professionals, whether incorporated or not, are contributing to a retirement plan for the benefit of their employees as well as themselves. Participation is involuntary and the plan is called the Social Security Act. Required contributions are based upon a maximum taxable wage multiplied by 5.85%. The maximum taxable wage base in 1973 was $10,800, $13,200 in 1974, and further increased to $14,100 in 1975.

Thus, if in 1975, a professional employs nurses A and B, whose salaries are $10,800 and $8,000 respectively, then he must contribute $631.80 for nurse A and $468 for nurse B. However, the benefits received and the contributions required are determined by maximum taxable wage base, not the salary received by an employee if higher than the maximum wage base. Therefore, if the professional receives a salary of $60,000, his contribution to the Social Security Act ($824.85) represents 1.37% of his salary.

As a result of this disparity, an employer may adopt the retirement plan which supplements the contribution or benefits under the Social Security Act. This is called integration. "Integration of pension and profit sharing plans is a process of correlating the benefits or contributions under a plan with those under a governmental program so that the total will constitute a unified and non-discriminatory arrangement satisfying the requirements for tax qualification."[53] In effect, the government's plan is treated as part of employer's plan, and the employer's plan picks up where the government's plan leaves off. The rate of benefit under the governmental program, as a percentage of compensation, is the maximum rate that may be used under the employer's plan.[54]

Therefore, if a plan is properly integrated, a classification that excludes all employees who are compensated below the compensation level used for integration purposes will not be considered discriminatory solely because the contributions or benefits based on that part of excluded remuneration differ from contributions or benefits based on the part of remuneration that is not so excluded. In addition, if the plan is properly integrated, the plan will not be discriminatory if it excludes all employees below the maximum taxable wage base.[55]

WATCH THIS

The Pension Reform Act provides that once a participant or his beneficiary is receiving benefits under the plan, or in the case of a participant who has separated from service and has nonforfeitable defined benefits, such benefits may not be decreased by any increase in Social Security benefits.[56] This rule will not prevent the plan from reducing benefits of active particpants if Social Security benefits increase.

Defined Benefit Plans

The basic integration rate for defined benefit plans is 37½%. The value of the Social Security benefits paid by the employer is considered to be 37½% of the employees' wages subject to the Social Security tax. Thus, an integrated defined benefit pension plan may provide a normal retirement benefit equal to 37½% of a professional's average salary which exceeds the applicable integration level used by the plan.[57]

Example

Assume a professional with a monthly salary equal to $5,000. His monthly retirement benefit based upon a 37½% integration rate in excess of $10,800 would be $1,537.50 or $18,450 annually for life.

$5,000 (monthly compensation) minus $900 (monthly equivalent of $10,800 x 37.5%)

WATCH THIS

The above benefit will not be considered discriminatory where the following provisions are provided:[58]

1. Average Compensation is defined to mean the average compensation over the highest five consecutive years.[59]
2. There are no benefits payable in the event of death before retirement.
3. The normal form of retirement benefit is a straight life annuity.
4. If a participant retires before completing 15 years of service, the rate of his normal retirement benefit will not exceed 2½% for each year of service.

5. Benefits payable in the event of early retirement or for any other reason which causes severance of employment cannot exceed the actuarial equivalent of the maximum normal retirement benefit.
6. Retirement age is not less than age 65.

If an integrated plan provides for a pre-retirement death benefit or for a retirement benefit other than a straight life annuity, then the integration rate must be reduced from 37½%. The amount the benefit must be reduced by will depend upon the benefits provided by the plan.

If a pre-retirement death benefit is provided, the retirement benefit may not exceed 8/9 of the benefit which would have been provided if the plan did not provide for such death benefits, and if the retirement benefit is an annuity guaranteed for ten years, then the retirement benefit must be reduced by another 10%

Example

Assume the facts in our previous example where the professional's annual retirement benefit is a straight life annuity equal to $18,450. If the plan provides for a death benefit, the annual annuity would be reduced to $16,400 (8/9 x 18,450). If the plan provided a guaranteed annuity for ten years certain, then the benefit would be further reduced to $14,760 (90% x 16,400).[60]

MONEY PURCHASE PENSION PLANS AND PROFIT SHARING PLANS

An integrated money-purchase pension plan and profit sharing plan may provide for an excess contribution for compensation in excess of an applicable wage base in an amount equal to 7%. Thus, in designated yearly a money-purchase pension plan may provide a contribution formula of 10% of the first $14,100 of compensation and 17% of the excess.

WATCH THIS

The practitioner should be aware of the following:

1. It is not necessary to use the maximum wage base for integration purposes. In fact, in many cases, it will often provide larger contributions if a lower wage base is used.

Example

Assume the following:

Professional - Salary of $60,000
Secretary - Salary of $ 7,200
Contribution Formula: 13% of first $14,100 of
compensation, 20% of excess

In such a case, the professional's contribution will be equal to $11,013. However, if the contribution formula was 13% of the first $7,200 and 20% of the excess, then the professional's contribution will be equal to $11,496, or an additional $483.00 annually.

2. There can be no provisions made for withdrawals under an integrated profit sharing plan.[61] Since this is one of the most favorable features of a profit sharing plan, integrating should be seriously considered before doing so.
3. If a corporation adopts both a pension and profit sharing plan, only one plan can be integrated, if all the employees of the corporation are participating in both plans.[62]

SEGREGATED INVESTMENT ACCOUNTS

In a retirement plan consisting of two or more professional participants, serious problems may arise if each has strong feelings as to how the retirement funds should be invested to provide the maximum benefits. One may wish to invest in speculative or high risk securities whereas the other may feel that a more conservative approach is the best investment policy to follow. Unless this problem is resolved, serious friction will develop between the professionals and may even cause the breakup of the corporation.

Fortunately there is a simple solution to this dilemma. The retirement plan should provide that the participants shall have the right to direct the trustees as to how they would like to have the money allocated to their respective accounts invested. Thus, each participant can invest his funds as aggressively and conservatively as he chooses, and the earnings and losses will only be allocated to his account. Therefore, the conservative investor need not be concerned that the speculative investing philosophy of his colleague will diminish his retirement account, and the professional who is willing to take high risks to obtain high returns does not have to be deterred because of the conservativeness of his associates.

If the plan provides for segregated accounts or earmarked investments, then this right must apply to all participants. If only the professional employees have a right to direct the trustees as to how their allocations are to be invested then the plan will be considered discriminatory and will not qualify.[63]

Segregated accounts may prove to be an administrative headache in large professional corporations, and the professionals should be aware of additional costs for maintaining many different accounts. Nevertheless, earmarked investments may prove to be one of the most important features of the retirement plan and should certainly be used in plans consisting of two or three professionals.

TRUSTEES' LIABILITY FOR PARTICIPANT'S SEGREGATED ACCOUNT

If a participant instructs the trustees as to how he would like his funds invested, such trustee shall not be responsible for any loss because of a failure to diversify or because the investment does not meet the prudent man's standards. However, the investment must not contradict the terms of the plan.[64]

RECEIVING RETIREMENT BENEFITS WHILE STILL WORKING

A common feeling among many professionals is that they never intend to retire. Many feel they will probably reduce their work week but do not intend to entirely stop working, and as a result, they become concerned that they may never receive their retirement funds.

This concern can be alleviated. It is not necessary to postpone receipt of retirement benefits until actual retirement from the corporation. It is permissible for a participant to continue to work beyond his normal retirement date and to receive retirement benefits at the same time.[65]

Thus, a professional may supplement his reduced income as a result of his shorter work week with his retirement benefits. Remember, this right to receive retirement benefits while still working beyond the normal retirement date applies equally to non-professional employees.

PROTOTYPE RETIREMENT PLAN VERSUS INDIVIDUALLY DESIGNED PLANS — WHICH TO CHOOSE

A prototype is a plan which has been designed by an insurance company, mutual fund company or bank which has already been approved by the Internal Revenue Service. A corporation which adopts a prototype plan completes an adoption agreement which permits the corporation, in many cases, to elect the vesting schedule, the eligibility requirements and the contribution formula. The plan together with the adoption agreement is then submitted to the Internal Revenue Service for approval.

The advantages of prototype plans are that the professional will be able to save the legal fees in drafting a tailor-made plan, and in some cases, the sponsoring company will administer the plan for a nominal fee, rather than being required to have the plan administered by the accountant, lawyer or independent actuarial firm at a much larger fee.

However, in the author's opinion, the price that the professional will subsequently pay for saving these initial fees is not justified. A prototype plan, in almost all cases, will not provide the flexibility discussed in this chapter. That is, loans, withdrawals, segregated accounts and postponed distribution of funds in the event of termination is almost never found in a prototype plan. In addition, the professionals adopting a prototype plan become "locked" into the sponsoring company's investments. If an insurance company is involved, then all the participants must purchase a certain amount of insurance which is usually based upon a percentage of their accounts, whether insurance is desired or needed by all the participants. (In insurance company plans, the auxiliary fund can usually be invested as the trustees select.) If a mutual fund company plan is adopted, then a certain percentage of the total plan must be invested in that company's shares each year, irrespective of investment performance.

This is a high price to pay for saving a one-time installation fee, since the success of the retirement plan often results from the flexibility which can be built into a tailor-made plan. The practitioner should be absolutely positive that such flexibility is not required before adopting a prototype plan for his clients.[66]

FOOTNOTES

[1]See Russell Carpenter "How to set up a cash option profit sharing plan that satisifies IRS requirements" JTAX, August, 1971.

[2]Reg. §1.401-3(c); 1.401-4(a) (1) (ii).

[3]Rev. Rul. 56-497; 1956-2 CB 284.

[4]Ibid.

[5]See Note 1.

[6]I. Goodman "Panel on Qualification and Operating Requirements for Pension and Priofit Sharing Plans," January 5, 1973, Question No. 11.

[7]Rev. Rul. 55-423; 1955-1 CB 41; I. Goodman "Recent Developments in Tax Treatment of Pension and Profit Sharing Plans," October 4, 1962; Prentice-Hall Pension Library - New Form and Ideas, Para, 25,026.

[8]Rev. Rul. 63-180 IRB 1963-34; Byron A. Hicks v. U.S. 205 Fed. Supp. 343 (1962).

[9] Prop. Regs. §1.402(a) - 1(a) (1) (i); 37 F.R. 25938 (1972).

[10]ERISA §2006(b).

[11]ERISA §2006(d).

[12]ERISA §2006(a).

[13]Ibid.

[14]Ibid.

[15]Rev. Rul. 73-340, IRB 1973-34.

[16]Rev. Rul. 69-421 IRB 1969-32; Part 5(0); "Guides for Quailificaiton of Pension, Profit Sharing and Stock Bonus Plans," IRS Publicaiton 778 (2-27), Part 5(0).

[17]Rev. Rul. 67-288 IRB 1967-36; Ibid.

[18]Ibid.

[19]Rev. Rul. 71-437 IRB 1971-40.

[20]Ibid.

[21]"Pension Trust Audit Guidelines," IR Manual 45 (10)5-1 (12-4-72) §612.2(1) (a); Rev. Proc. 72-6 IRB 1972-1§8.02; Regs. §1.503(c)-1(b)(1).

[22]Ibid, IR Manual §612(2)(1)(b); Regs. §1.503(c) - 1(c).

[23]Prentice-Hall, Inc. Pension Library "Forms," Para. 25,126.

[24]IRC §4975(d) (1).

[25]Rev. Rul. 69-421 IRB 1969-32, Part 5 (m); "Guides for Qualification of Pension, Profit Sharing and Stock Bonus Plans," IRS Publication 778 (2-72) part 5(m).

[26]Ibid.; Rev. Rul 71-244 IRB 1971-23.

[27]Rev. Rul. 71-295 IRB 1971-28.

[28]Rev. Rul. 68-24 IRB 1968-3.

[29]See Note 25.

[30]Rev. Rul. 69-4 IRB 1969-2 §14.03; Rev. Rul. 71-446 IRB 1971-41 §15.03.

[31]Rev. Rul. 71-224 IRB 1971-20.

[32]Rev. Rul. 71-332 IRB 1971-30.

[33]Ibid.

[34]Rev. Rul. 55-424; 1955-1 CB 42.

[35]Rev. Rul. 55-423; 1955-1 CB 41.

[36]Rev. Rul. 58-230; IRB 1958-20.

[37]I. Goodman "Tax Treatment of Employees Under Pension and Profit Sharing Plans," April 24, 1965.

[38]See Note 35.

[39]Rev. Rul 57-587 1957 CB 260.

[40]Rev. Rul. 69-217 IRB 1969-18; Rev. Rul. 69-421 IRB 1969-32, part 4(h).

[41]Rev. Rul. 69-627 IRB 1969-51.

[42]IRC §411(a) (1).

[43]Private Revenue Ruling, Prentice-Hall Pension Library Para. 11,977.

[44]Rev. Rul. 69-277 IRB 1969-22; Rev. Rul. 60-323, 1960,2 CB 148.

[45]IRC §411(b) (2) (A).

[46]IRC §411(b) (2) (B).

[47]IRC §411(d) (5).

[48]See Note 51, infra.

[49]IRC §411(c) (2) (A) (i).

[50]IRC §411(c) (2) (A) (ii).

[51]IRC §411(c) (2) (B).

[52]Wilf, "Limitation on benefits and contributions for corporate employees under new pension law," 41 JTAX 280 Footnote 13.

[53]I. Goodman, "Integrating Pension and Profit Sharing Plans For Tax Qualifications," October 18, 1969.

[54]Ibid.

[55]IRC §401(a) (5); Regs. §1.401-3(e) (1); IRS Publication 778 "Guides for Qualification of Pension, Profit Sharing and Stock Bonus Plans," (2-72), part 5(a).

[56]IRC §401(a) (15).

[57]Rev. Rul. 71-446, IRB 1971-41.

[58]Reg. §1.401-3(e) (2) (ii).

[59]See Rev. Rul. 72-276, IRB 1972-23, which indicates that compensation may be averaged over three or four years if the integration limit is multiplied by 90% and 95%, respectively.

[60]See Note 57, §§8-12 for detailed explanation.

[61]See Note 30.

[62]See Note 57, 517.

[63]Rev. Rul. 70-370, IRB 1970-29; Rev. Rul. 69-421, IRB 1969-32, Part 5(r).

[64]ERISA §404(c)(2); See chapter 11 "Handling Investments and Life Insurance in the Retirement Plan," section entitled "What are the Duties of the Trustee," p. 195.

[65]Rev. Rul. 71-24 IRB 1971-3; "Guides for Quailification of Pension, Profit Sharing and Stock Bonus Plans," IRS Publication 778 (2-72), Part 5 (g).

[66]Gorlick, "Running Corporate pension plans: What help is needed?" Medical Economics, January 21, 1974, pps. 133, 141. "You can probably get the investment, actuarial, and other services you need for a pension and profit sharing plan cheaper if you buy them as a unit through a master or prototype plan. Such plans are usually offered by insurance companies, banks and mutual funds.

These services are offered cheaply because their sponsers are anxious to handle the investment of your money. In fact, many master and prototype plans lock you into a specific mutual fund or insurance plan. That's the most serious drawback to these arrangements. Once you put your money in, there's usually no way to change the investment program without starting all over with a new plan. Even if there are options, they may be too limited to meet changing conditions—a new colleague, for example, who wants to make his own investment choices."

11

HANDLING INVESTMENTS AND LIFE INSURANCE IN THE QUALIFIED PLAN

Subject to certain restrictions which are subsequently discussed, the Internal Revenue Code does not place any specific limitation upon the investments which can be made by the retirement plan, and generally, the contributions to the plan may be used to purchase any investments permitted by the trust agreement to the extent allowed by local law.[1] Thus, the corporate retirement program provides a unique opportunity for the professional to develop his investment portfolio and fulfill his life insurance needs. For example, the pension or profit sharing plan may invest in common stock, preferred stock, bonds, convertible bonds, mortgages, real estate, mutual funds, commercial paper, treasury notes, annuities, oil and gas units, commodities, options and life insurance.

Despite the wide discretion available to the professionals in regard to plan investments, there are certain restrictions placed upon some investments, and there are many requirements which must be complied with in regard to the operation of the plan. Therefore, the practitioner must advise his clients on a continual basis if unexpected adverse tax consequences are to be avoided. In addition, proper planning in regard to the funding of the plan as well as its operation will maximize the professional's tax savings.

Some of the topics discussed in this chapter, which are designed to enable the practitioner to properly advise his clients in regard to the funding and operation of the retirement plan, are as follows:

1. The restrictions which are placed upon plan investments.
2. Whether or not the professionals should be the trustees of their retirement plan.
3. The duties a trustee assumes and his liability for the breach of these duties.
4. The advantages and disadvantages of life insurance in the retirement plan.

5. When to purchase life insurance in the retirement plan to maximize tax savings.
7. How to handle the professional's personally-owned insurance.
7. How to handle the professional's Keogh plan after incorporating

FUNDING THE RETIREMENT PLAN

The choice of funding medium will directly affect the method by which these investments may be made. That is, if the professionals wish to establish a retirement plan where contributions are invested in securities, life insurance or other such investments, then a trust will be required in order to make such investments.[2] This is often referred to as the "self-administered plan" or "trusteed plan." On the other hand, if the professionals only wish to purchase annuity contracts or other such insurance contracts providing retirement benefits, then a trust may not be required.[3] This type of plan is often referred to as an "insured plan."

The Insured Plan

The following are some of the vehicles available for providing benefits under an insured plan:

Individual policies

Under this method, the corporation purchases a separate annuity contract or retirement income policy in the name of each participant in an amount which will provide the required retirement income.[4] When individual policies are purchased a trust is generally used, although not required, unless retirement income or endowment policies are involved, in which case a trust is required.[5]

The primary disadvantage with this funding vehicle is that if there is a high turnover the corporation will recover only the cash value which has accumulated, if any, in the policy. Thus, the corporation will sustain a monetary loss with every employee who terminates his employment.

Group annuity plans

When a plan is funded with group annuities, the corporation enters into a contract with the insurance company by means of a master contract, whereby premiums are paid to the insurance company for the purchase of deferred annuities. The insurance company agrees to provide specified benefits for the designated purchase payments. A minimum number of participants is required and no trust instrument is normally used.

Group permanent insurance plans

A group permanent plan combines group life insurance with group annuities into one contract on a level premium basis. Unlike group life insurance, a group permanent contract has a cash value that can be converted into an annuity on the employee's retirement. The employee has life insurance protection until retirement, at which time the annuity portion of the contract becomes operative.

The group permanent plan is ordinarily available only when there are at least fifty eligible employees and at least $250,000 face amount of insurance.[6] Therefore, the funding vehicle is not applicable to almost all professional corporations.

Group deposit administration contracts

A deposit-administration contract is used to accumulate funds at interest with an insurance company, which is then used to purchase a single premium annuity when an employee retires. This is distinguished from the other deferred annuity contracts where payments are applied immediately to provide annuities on the employees. The employer's annual contribution to the deposit-administration fund is determined by the benefits to be provided, the cost of annuities at retirement, and other factors, such as the age, sex and compensation of the participants. No trust is used in this type of contract.

Variable annuities

The above insured benefits all provided the employee with a stated fixed payment over his lifetime after retirement. However, in the age of rising inflation the retirement benefits received by the employee in fact may not provide him a satisfactory replacement for his earnings. To cure this defect, the variable annuity was created. Instead of a specified dollar amount, the employee is provided with a given number of units. These units have an initial dollar value, but the value is varied depending upon the change in the value of the funding vehicle which is providing the benefits. Normally, the funds are invested in common stocks. Unfortunately, the benefits may be lower than anticipated in a declining market.

Variable annuity plans may be either trusteed or non-trusteed.

The Self-Administered or Trusteed Plan

Professionals who wish to have the contributions which are made to their retirement plan invested in a variety of investments, other than in insurance products, must establish a trust. Generally, a plan will be "split funded" whereby the trust invests a portion of the contributions in securities and a portion for life insurance which will serve as a death benefit as well as accumulate cash value for retirement. The principal difference between the uninsured plan and the trusteed plan is that in the latter, contributions are made directly to the trustees, who are then responsible for investing these funds pursuant to the terms of the trust, and in the former, payments are made directly to the insurance company.

The usual arrangement is to have two instruments: the plan and the trust. However, both are often combined into one instrument. The plan usually provides the eligibility requirements, retirement benefits as well as requirement for disability and death benefits and the various rights of the participant. The trust is established in accordance with applicable local law and is an agreement between the corporation and the trustees. The trust defines the trustees' duties and responsibilities and how the funds should be invested.

WHAT RESTRICTIONS ARE PLACED UPON RETIREMENT PLAN INVESTMENTS

Although the investments permitted in a retirement plan are varied, there are certain limitations and restrictions which are placed upon plan investments and transactions by the Internal Revenue Code, and if the trustees are not careful, the qualification of the trust may be jeopardized, the income which is otherwise exempt from tax will now be taxable to the trust, or certain parties may be held liable for certain actions. To avoid these results the following requirements must be met:

1. The investment policies of the trust must be for the exclusive benefit of the employees or their beneficiaries.[7]
2. The investments must not constitute a prohibited transaction.[8]
3. The trust must not derive income from any unrelated trade or business.[9]
4. The investments must not be used to operate a feeder organization.[10]

Most professional corporations should not have any difficulty in maintaining their exempt status and qualification of their retirement plan and trust. Nevertheless, it is possible for the unwary to fall within one of the above pitfalls without being cognizant that the plan's qualification or the trust's exempt status is in jeopardy. For this reason, these four requirements are discussed below in more detail.

Exclusive Benefit of Employees

Investments of an exempt employee's trust which are part of a qualified plan must be made in such a manner that they comply with the requirement that the plan be maintained for the exclusive benefit of the employees or their beneficiaries. Where, however, the investments are made as to result in preferential treatment for the prohibited group or if the funds of the retirement plan are being used by the creator-employer of the plan, in a manner which is inconsistent with the "exclusive benefit rule," then the plan will lose its qualification.

The Internal Revenue Service has established certain requisites which must be compiled with if the exclusive benefit rules are to be met, which are as follows:[11]

1. The cost of the investment must not exceed its fair market value at the time of its purchase.
2. The investment must provide a fair return commensurate with the prevailing rate.
3. Sufficient liquidity must be maintained by the trust to permit distribution in accordance with the terms of the plan.
4. The safeguards and diversity that a president investor must adhere to must be followed by the trustee.

In general, almost all professional corporations should not have any difficulty in meeting these requirements provided the trust assets are not primarily benefiting the professional employees to the detriment of the lower paid employees and that the corporation is not using the funds of the trust for purposes which are inconsistent with the exclusive benefit rule.

PROHIBITED TRANSACTIONS

Prior to the Pension Reform Act, a qualified trust and the corporation which created it were not precluded from entering into a business arrangement provided the terms of the arrangement were similar to those which would be negotiated between unrelated parties in an arm's length transaction.[12] The most common situations which arose were the loan of retirement funds to the corporation or a lease or sale of personal or real property by the trust to the corporation or from the corporation to the trust.

The Pension Reform Act now prohibits certain specified transactions, including those mentioned in the above paragraph, between the retirement plan and persons referred to in the Act as "parties in interest" or disqualified persons." The following are prohibited transactions:[13]

1. The sale or exchange, or leasing of any property between a plan and a disqualified person.
2. The lending of money or other extension of credit between a plan and a disqualified person.
3. The furnishing of goods, services or facilities between a plan and a disqualified person.
4. The transfer to, or use by or for the benefit or, a disqualified person of the income or assets of a plan.
5. The acquisition, on behalf of the plan, of employer securities or real property which results in more than 10% of the plan's assets being invested in such securities or real property.

WATCH THIS

Outside of certain exceptions, the Pension Reform Act has effectively eliminated all business arrangements between the retirement plan and the professional corporation and the professional shareholders of the corporation. The penalities for engaging in such a transaction are severe, and the fact that a disqualified person did not know he had engaged in a prohibited transaction would not negate his liability for the penalities imposed under the Internal Revenue Code.[14]

Who is a "party in interest" or "disqualified person"

The term, "party in interest," is used in the labor side of the Pension Reform Act, and the term, "disqualified person," is used in the tax side of the Act. The terms are synonomus, and this author refers to "disqualified persons" in this chapter merely because of its use in the tax side of the Act. Examples of a "party in interest" or "disqualified person" are as follows:[15]

1. A fiduciary

The Pension Reform Act defines the term fiduciary to be any person who exercises any discretionary authority or control respecting the management of the plan, exercises any authority or control respecting the management or disposition of its assets or has discretionary authority or responsibility in the administration of the plan.[16]

respecting the management or disposition of its assets or has discretionary authority or responsibility in the administration of the plan.[16]

2. A person providing services to the plan.
3. An employer whose employees are covered by the plan.
4. An officer, director (or an individual having powers or responsibilities similar to those of officers or directors), a ten percent or more shareholder, or a highly compensated employee (earning ten percent or more of the yearly wages of the employer) of the employer who adopted the plan.

WATCH THIS

Not only are the professional corporation, its officers, directors, most of its shareholders, and the trustees of the retirement plan included within the term ''party in interest'' or ''disqualified person,'' but the term will also encompass those individuals who render investment advice for a fee and those individuals to whom ''discretionary duties'' have been delegated by named fiduciaries.[17] Attorneys and accountants will not normally be included in the definition of the terms unless their duties give them discretionary authority or control over the plan's assets.[18]

Exemptions to the prohibited transaction rules

The Pension Reform Act provides that the following transactions between the retirement plan and a disqualified person will not be considered prohibited transactions. There are exemptions other than those listed below, but because of their inapplicability to professional corporations, they will not be discussed.[19]

1. Loans made by a plan to a disqualified person who is a participant or beneficiary of the plan if certain requirements are met.[20]

2. Any contract or reasonable arrangement with a disqualified person for office space, or legal, accounting or other services necessary for the establishment or operation of the plan, if no more than reasonable compensation is paid therefor.[21]

3. If certain requirements are met, a trustee bank may invest plan funds in its pooled investment fund, if the plan specifically so provides.[22]

4. Receipt by a disqualified person of any benefit under the plan to which he may be entitled as a participant or beneficiary, provided the benefit paid is entitled as consistent with the terms of the plan as applied to all other participants and beneficiaries.[23]

5. The receipt by a disqualified person of any reasonable compensation for services rendered, or for reimbursement of expenses properly and actually incurred. However, if a disqualified person receives full-time pay from the corporation whose employees are participating in the plan, then he shall only be entitled to be reimbursed for expenses actually incurred by him.[24]

6. Service as a fiduciary in addition to being an officer, employee, agent or other representation of a disqualified person.[25]

7. The Secretary of Labor may grant exemptions at his discretion if he finds that such exception is (a) administratively feasible; (b) is in the interests of the plan and of its participants; (c) will not affect the rights of the participants and beneficiaries of such plan.[26] It is doubtful that this exemption will be applicable to professional corporations.

Penality and liability of ''party in interest'' or ''disqualified person'' for involvement in a prohibited transaction

Prior to the Pension Reform Act, a trust which engaged in a prohibited transaction would lose its exempt status. This generally was detrimental to the plan participants since their future benefits under the plan came to an end because, in such cases, the plan was usually terminated. To eliminate this result, instead of disqualification, the Pension Reform Act now imposes a penalty tax, under the tax side of the Act, on disqualified persons who engage in a prohibited transaction,[27] and, under the labor side of the Act, a fiduciary is liable for any losses incurred as a result of the prohibited transaction in which he engaged or if he profited from such transaction, then he must reimburse the trust by the amount of profit he realized.[28] In addition, a fiduciary may be subject to civil liability.[29]

The tax imposed upon disqualified persons who engage in prohibited transactions is on two levels:

1. *Level One:* A tax equal to 5% of the amount involved with respect to the prohibited transaction for each year in the taxable period.[30]

This tax is imposed automatically without regard to whether the violation was inadvertent.

2. *Level Two:* If the prohibited transaction is not corrected within 90 days after the mailing of the notice of deficiency for the tax imposed under level one, then a tax equal to 100% of the amount involved will be imposed.[31] This tax may be waived by the Secretary of Treasury.[32]

To correct a prohibited transaction, the transaction must be undone to the extent possible, but in any case, the final position of the plan must be no worse than it would have been if the disqualified person were acting under the highest fiduciary standards.[33]

WATCH THIS

A fiduciary will not be subject to these penalty taxes if he is acting in his capacity as such. However, if when the prohibited transaction was committed he was acting in a capacity other than that of a fiduciary or in a capacity in addition to that of a fiduciary, then he will be treated as other disqualified persons and subject to the tax.[34]

Effective date

The effective date of these provisions was January 1, 1975.[35] However, if a plan was engaged in an activity which was in effect on July 1, 1974 and was not prohibited under prior law but is now disallowed, it can generally be continued until July 1, 1984.[36]

Unrelated Trade or Business Income

Although a qualified retirement trust is part of a plan which meets all applicable requirements for qualification, and itself is a qualified trust, it may nevertheless be denied exemption if it is operated for the primary purpose of carrying on a trade or business for profit.[37]

Passive investment income such as interest, dividends, annuities, and royalties will be exempt from tax,[38] and generally rents from real estate owned by the trust will also be exempt.[39] On the other hand, rent from personal property which is not part of real estate, which is being leased, will be taxed to the trust.[40]

However, if the trust engages in a trade or business which is regularly carried on, then the income generated from such trade or business will be taxable to the trust.[41] It should be noted that only income derived from the direct operation of a trade or business is subject to tax. If the trust owns all the stock of a corporation which directly operates a trade or business, the dividends received by the trust are not taxed.

Furthermore, if investments are purchased with loaned money, referred to as "debt-financed investments," the income derived from such investments will be taxed to the trust.[42] Income from such investments will be taxed to the trust in the same proportion that the debt bears to the average amount of adjusted basis of the property during the taxable year.[43]

For example, part of the income derived from or gain derived from the sale of stock purchased on margin will be taxable to the trust.[44]In addition, the gain from the sale of mortgaged real estate will also be taxable to the trust to the extent of the highest amount of acquired indebtedness. Thus, if the trust purchased raw land, borrowing 50% of the sales price the trust would nevertheless pay a tax on 50% of the gain from the sale of such land even though the indebtedness had been decreased to 30%.[45]

In addition, the trust that participates in a partnership as a partner will be taxed on income earned from debt-financed investments,[46] and rental income from real property is taxed when it arises from debt-financed property.

Feeder Organizations

A feeder organization is an employee trust that is operated for the primary purpose of carrying on a trade or business for profit and pays such profits to an exempt organization. Such an organization is denied exemption under §502 of the Internal Revenue Code even though an exempt organization benefits from the profits.[47] This restriction is really academic in regard to professional corporations.

On the other hand, a profit sharing plan which provides its funds to meet the required contribution of a pension plan covering the same employees is called a feeder plan. Therefore, if a professional corporation maintains both a pension and profit sharing plan, and the corporation for one reason or another cannot meet its required contribution to the pension plan, the profit sharing plan cannot use its funds to meet this obligation. Such a plan will not qualify since it is not being operated for the exclusive benefit of the employees because it relieves the corporation of its obligations.[48] This also should not pose a serious threat to the professional corporation because the problem can very easily be avoided.

TRUSTEES

Who Should Be the Trustees of the Retirement Plan

Subject to applicable state law, a professional corporation may appoint any individual or other entity to be trustee of its retirement plan. Therefore, the trustee(s) may be either the professionals themselves, a bank, a commercial trust company or other entity which is legally authorized to perform such services.

As a general rule, most professionals elect to administer the retirement plan themselves and assume the duties of being trustee. Their reasoning is that they will retain complete control over the plan and will avoid expensive professional trustee fees. This author has come to question the wisdom of such a decision and whether the "do-it-yourself approach" is truly less expensive than employing an outsider to act as trustee. The reasons for not having the professionals themselves serve as trustees are as follows:

1. Most professionals do not have the time to devote to their investments and the experience to make sound investments.
2. Most professionals because of time limitations do not keep adequate records of retirement plan transactions, which makes the job of the accountant or attorney who prepares the trust allocation and Internal Revenue Service reports more difficult, and consequently, more expensive.
3. Professionals who serve as trustees may inadvertently use the trust funds for purposes other than for the "exclusive benefit of employees." This problem would effectively be eliminated if a corporate trustee was appointed.
4. The problem of whether loans are being granted on a uniform and nondiscriminatory basis among all employees is eliminated if a corporate trustee is chosen.
5. The problem of constructive receipt which might arise, for example, under the withdrawals provision of the profit sharing plan, is largely eliminated if a bank or other such entity is serving as trustee rather than the professionals who would themselves decide whether or not they are entitled to withdraw a portion or all of the contribution which has been allocated to their account.
6. The fees charged by a bank for administering the plan will generally not be more expensive than

the fees charged by the professional corporation's attorney or accountant for the same services.

7. Even though a corporate entity may be chosen to serve as trustee, the professional corporation would still be able to review the work of the corporate trustee, give investment advice and objectives, and always has the authority to remove the corporate trustee.
8. If the retirement plan only has one participant which is the professional, who is also serving as trustee, then it is possible that the Internal Revenue Service may hold that there is no valid existing trust under the Doctrine of Merger. A corporate trustee would avoid this problem.[49]

On the other hand, there are some professionals who are financially sophisticated, keep good records, and comply with the plan's provisions. In such cases, there is no reason why they should not serve as trustee if they feel they can achieve better investment results than a bank or other such institution.[50]

What are the Duties of a Trustee

The Pension Reform Act of 1974 imposes the following duties and responsibilities upon the trustees of the plan.

1. Each trustee must act solely in the interests of the plan's participants and beneficiaries and exclusively to provide benefits to these participants and beneficiaries.[51]
2. Each trustee is required to act with the care, skill, prudence and diligence under the circumstances then prevailing that a prudent man acting in a like capacity and familiar with such matters would use in conducting an enterprise of like character and with like aims.[52]
3. The Trustee must diversify the investments of the retirement plan so as to minimize the risk of large losses, unless under the circumstances it is clearly prudent not to do so.[53]

The degree of investment concentration that would violate this requirement to diversify cannot be stated as a fixed percentage, since the nature of the investments will depend upon the facts and circumstances of each case. The factors to be considered include:[54]

1. The purpose of the plan
2. The amount of plan assets
3. Financial and industrial conditions
4. The type of investment, whether mortgages, bonds or shares of stock
5. Distribution as to geographical location
6. Distribution as to industries
7. Dates of maturity

In this regard, a trustee should usually not invest the whole or an unreasonably large proportion of the trust property in a single security or in various types of securities dependent upon the success of one enterprise or upon conditions in one locality, since the effect is to increase the risk of large losses. Thus, although the trustee may be authorized to invest in industrial stocks, he should not invest a disproportionate amount of the plan assets in shares of corporations engaged in a particular industry.

The above was a list of affirmative duties and responsibilities which a trustee assumes in his capacity as such. The following is a list of transactions which a trustee must not do if he is not to be in breach of his fiduciary obligations to the plan participants and beneficiaries.[55]

1. Deal with the assets of the plan in his own interest or for his own account.
2. Receive consideration for his own personal account from any party dealing with the plan in connection with the transaction involving the income or assets of the plan.
3. Acting in any transaction involving the plan on behalf of a person whose interests are adverse to the interests of the plan or of its participants or beneficiaries.

Trustee's Liability for Breach of Fiduciary Duty

A trustee will be responsible for any losses incurred as a result of his failure to meet the standards set forth in the preceding section.[56] However, a trustee will not be responsible for any breach of fiduciary duty if such breach was committed before he became a trustee or after he ceased to be a trustee.[57]

In addition, exculpating provisions which relieve a trustee of responsibility or liability are void and have no effect.[58]

Furthermore, a trustee is liable for the breach of fiduciary responsibility by another trustee in the following circumstances:

1. If he knowingly participates in a breach of duty committed by the other trustee.[59]
2. If he knowingly undertakes to conceal a breach committed by the other trustee.[60]
3. If he enables the other trustee to commit a breach through his failure to exercise prudence in carrying out his specific responsibilities.[61]

Example

> A and B are co-trustees and are to jointly manage the plan assets. A improperly allows B to have sole custody of the Plan assets and makes no inquiry as to his conduct. A will be responsible for any breach of fiduciary duty committed by B.

4. If he knows that another trustee of the plan has committed a breach and he doesn't take any steps under the circumstances to remedy the breach.[62]

However, a plan may allocate certain responsibilities between the trustees, in which event, one trustee will not be responsible for the breach of the other which was incurred while said other trustee was performing his specific duties.[63]Furthermore, if an investment manager is appointed, a trustee will not be responsible for any acts or omissions of such investment manager.[64]

OBSERVATION

Most trustees of a professional corporation's qualified retirement plan will have little difficulty in meeting responsibilities and obligations as such. However, there are many attorneys and accountants who are trustees of many plans in name only, and perform no duties as a trustee and never intended to actively undertake the duties of a trustee. Practitioners in this situation should now reevaluate their position in view of their potential liability for the acts or omissions of their co-trustees. Language to the effect that one co-trustee will not be liable for the acts or omissions of the other co-trustee has no effect under the Pension Reform Act as was discussed above. Thus, the practitioner must now take a more active role than he intended when he agreed to become one of the trustees, if he is going to reduce his liability to plan participants. Furthermore, the practitioner may find himself in a very awkward situation if he becomes aware of a breach of duty of a co-trustee, who happens to be the professional whose practice he incorporated or for whom he renders other professional services. In this instance, the practitioner may be required to report this breach to the Secretary of Labor or the Secretary of Treasury, whichever is appropriate, if he is to be relieved of his liability for this breach.

If the purpose of the practitioner for becoming a co-trustee was merely to resume duties as such in the event of the incapacity of the other co-trustee, then this should be stated in the trust. If the practitioner is required to perform only limited services as co-trustee, then these duties should be specified. In this manner, the practitioner's liability is limited to the duties he agrees to assume, rather than for the entire management of the trust.

Requirements for bonding

Unless exempted by the Secretary of Labor, or unless other standards are met as may be established by the Secretary of Labor deemed to protect the interests of plan participants and beneficiaries, every fiduciary of a qualified retirement plan and every person who handles the funds or other property of the plan is required to be bonded. The bond shall represent no less than 10% of the amount handled, but in no case shall the bond be less than $1,000.[65]

INSURANCE IN THE RETIREMENT PLAN

How Much Insurance Can the Plan Purchase?

A qualified plan is a plan of deferred compensation whose primary purpose is to provide retirement benefits. Therefore, a plan which calls only for the purchase of ordinary life insurance policies will not be a qualified plan, since the reserve accumulated on the policy will only provide a small annuity, and its primary purpose is to provide insurance protection.[66] However, a qualified retirement plan, whether pension or profit sharing, may provide for the purchase of ordinary life insurance provided the insurance purchased is incidental to the plan's primary purpose.[67]

Several rules have developed regarding what constitutes "incidental" for the various types of retirement plans. These rules are of extreme importance, because if the amount of insurance which is purchased exceeds what is considered "incidental," the plan will be disqualified.

Defined benefit pension plan

Until recently, the Internal Revenue Service took the position that a pre-retirement death benefit in a defined benefit pension plan would be only considered incidental if such benefit was no greater than (1) 100 times the anticipated monthly normal retirement benefits, or (2) the reserve under the life insurance policy and the auxiliary fund.[68] There is no relationship between the cost of the insurance protection to the total contribution allocated to the particular employee's account, and under this rule, it is possible to spend more than 50% of the total contribution for insurance.

The most serious problem created with this definition is that it is possible that forfeitures may result. For example, if a plan has provided a death benefit equal to 100 times the monthly retirement benefit, which is fully funded with life insurance, the auxiliary fund will be forfeited since it cannot be paid out as an additional death benefit.[69] In such an event, the forfeitures will be used to reduce the following year's contribution to the plan. If the plan is terminated upon the death of the key professional employee, the forfeiture will be used to fund the benefits of all remaining participants. Any balance will then revert back to the corporation as an "erroneous actuarial computation" which will be taxed as ordinary income to the corporation. Thus, the limitation of the death benefit would have extremely undesirable results.

However, in a recent revenue ruling, the Internal Revenue Service modified its position and now provides that in addition to the "100 times" test a death benefit will be considered incidental if less than 50% of the employer's contribution credited to each participant's account is used to purchase ordinary life insurance, even if the total death benefit consists of both the face amount of the policies and the amount credited to the participant's auxiliary account at the time of death.[70]

Thus, the most serious disadvantage of a defined benefit plan has been eliminated, and with the limitation placed upon contributions to money-purchase pension plans, and target benefit plans by the Pension Reform Act of 1974, greater use may not be made of defined benefit plans, whereas previously they were generally avoided because of the limitation of death benefits.[71]

Money-purchase and target-benefit pension plans

The purchase of life insurance in a money purchase pension plan will be deemed incidental if either of the following two tests are met:

1. The death benefit is either the greater of (a) 100 times the anticipated monthly normal retirement benefit or (b) the reserve under the policy and the auxiliary fund; or

2. The aggregate of the premiums paid for life insurance in the case of each participant is less than one-half of the aggregate of the contributions allocated to him at any particular time, and the plan requires the trustee to convert the entire value of the life insurance contract at or before retirement into cash, to provide periodic income so that no portion of such value may be used to continue life insurance protection beyond retirement, or to distribute the contract to the participant at retirement.[72]

Almost all professional corporations should use the limitation provided in the second test since the trust will be able to distribute the entire amount allocated to the deceased participant's account, including the proceeds of life insurance and the auxiliary fund to his beneficiary named under the plan or as designated by the participant, whereas under Test One a forfeiture would be created.

Profit sharing plans

A profit sharing plan may provide for the distribution of the funds accumulated in the plan after a fixed number of years, which has been defined to mean not less than two years.[73] Thus, funds which have accumulated for at least two years may be used to purchase ordinary life insurance policies without regard to whether the cost is incidental.[74]

However, when ordinary insurance is purchased with current contributions, the insurance must be incidental to the primary purpose of the plan. The purchase of ordinary life insurance will be considered incidental if less than 50% of the employer's contribution, including forfeitures credited to each participant's account, is used to purchase ordinary life insurance policies on the participant's life, even though the total death benefit consists of both the face amount of the policies and the amount credited to the participant's account at the time of death.[75] This test is expressed in terms of contributions, and the earnings, capital gains, or losses of the trust are not taken into account in determining the amount of trust funds which may be used to pay premiums.[76]

Should Life Insurance be Purchased in a Profit Sharing Plan

The professionals should limit the amount of insurance which they purchase through the profit sharing plan. Since the premium paid for insurance out of current contributions must be less than 50% of the total contribution allocated to the particular employee's account, the corporation becomes obligated to make a certain fixed contribution to the plan each year in order to meet the incidental test. The larger the percentage of insurance which is purchased creates a larger required contribution which must be made to the plan by the corporation. Thus, the flexibility of being able to vary the contributions to a profit sharing plan is lost. As a result, it is usually recommended that insurance be purchased through a pension plan other than through a profit sharing plan, and if insurance is purchased through the profit sharing plan, the amount purchased should represent a small percentage of the total contribution.

Voluntary Contribution Used to Purchase Life Insurance

The "incidental test" only applies to the contributions which are made by the corporation to the plan and does not apply to a participant's voluntary contributions. Therefore, even though a retirement plan has already purchased the maximum amount of life insurance permitted under the "incidental test," a participant may direct that his voluntary contributions be used to purchase additional amounts of ordinary life insurance.[77]

What Happens if the Premiums paid for Life Insurance Exceeds the 50% Test

If the "incidental test" is not met, then the plan will lose its qualification. However, it is possible, by error or otherwise, that in one particular year, an amount in excess of what is considered "incidental" will be spent for ordinary life insurance policies. This will not, in itself, necessarily cause the plan to lose its qualification if the aggregate amount of life insurance premiums in the case of each participant is less than one-half of the contributions allocated to him at any particular time.[78] Thus, if insurance is not purchased until the second plan year, and the premium paid represents 55% of the participant's contribution, the plan will not be disqualified since in the aggregate, the total premium paid in relation to the total participant's allocated contribution for the two plan years, is less than 50%.

Can A Qualified Retirement Plan Purchase Term Insurance

A qualified pension or profit sharing plan may purchase term insurance on the lives of its participants or any particular participant. However, the amount which can be applied for such insurance may not exceed 25% of the participant's account.[79] However, since the employee will have to include the total premium paid for the insurance in his gross income, its attractiveness is reduced.[80]

Taxation of life insurance purchased under a qualified retirement plan

Income Tax

The cost of pure life insurance protection is treated as a current distribution from the plan to the employee for whom life insurance has been purchased, and such cost must be reported as income by such employee on his personal income tax return in the year in which the premium is paid.[81]

"Pure insurance protection" is the difference between the face amount of the policy and its cash value at the end of the policy year,[82] and the cost of such protection is determined by multiplying this amount by the Internal Revenue Service's one-year premium term rate at the employee's age as published in Revenue Ruling 55-747 CB 1955-2,228. These rates have become known as the P.S. 58 table. If group term insurance is purchased, it appears that the employee will have to include in income the actual premium paid for such coverage, and that the "P.S. 58 Table" is not applicable.[83] If the insurance company's rates for one-year individual term policies to all standard risks is lower than the Internal Revenue Service's rates, then the insurance company's rates may be used.[84]

The Internal Revenue Service's rates are as follows:

Uniform One Year Term Premiums for $1,000 Life Insurance Protection
(Based on Table 38, U.S. Life Tables and Actuarial Tables (U.S. Government Printing Office, Washington, D.C.—1946), and 2½% of interest.)

Age	Premium	Age	Premium	Age	Premium
15	$1.27	36	3.41	57	16.18
16	1.38	37	3.63	58	17.56
17	1.48	38	3.87	59	19.08
18	1.52	39	$4.14	60	$20.73
19	1.56	40	4.42	61	22.53
20	1.61	41	4.73	62	24.50
21	1.67	42	5.07	63	26.63
22	1.73	43	5.44	64	28.98
23	1.79	44	5.85	65	31.51
24	1.86	45	6.30	66	34.28
25	1.93	46	6.78	67	37.31
26	2.02	47	7.32	68	40.59
27	$2.11	48	7.89	69	$44.17
28	2.20	49	8.53	70	48.06
29	2.31	50	9.22	71	52.29
30	2.43	51	$9.97	72	56.89
31	2.57	52	10.79	73	61.89
32	2.70	53	11.69	74	67.33
33	2.86	54	12.67	75	73.23
34	3.02	55	13.74		
35	3.21	56	14.91		

Example

Assume that the retirement plan of which Dr. Smith, age 45, is a participant, has purchased a $100,000 ordinary life insurance policy on his life. At the end of the first year, the policy has a cash value of $1500. The amount which Dr. Smith must include in income is computed as follows.

1. 100,000 (face amount) – 1500 (cash value) = 98,500 (pure protection)
2. 98,500 ÷ 1000 = 98.5
3. 98.5 x 6.30 (pure insurance cost for each $1000 of insurance at age 45) = 620.55
4. $620.55 is the amount which Dr. Smith must include in his gross income.

How to Time the Purchase of Life Insurance to Maximize Tax Savings

If the trust purchases life insurance on an employee's life in December, paying the first year's premium in full at that time, and the employee's tax year is the calendar year, then the employee will include in income the full "P.S. 58" cost for that year. No apportionment is permitted. However, if the trust only paid a portion of the total premium, the cost may be apportioned.[85]

Therefore, the trust should pay the premium either monthly, quarterly, semi-annually, or in full, depending upon when the policy is purchased.

For example, if the policy is purchased in June, the trust should pay for the insurance semi-annually rather than in full. This will reduce the P.S. 58 cost by 50% to the employee. By referring to the above example, Dr. Smith would reduce his "cost" by $310.27 and assuming Dr. Smith is in the 50% tax bracket, he will save $155.13. If the policy is purchased in December, only the first month's premium should be paid, in which case Dr. Smith would only include in his gross income $51.71.

Estate Tax

A death benefit which includes the face amount of life insurance purchased on the life of a deceased employee, payable under a qualified retirement plan is not included in the decedent's gross estate provided the benefit is not made payable to the decedent's executor or otherwise made available for the benefit of his estate.[86] The exclusion does not apply to that portion of the death benefit which is attributable to the employee's contributions.[87]

The exclusion is available only if the death benefit is received under the retirement plan. Therefore, if the employee elects a lump sum distribution at retirement, the remaining balance at his death will be included in his gross estate. However, if the employee elects a joint and survivor annuity at retirement, the exclusion will apply to the remaining payments the survivor receives upon the employee's death.[88]

Because of the estate tax savings available from death benefits payable under a qualified plan, many individuals who, because of other sources of income, seek to postpone the receipt of their retirement funds by electing a distribution which will result in most of the funds passing to their beneficiaries estate tax free. The Internal Revenue Service, as a result, has placed restrictions on the manner in which an employee's account may be paid out on his retirement. For example, an employee cannot elect to have his retirement benefits paid to his beneficiary without receiving any of the benefits himself[89] or alternatively, the employee cannot elect to just receive the interest earned on his account and leave the principal to his beneficiary.[90] On the other hand, the Internal Revenue Service will generally allow any settlement option provided the participant always receives more than one-half of the funds accumulated for his benefit at retirement.[91]

Careful Planning Can Maximize Estate Tax Savings

It is possible with careful planning not only to keep the retirement death benefit out of the employee's estate, but out of the estate of his wife as well. The professional, instead of naming his wife as direct beneficiary of his death benefit, designates the non-marital portion of his revocable "marital deduction'' trust as beneficiary. Since the non-marital portion is not includable in his wife's estate at her death, the professional has effectively by-passed two estate taxes. In addition, the estate tax exclusion will apply even if a testamentary trust is named as beneficiary.[92]

It is important, however, to be certain that these funds cannot be used to pay estate taxes, administration costs and other miscellaneous expenses and debts of the deceased employee. If the funds or any portion of them are used for such purposes, the total death benefit will be included in his gross estate.[93] Therefore, language in the employee's trust should specifically prohibit the use of the funds for these purposes. Suggested language which might be used is as follows.

> Nothwithstanding anything herein contained to the contrary, no such payment of debts, expenses, or legacies, and no payment of taxes shall be made by the Trustees from the proceeds received from any employees' pension, stock bonus, or profit sharing plan or from any retirement annuity contract if such proceeds are excludable from the gross estate of the Donor for Federal tax purposes pursuant to the provisions of Section 2039 of the Internal Revenue Code of 1954 or any amendment thereto.

OBSERVATION

Whether or not a professional should be advised to name the non-marital portion of his inter vivos trust will depend upon the facts in the particular case. Since the principle of the non-marital portion will only be available to the surviving spouse at the discretion of the trustee, the professional, if his estate is otherwise small, may wish to leave a portion of the death benefit to the marital portion of his trust in order that his wife may have readily available funds. On the other hand, if his estate is large, then it might be advisable to designate the non-marital portion as beneficiary, since the ''marital portion'' will be adequately funded. In any case, the professional's estate must be analyzed, and the consequences of the choice of beneficiary completely discussed with the professional and his wife.

Should Life Insurance Be Purchased In A Qualified Retirement Plan

Much has been written on the subject of whether or not insurance should be purchased in a qualified plan.[94] Unfortunately as with so may other decisions facing the practitioner in the area of professional corporations, there are no established rules which can be applied in all cases, and the decision will often be based upon the facts in the particular case. The issue is further complicated by the fact that many of the advantages of life insurance are often considered disadvantages by its critics, and similarly, disadvantages are often considered advantages by the advocates of the use of life insurance in the plan. The following chart lists some of the advantages and disadvantages of life insurance as a plan investment.

SHOULD LIFE INSURANCE BE PURCHASED IN A QUALIFIED PLAN?

Advantages	*Disadvantages*
1. The premiums for life insurance are purchased with tax deductible dollars except for the P.S. 58 cost.	**1.** The P.S. 58 cost which must be included in the employee's income each year becomes rather substantial for the older employee.
2. P.S. 58 costs, although reported as income by the employee, are offset against amount beneficiary must report as income upon receipt of death benefit.[95]	**2.** Although the P.S. 58 cost is offset from death or retirement benefits, the initial cost was paid while the employee was in a high tax bracket, whereas the credit is used against presumably the lower income tax bracket of the employee's beneficiary or the employee's retirement income.

	Thus, the P.S. 58 cost may never actually be recovered in its entirety.
3. The proceeds from the life insurance are not included in the gross estate of the employee if not made payable to his executor.	**3.** The funds which are used to purchase life insurance reduce the amount available for equity investments, thus reducing the employee's retirement benefit.
4. Difference between face amount of policy and its cash value is income tax free.[96]	**4.** Corporation will usually not recover back premiums paid for an employee terminating his employment. If there is a rapid turnover of employees, cash value will probably never equal premiums paid, thus making cost of insurance prohibitive.
5. The cash value accumulation represents a fixed dollar balance to the retirement plan.	**5.** Cash value accumulation has no chance of capital appreciation and the cash value would build up tax free if life insurance was purchased outside the plan.
6. Cash value will provide annuity guaranteed at today's annuity rates. This will be very favorable to employee since advances in medicine will prolong one's life expectancy.	**6.** The guaranteed present annuity rates are really not that attractive since "... the annuity payout guarantees are so far discounted as to have little meaning."[97]
	7. Employee at retirement must either convert the policy into annuity using its cash value, or elect to have the policy distributed to him, in which event he will pay a tax on the cash value.[98] If the first alternative is selected, employee's insurance program may be eliminated or rendered insubstantial. If the latter choice is selected, the employee's income tax liability is increased in year policy is distributed.
	8. Beneficiary of proceeds will report the cash value as income on her income tax return. Only difference between face amount and cash value will be received income tax free.[99] If insurance is purchased outside plan, entire proceeds are received income tax free.

OBSERVATION

As one can readily observe, it is often difficult to clearly determine whether a particular result or consequence of purchasing life insurance in the qualified plan is an advantage or a disadvantage, and one can become bewildered with the number of alternative methods which can be suggested for providing the professional's life insurance needs.

For example, frequently those who oppose the purchase of life insurance advocate the purchase of term insurance as the sole means of fulfilling one's insurance program. The difference between the cost of an equivalent amount of whole life insurance and the cost of the term insurance is then invested in securities which are supposed to produce a greater return than the cash value accumulation of the whole life policy. The problem with this approach is that it may work well in principal, but not in practice. This author knows many professionals who, in hindsight, would rather have the cash value of an insurance policy as opposed to the losses they have incurred in the current securities market. In addition, the premiums on term insurance become very expensive as the employee grows older and, as a result, the professional often drops his coverage before his needs for insurance have elapsed.

On the other hand, this author does not believe that the professional's entire insurance program should be provided through the retirement plan, since if the policy is converted into an annuity at retirement, the employee's entire insurance program is lost.

Alternatively, it is suggested that the professional continue to purchase his insurance outside the plan, but to borrow the cash value of the policy to pay the premiums. This is often referred to as "minimum deposit" insurance. In this manner, the interest payments are tax deductible to the professional, thus producing the same tax deductible result as if the insurance was bought through the retirement plan. The potential problem with this solution is that if the policy is maintained for a long period of time, the interest payments can become prohibitive. Furthermore, if group term insurance is utilized, it is quite possible that the cost of providing insurance benefits for the other employees may offset the tax deductible features of such insurance to the professional and actually increase the cost of his own coverage when considering the premiums paid for these other employees. This author believes that life insurance will, in many cases, be a wise investment choice and should not be rejected because of its supposed disadvantages. The first step is to determine the professional's insurance needs, then determine the best method of satisfying these needs. Usually a balance between personal, group term and qualified plan insurance will provide the best results. Unfortunately, because there are so many variables, no set rules can be established and each professional's circumstances, retirement objectives, and investment philosophy must be carefully analyzed.

Is Every Plan Participant Required to Purchase Insurance If One Participant Purchases Insurance?

The answer to this question is clearly "no." The plan should be so drafted that each participant will have the election whether he would like to purchase life insurance with the amount which is allocated to his account. Therefore, each employee's insurance objectives can be met independently of the other employees. Thus, one employee may elect to use 40% of his contribution to purchase insurance and another might use only 20% and a third may elect not to purchase any insurance.

How to Handle Personally-Owned Insurance After Incorporating[100]

As previously discussed, one of the attractive features of a qualified retirement plan is the ability to purchase one's life insurance with tax deductible dollars, other than the P.S. 58 cost. As a result, many professionals have sought to transfer their personally owned ordinary life insurance to their retirement plan which would then assume the premium payments. The advantage of such a transfer is that the contestability period of the transferred policy normally has expired at the time of transfer and the premiums will be lower than the premiums for a new policy at the employee's older age.

However, until recently, most practitioners, as a result of a series of private rulings on the issue,[101] adopted the position that personally owned ordinary life insurance should not be transferred by an employee to a qualified plan for the following two reasons:

1. A transfer of a personally owned ordinary life insurance policy to a qualified plan, either directly to the trust or to the corporation which would then transfer the policy to the trust, would not come within the exception of the "transfer for value" rule under Internal Revenue Code §101(a) (2), and thus the proceeds would be taxable to the beneficiary to the extent the proceeds received exceeded the consideration paid and

2. A transfer of personally owned life insurance to a qualified plan might be considered discriminatory by the Internal Revenue Service and thus jeopardize the qualification of the plan.[102]

WATCH THIS

It should be noted that the issue of "transfer for value" and "discrimination" was raised only when an employee desired to transfer an ordinary life insurance policy to the trust. On the other hand, if the employee owned a term life insurance policy, he could have it converted to ordinary life policy, which would then be issued and paid by the trust. It is felt that since the only benefit in being transferred is the employee's guarantee of insurability, then the transfer should not be considered a transfer for value.[103]

The issuance of revenue ruling 73-338 IRB 1973-34 p. 5 removed much of the hesitancy that practitioners had against transferring personally owned life insurance to a qualified trust.

This ruling held that the purchase by an employer of an employee's personally owned life insurance policy for its cash value, with its subsequent transfer by the employer to its qualified trust would not be considered a transfer for value. The ruling concluded that since: (1) the proceeds of the policy had to be paid to the employee's designated beneficiary upon his death; (2) the corporation retained no rights over the policy or to the proceeds; and (3) the trust had no right to retain the insurance proceeds, that no significant change in the beneficial ownership of the proceeds occurred, and thus, such a transaction would not constitute a transfer for value. Although the ruling specifically referred to a transfer by the employee to the corporation and then to the trust, there is no reason why the conclusion reached in this ruling would not be equally applicable to a transfer by the employee directly to the trust.

Unfortunately, this revenue ruling did not discuss the issue of whether discrimination, which was raised in previous private rulings, would continue to be an issue, and one well-respected attorney in an article seriously questions whether an employee can still safely transfer his personally owned ordinary life insurance policy.[104] However, the discrimination issue was raised in a case where the cash value had been borrowed by the employee, who was a member of the prohibitive group, and the interest was going to be paid by the trust. If there had been no loan against the policy, it is questionable whether the issue of discrimination would have been raised.

However, a more recent revenue ruling[105] has expanded the permissible methods of transferring a life insurance policy by an employee to a qualified trust, and as a result, this author feels much less hesitant to transfer a policy at present time even though the issue of discrimination has not yet been fully answered. This latest ruling provided that a participant could transfer his personally owned life insurance policy to the trust as a voluntary contribution in lieu of a voluntary cash contribution. The ruling held that if (1) the insurance proceeds are payable to the employee's designated beneficiary at death, and (2) the cash surrender value of the policy is payable to the participant upon his normal retirement date or termination of employment, if earlier; there is no significant change in the beneficial ownership of the life insurance policy and that such a transfer would not constitute a transfer for value.

If a life insurance policy is transferred by this method, care must be taken to insure that the value of the policy does not exceed the employee's permitted voluntary contribution limit of 10% of his aggregate compensation for the years that he has been a participant in the plan.

A NINE-POINT CHECKLIST ON HOW TO AVOID POTENTIAL PITFALLS IN TRANSFERRING PERSONALLY OWNED INSURANCE TO QUALIFIED PLAN

1. Provide language in trust authorizing trustees to purchase insurance from plan participants or allowing a participant to transfer his personally owned insurance to the trust.
2. Provide that the participant has the right to designate the beneficiary of the policy proceeds.
3. Provide that the corporation will retain no right over the policy or to its proceeds.
4. Provide that the trust will have no right to retain its insurance proceeds, if paid to the trust.

5. Avoid transferring policies having loans outstanding which will obligate trust to pay the interest on the loan. These loans should be paid off before the policy is transferred.
6. Provide that all employees participating in the plan shall have the right to transfer their personally owned life insurance policies to the trust. This right should not be limited to members of the prohibitive group.
7. Provide that the cash surrender value of the policy must be paid to the employee's designated beneficiary or is payable to the employee upon his retirement.
8. Be sure that policy that is being transferred does not exceed "incidental" rules.
9. Be sure to determine the true value of the policy that is being transferred. Otherwise, a voluntary contribution of the policy to the plan may exceed the permitted voluntary contribution limits. Alternatively, if the consideration received by the employee exceeds its value, the Internal Revenue Service could argue that a prohibitive transaction occurred, which could jeopardize the qualification of the plan.

HOW TO HANDLE THE KEOGH PLAN AFTER INCORPORATING

If the funds in a Keogh plan are distributed to an owner-employee prior to his attaining age 59½, other than for death or disability, the owner-employee will include in income the value of the amount received and pay a penalty tax for a premature distribution.[106] As a result, most professionals when they incorporated their practices, normally "froze" their Keogh plan and left the assets in the plan until they could be withdrawn without a penalty. If the professional's Keogh plan was invested solely in securities or mutual funds, the "freezing" of the plan generally did not create any problems for the professional. On the other hand, if the professional had purchased life insurance in the Keogh plan, his only available options, if he did not wish to have the assets, including life insurance policy, distributed to him, was to put the policy on a paid-up basis or cash in the policy, and invest the proceeds in securities or mutual funds. In most cases, if either alternative was adopted, the professional never received back the total premiums paid for the policy, since the accumulated cash value never equaled the total premiums paid when the policy was terminated. Thus, the incorporating professional incurred, in such cases, a financial loss which increased the cost of incorporating his practice.

Fortunately, two recent revenue rulings have effectively eliminated this additional "cost" to the professional who had purchased life insurance in his Keogh plan and who now elected to incorporate his practice.

The first revenue ruling[107] provided that a partnership, who had adopted a Keogh plan, and then subsequently incorporated and adopted a corporate retirement plan, could transfer the funds of the first plan to the latter, provided that the restrictions which applied to the Keogh assets continued to apply to the transferred assets after they were transferred to the corporate plan. These requirements are:

1. The trustee must be a bank;
2. Separate accounts must be maintained for the funds transferred on behalf of each owner-employee;
3. No payment of benefits can be made from the transferred account before the owner-employee attains the age of 59½ or becomes disabled;
4. The distribution of the transferred funds must begin prior to the end of the taxable year in which he attains the age of 70½.

As a result of this ruling, a professional who incorporated now had an accepted method by which he could then transfer his Keogh assets, including life insurance purchased therein to the new corporate retirement plan. However, the requirements of the ruling resulted in additional administrative work for the plan administrators, since separate accounts had to be kept for both the transferred Keogh assets and corporate contributions, and a bank had to be trustee. Consequently, many professionals found it less expensive in the long run and less confusing to "freeze" their Keogh assets than to transfer them to the new corporate plan.

Fortunately, a more recent ruling has eliminated the above problems as far as the transfer of life insurance is concerned. This ruling[108] provided that the trustee of a Keogh plan could transfer life insurance policies on the lives of its participants to the trustee of a corporate retirement plan in exchange for its cash surrender value. In addition, there was no requirement that the Keogh restrictions be placed on the transferred policies, since the assets of the Keogh plan still remained intact after the transfer.

Thus, life insurance in a Keogh plan does not have to be put on a paid-up basis or cashed in after incorporating, but can be maintained by merely transferring the policy to the corporate retirement trust for its cash surrender value.[109]

HOW TO AVOID CONSTRUCTIVE RECEIPT IN TRANSFERRING KEOGH ASSETS TO THE CORPORATE RETIREMENT PLAN

It is important that the transfer of assets from the Keogh plan to the corporate plan be carried out in such a manner that the transfer is not considered a distribution to the professional. If the transfer is considered as being distributed, then the professional will include the value of transferred assets as income as well as being subject to a penalty tax. For example, the Internal Revenue Service holds that a distribution will occur when an employee receives the Keogh assets, even though he immediately transfers these assets to the trustees of the corporate retirement plan.[110] Thus, it is important that the assets be transferred directly from the trustees of the Keogh Plan to the trustees of the corporate plan.[111] If this is done, there will be no problem of constructive receipt.

FOOTNOTES

[1]Regs. §1.401-1(b) (5) (i).

[2]ERISA §403(a).

[3]ERISA §403(b).

[4] A retirement income policy provides a death benefit whereas the annuity policy doesn't. Normally, a retirement income policy will be purchased at a higher premium than an annuity, unless the employee is uninsurable.

[5]Prentice-Hall Pension Library, §2112.

[6]Prentice-Hall, Pension Library, §2131.

[7]Pension Trust Audit Guidelines, IR manual 45(10) 5-1 (12-4-73) §611.1; Rev. Rul. 69-421, IRB 1969-32 Part 2(K) (1), ERISA §404(a)(1)(A)(i).

[8]Ibid., IR Manual §612.1, Rev. Rul. 69-421, Part 2 (K) (2). ERISA §2003(c).

[9]Ibid., IR Manual §613, Rev. Rul. 69-421, Part 2(K) (3).

[10]Rev. Rul. 69-421, Part 2(K) (4).

[11]Rev. Rul. 69-421, Part 2(K)(1); Rev. Rul. 69-494 IRB 1969-38; Congressional Reports, Prentice Hall-Handbook on Pension Reform Law, September 6, 1974, Bulletin No. 8, ¶845, p. 622.

[12]Pension Trust Audit Guidelines, IR Manual, 45(10)5-1 (12-4-72), §611.2.

[13]IRC §4975(c); ERISA 406(a).

[14]IRC S4975(a); Under the Labor side of the Act, a fiduciary will only be liable if he knew or should have known that he enjoyed in a prohibited transaction. (ERISA § 406(a))

[15]ERISA §3(14); IRC §4975(e)(2).

[16]IRC §4975(e)(3); ERISA §3(21)(A).

[17]Matthew Bender, Federal Pension Law Service, 1974, SR 101-53.

[18]Ibid.

[19]IRC §4975(d); ERISA §408.

[20]IRC§4975(d)(1); ERISA §408(b)(1); see chapter 10 "Retirement Plan Drafting Techniques," Section entitled "Loans", p. 176

[21]IRC §4975(d)(2); ERISA §408(b) (2).

[22]IRC §4975(d)(8); ERISA §408(b) (8).

[23]IRC §4975(d)(9); ERISA §408(c)(1).

[24]IRC §4975(d)(10); ERISA §408(c) (2).

[25]IRC §4975(d)(11); ERISA §408(c)(3).

[26]IRC §4975(c)(2); ERISA §408(a).

[27]IRC §4975(a), (b).

[28]ERISA §409(a).

[29]Ibid.

[30]IRC §4975(a).

[31]IRC §4975(b).

[32]ERISA §3003(a).

[33]IRC §4975(f)(5).

[34]IRC §4975(a).

[35]ERISA §2003(c) (1) (A).

[36]ERISA §2003(c)(2).

[37]IRC §501 (b) (1). Rev. Rul. 69-421 IRB 1969-32, part 2(k)(3).

[38]IRC §512(b)(1).

[39]IRC §512(b)(3)(A)(i); Regs. §1.512(b)-1(c)(2).

[40]Rev. Rul. 60-206, 1960-1 CB 201; Cooper Tire and Rubber Company Employees' Retirement Fund, 306 F2d 20 (CA 6, 1962).

[41]Regs. §1.513-1.

[42]IRC §512(b) (4) and §514(a) (1); Rev. Rul. 74-197 IRB 1974-18, p. 11- Rev. Rul. 71-311 IRB 1971-29.

[43]IRC §514(a).

[44]Pension Trust Audit Guidelines, IR Manual 45(10)5-1(12-4-73) §613.4.

[45]See Kopple "Some Investments Cause Tax Problems," Pension and Welfare News, August, 1972; See also Gorlick, "The time bomb in corporate retirement plans," Medical Economics, June 25, 1973.

[46]Rev. Rul. 74-197, IRB 1974-18; Pension Trust Audit Guidelines; IR Manual (10) 5-1, (12-4-72) §613.4(3) (d).

[47]Rev. Rul. 69-421, IRB 1969-32, Part 2(K) (4).

[48] Ibid., part 2(q).

[49]Antin, "The Horrors of the Individual as Trustee of a Retirement Plan," Pension and Welfare News, November, 1972, p. 72; Although some Internal Revenue Service offices have held differently, there appears to be no requirement that a pension or profit sharing plan must have at least two trustees when there is more than one participant. See I. Goodman, "Establishing a Successful Retirement Program," November 12, 1971, Questions and Answers, Question No. 6.

[50]See Gorlick, "Running Corporate Pension Plans: What Help is Needed?" Medical Economics, January 21, 1974, p. 133.

[51]ERISA §404(A1)(1)(A)(i); Rev. Rul. 73-532 IRB 1973-49, p. 11.

[52]ERISA §404(a)(1)(B).

[53]ERISA §404(a)(1)(C); James Morrissey v. Curran CA2 CCH Pension Service, ¶20,388.

[54]Congressional Reports, Prentice-Hall Handbook on Pension Reform Law, September 6 1974, Report Bulletin No. 8, §854, p. 622.

[55]ERISA §406(b).

[56]ERISA §409(a); A trustee will not be responsible for losses incurred in a participant's segregated account, if such investment is permitted under the plan. (ERISA §404(c)(2))

[57]ERISA §409(b).

[58]ERISA §410(a).

[59]ERISA §405(a)(1).

[60]Ibid.

[61]ERISA §405(a)(2).

[62]ERISA §405(a)(3).

[63]ERISA §405(b)(1)(B).

[64]ERISA §405(d)(1).

[65]ERISA §412.

[66]Rev. Rul. 54-67 CB 1954-1, 149; On the other hand, a plan may be entirely funded with retirement income contracts or endowment contracts, even though such policies provide insurance protection, since such policies develop substantial cash values which can be used to provide retirement benefits.

[67]Regs. §1.401-1(b)(1)(i).

[68]Rev. Rul. 68-453 IRB 1968-34) Rev. Rul 73-01 IRB 1973-47, p. 9.

[69]Ibid.

[70]Rev. Rul. 74-307 IRB 1974-26.

[71]In plans consisting of many participants, the forfeitures created by the limitation in the death benefit help to reduce the cost to the employer, and such forfeitures are considered in determining the employer's required annual contribution. However, this will almost never be the objective in a professional corporation.

[72]Rev. Rul. 66-143 IRB 1966-22; Rev. Rul. 68-31 IRB 1968-4.

[73]Rev. Rul. 54-231 CB 1954-1,150; Rev. Rul. 71-295 IRB 1971-28.

[74]Rev. Rul. 60-83, 1960-1 CB 157.

[75]Rev. Rul. 57-213 IRB 1954-21; Rev. Rul. 73-501 IRB 1973-47, p. 9.

[76]Rev. Rul. 57-213 ibid.

[77]Rev. Rul. 69-408 IRB 1969-30.

[78]Rev. Rul. 54-51 CB 1954-1, 147.

[79]Rev. Rul. 66-143 IRB 1966-22.

[80]See this chapter, section entitled "Taxation of Life Insurance Purchased Under a Qualified Retirement Plan" p. 199.

[81]Rev. Rul. 56-634 IRB 1956-50; IRC §72(m)(3)(B); Regs. §1.72-16(b); This cost is only reportable as income to the affected employee when the proceeds of the policy are payable to a beneficiary of the employee (other than the retirement trust) or when the proceeds are payable to the trust, and the plan requires the trustees to pay said proceeds to a beneficiary of the employee. The employee will not be taxed if the trustee has any right to any of the proceeds. (Regs. §1.72-16(b)(6)).

[82]Regs. §1.72-16(b)(3).

[83]I. Goodman "Tax Treatment of Employees Under Pension and Profit Sharing Plans" April 24, 1965, Q and A, Q No. 10; Although the question pertained to group term insurance purchased through a qualified plan, it would seem that the same principle would apply if individual term policies were purchased.

[84]Rev. Rul. 66-110 IRB 1966-20.

[85]Private Revenue Ruling, letter signed E. I. McLarney, Deputy Commissioner, 4/30/46 Prentice-Hall ¶12,707A; I. Goodman "Development of Limitations on Deductions Under Pension and Profit Sharing Plans" February 14, 1972, Questions and Answers, Question No. 1

[86]Regs. §20.2039-2(b).

[87] §2039(c).

[88]Rev. Rul. 72-240 IRB 1972-20.

[89]Rev. Rul. 56-656 IRB 1956-51.

[90]Regs. §20.2039-2(b) example 4.

[91]Rev. Rul. 72-241 IRB 1972-20; Rev. Rul. 73-445 IRB 1973-44, p. 7; (this ruling held that a plan will not qualify where its participants could elect a $100 a month retirement benefit with balance going to their beneficiary because employee would not receive at least 50% of his account prior to his death; see also Rev. Rul. 74-325 IRB 1974-27, p. 14.

[92]Rev. Rul. 73-404 IRB 1973-40, p. 6.

[93]Ibid.

[94]Budnitz "Should Tax Sheltered Permanent Life Insurance Be Put in HR 10 or Professional Corporation Qualified Plans?" Vol. xxvii CLU Journal No. 4, October 1973, p. 14; Gorlick, "Best buys in life insurance after you incorporate" Medical Economics, December 6, 1971, p. 186; Reserach Institute of America, "Estate planning for Executive Fringe Benefits" Tax Coordinator, Special Study, April 27, 1972; Lynch, "The Use of Life Insurance in Qualified Pension or Profit Sharing Plans," The Financial Planner, May/June, 1974, p. 14; Eads "Taxation of Life Insurance Bought Under a Corporate Qualified Plan" The Financial Planner, February/March.

[95]Regs.§ 1.72-16(b).

[96]Regs. S1.72-16(c)(2)(ii).
[97]Lynch, Note 59.
[98]Regs. §1.402(a)-1(a)(2).
[99]See Note 96.

[100]The Pension Reform Act of 1974 prohibits the transfer of a professional's personally-owned life insurance policies to a qualified plan in which he is a participant as a result of Internal Revenue Code §4975(c), which prohibits the sale or exchange of any property between a plan and a disqualified person. However, as this book went to press, there has been much discussion regarding the unexpected results occurring from the literal interpretation of this section of the Act, and certain committees in Congress have already begun to examine the advisability of minimizing the severity of this Section. This author is of the opinion that the restrictions against all transactions between a qualified plan and a disqualified person will be liberalized and that certain sales or exchanges will be permitted. Since such transfers will most probably be permitted in the future and since the question of whether or not personally-owned life insurance can in fact be transferred to a qualified plan has already been a subject of much debate, this issue will be discussed in detail.

[101]The most common method of transfer discussed by these rulings was (1) a transfer by the employee directly to the trust in exchange for the policy's cash value at the time of transfer and (2) a transfer of the policy to the corporation for its cash value, whereupon the corporation would contribute the policy to the trust as part of its required contribution. At times, the employee would have borrowed the cash value prior to the transfer, in which case the interest on said loan would be paid for by the trust.

[102]For an excellent discussion of the history of this problem, see Simmons "Rev. Rul. 73-338: Does it solve the question of policy transfers to employees' trusts?" J Tax December, 1973 p. 372.

[103]Prentice-Hall Professional Corporation Guide ¶22,056 citing Private Ruling signed by Wm. W. Wharton, Jr., Chief, Review Staff, Internal Revenue Service, February 10, 1971.

[104]Simmons, see Note 102.
[105]Rev. Rul. 74-76 IRB 1974-7, p. 8.
[106]Regs. §1.72-17(e).
[107]Rev. Rul. 71-541 CB 1971-2.
[108]Rev. Rul. 73-503 IRB 1973-47, 11.

[109]The assets in a Keogh non-trusted annuity plan may not be transferred to the corporate retirement trust because Internal Revenue Code §401(g) prohibits the transfer of annuity contracts issued after 1962. See I. Goodman "Development of Limitations on Deductions Under Pension and Profit Sharing Plans" February 25, 1972, Questions and Answers, Question No. 3. However, Revenue Ruling 73-259 IRB, 1973-24, 9 provides that it is permissible to surrender the annuity contract to the insurance which could then reissue the identicial annuity contract to the trustees of the corporate plan. However, the normal Keogh restrictions will be applicable to these new annuity contracts.

[110]Rev. Rul. 69-254, 1969-1 CB 129.
[111]Rev. Rul. 68-160, 1968-1 CB 167.

12

THE ABC'S OF RETIREMENT PLAN VALUATIONS AND ALLOCATIONS[1]

The most frequently ignored aspect of servicing a professional corporation is the administration of the pension or profit sharing plan which has been adopted by the corporation. Every plan, whether pension or profit sharing, must provide for the annual valuation of the account and for the allocation of the participant's share of the realized and unrealized gains or losses plus the earnings of the plan assets for the plan year. If a profit sharing plan is involved, the plan must provide for the allocation of forfeitures among the remaining participants. Furthermore, the Pension Reform Act now requires that the Plan administrator inform each participant of his accrued benefit if the participant so requests.[2]

Failure to make such allocations on an annual basis will obviously be a cause for concern in the event of an audit by the Internal Revenue Service and will cause a nightmare for the professional or the practitioner when a vested participant terminates her employment and it becomes necessary to ascertain the portion of the pension or profit sharing account to which she is entitled.

The problem confronting most practitioners is their lack of experience in this area and the lack of written material on the subject which can assist them. This chapter will provide a step-by-step approach in making the valuations and allocations and the necessary formulas whereby the practitioner will merely have to substitute his figures in the appropriate places.[3]

The illustrated problems represent the typical situations which will confront almost all practitioners at one time or another. The allocation problems illustrated are as follows:

Problem One - Corporation makes required contribution to the pension plan, insurance is not a trust investment.

Problem Two - Corporation contributes an amount in excess of what is required.

Problem Three - Corporation makes required contribution to the pension plan, insurance is a trust investment.

Problem Four - Corporation fails to make the required contribution to the pension plan, insurance is not a trust investment.

Problem Five - Corporation fails to make the required contribution to the pension plan, insurance is a trust investment.

Problem Six - How to make the necessary allocation in profit sharing plans.

Terms

APC	Actual pension contribution
A	Appreciation
PC	Participant's contribution
PIP	Participant's insurance policy
PS of APC	Participant's share of actual pension contribution
PS of A	Participant's share of appreciation
PS of D	Participant's share of deficit
PS of PA	Participant's share of pension account*
PS of PA_c	Participant's share of pension account, current year*
PS of PA_p	Participant's share of pension account, previous year*
PS of TPA	Participant's share of total pension account
RPC	Required pension contribution
TIP	Total insurance premium
TPC	Total participant's contribution
TPA	Total pension account
VPA_c	Value of pension account, current year*
VPA_p	Value of pension account, previous year*

Appreciation - Shall also mean losses. In the event of losses, each participant's allocable share of the losses is subtracted from his account.

*Where applicable, these symbols will also mean profit sharing plans.

PROBLEM ONE — REQUIRED CONTRIBUTION MADE, NO INSURANCE

This problem assumes that the exact contribution that was required to be made by the corporation to the pension plan was in fact made, and that the pension account was only invested in securities, certificates of deposit, and other like investments, and that no insurance was purchased for the benefit of any participant.

Step One

Determine the appreciation or losses of the pension account, as of the last day of the plan's fiscal year.[4]

This is determined by subtracting the value of the pension account as of the last day of the previous plan year plus the contribution made to the plan for the current year from the value of the pension account as of the last day of the plan's current fiscal year.

$$VPA_c - VPA_p + TPC = A$$

Step Two

Determine each participant's share of the appreciation of the pension account as of the last day of the plan's fiscal year.

This is determined by computing the percentage increase in the value of the account from the last day of the previous fiscal year and the last day of the current fiscal year and then multiplying said percent by each participant's account.[5]

a. $\dfrac{A}{VPA_p + TPC}$ = percentage increase

b. percentage increase X PS of PA_p + PC = PS of A

Test one

After step two has been completed for each participant, the practitioner can check to see if the appreciation has been properly allocated among the participants by adding each participant's share of the appreciation. If done properly, the result will be equal to the appreciation for the year.

Step Three

Determine each participant's share of the entire pension account, including appreciation, for the current year alone.

This is computed by adding the participant's allocated contribution and his share of the appreciation.

$$\text{PC} + \text{PS of A} = \text{PS of PA}$$

Step Four

Determine each participant's share of the pension account for all years that he has been participating in the plan.

This is accomplished by adding the participant's share of the pension account for the previous year to the participant's allocation for the current year (Step Three result).

$$\text{PS of PA}_p + \text{PS of PA}_c = \text{PS of TPA}$$

Test two

To determine if the allocation of the total pension account has been made properly, add each participant's share of the total pension account. If computed correctly, this will equal the total value of the pension account as of the close of the current fiscal year.[6]

Example One

Money-purchase pension plan - 25% of first $9000 of compensation, 32% of excess

First Year

Two Participating Employees	*Salary*	*Contribution*
Doctor	$68,000	$21,130
Nurse	11,000	2,890
Required Contribution		$24,020
Amount actually contributed		$24,020
Value of Pension Account as of close of plan year		$25,995.00

Allocations:

Step One

25,995.00(VPA$_c$) - 24,020(TPC) = 1975(A)

Step Two

$$\frac{1975(\text{A})}{24{,}020(\text{TPC})} = .082223147$$

Doctor's Account

21,130(PC) x .082223147 = 1737.38(PS of A)

Nurse's Account

2890(PC) x .082223147 = 237.62(PS of A)

Test One

1737.38 + 237.62 = 1975

This corresponds to appreciation of pension account for current year.

Step Three

Doctor's Account

21,130(PC) + 1737.38(PS of A) = 22867.38(PS of PA)

Nurse's Account

2890(PC) + 237.62(PS of A) = 3127.62(PS of PA)

Test Two

22867.38 + 3127.62 = 25995.00

Allocation has been made correctly since this corresponds to value of account.

Example Two

Second Plan Year

Assume same facts as presented in example one, except that in the second year there is one additional participant.

Three Participating Employees	*Salary*	*Contribution*
Doctor	$68,000	$21,130
Nurse	11,000	2,890
Secretary	7,500	1,875
Required Contribution		$25,895.00
Amount Actually Contributed		$25,895.00
Value of Pension Account for both plan years		$54,115.00

Allocations:

Step One

54,115.00(VPA$_c$) - 25,995.00(VPA$_p$) + 25,895(TPC) = 2225(A)

Step Two

$$\frac{2225(A)}{25{,}995(VPA_p) + 25{,}895(TPC)} = .042879167$$

Doctor's Account

.042879167 x 22867.38(PS of PA$_p$) + 21,130(PC) = 1886.57(PS of A)

Nurse's Account

.042879167 x 3127.62(PS of PA$_p$) + 2890(PC) = 258.03(PS of A)

Secretary's Account

1955.40(PS of TPA)

Test Two

45,883.95 + 6275.65 + 1955.40 = 54,115.00

Allocations are correct, since the total of each participant's pension account equals the value of pension account.

PROBLEM TWO — EXCESS CONTRIBUTION, NO INSURANCE

Assume the same set of facts as presented in the above Example One, except that the corporation contributed $25,000 to the Pension Plan rather than $24,020, the amount which was required. In other words, the corporation made an excess contribution of $980.

In this event, the value of the pension account, including the excess contribution, is $26,975.00. However, when determining the participant's share of the pension account, the excess contribution should not be included in the value of the account. The reason for this is that if the plan were immediately terminated, the excess contribution would not be considered part of the plan assets, but would return to the corporation as an actuarial error. Thus, the excess contribution is not part of the trust assets. In addition, any allocation of the excess contribution to the participants would result in the participants receiving amounts to which they are not entitled.

Therefore, the excess contribution should not be included in the value of the pension account, the excess contribution should not be allocated to the participants, and the allocations should be made in the same manner as illustrated in Example One. The excess contribution will be considered part of the second year's contribution and will be allocated in that year.

Technically, it can be argued that part of the appreciation and earnings should be allocated to the excess contribution and, therefore, a pro rata portion of the appreciation and earnings should not be allocated among the participants. An excess contribution will be created, in most cases, on the last contribution to the plan, which in many cases will be very close to the end of the plan year. In this case, the earnings will be negligible and, if the contribution is placed in a checking account, there will be no earnings whatsoever. For this reason, this author makes no attempt to allocate a pro rate portion of the appreciation and earnings to the excess contribution. Excess contributions are treated as if there were no appreciation or earnings attributable thereto.

PROBLEM THREE — REQUIRED CONTRIBUTION MADE, WITH LIFE INSURANCE

This problem is very similar to the one set forth in Problem One, except that in this problem, the doctor has requested that the trustees purchase a life insurance on his life as an investment of his account. Therefore, the basic procedures established in Problem One will be followed in the problem.

Step One

Determine the appreciation or losses of the pension account as of the last day of the plan's fiscal year.

The formula set forth in Step One in Problem One is used here. However, when insurance is purchased, it is necessary to subtract the total insurance premiums paid for all participants from the contribution to the pension plan for the year to determine the amount of money which was available for investment.

$$CPA_c - VPA_p + (TPC - TIP) = A$$

Step Two

Determine each participant's share of the appreciation of the pension account as of the last day of the plan's fiscal year.

Appreciation in the pension account is generally attributable to the equity investments that have been made by the trust during the plan year. Although the cash value of an insurance policy is considered part of the total value of the plan, it is usually listed separately. That is, the total value of the pension plan is divided into two parts, the first representing the value of the equity investments and the second representing the cash value of the insurance policies.

Therefore, when computing the allocation of the appreciation when life insurance is a trust asset, it is necessary to determine the amount of money which was available for equity investments. Thus, when making the computations, it is necessary to deduct the amount of the insurance premium from each participant's account, since the amount expended for insurance was not available for investment purposes. If this was not done, the participant who purchased insurance as part of his account would be allocated an amount of the appreciation greater than he is entitled.

a. $$\frac{A}{VPA_p + (TPC - TIP)} = \text{Percentage Increase}$$

b. $$\text{Percentage Increase} \times PS \text{ of } PA_p + (PC - PIP) = PS \text{ of } A$$

Step Three

Determine each participant's share of the entire pension account, including appreciation, for the current year alone.

$$(PC - PIP) + PS \text{ of } A = PS \text{ of } PA$$

Step Four

Determine each participant's share of the pension account for all years that he has been participating in the plan.

$$PS \text{ of } PA_p + PS \text{ of } PA_c = PS \text{ of } TPA$$

Example

Target or assumed benefit plan - Target benefit of 95% of salary[7]

Two Participating Employees	*Salary*	*Contribution*
Doctor	$95,000	$33,753.50
Nurse	8,030	1,197.67
Required Contribution		$34,951.17
Amount Actually Contributed		$34,951.17
Trustees purchased a life insurance policy on the life of the doctor as an investment of his account.	Premium Cost	$ 5,550.00
Value of Account		$30,219.50[8]

Step One

30,219.50(VPA_c) - (34,951.17 - 5,550) (TPC - TIP) = 818.33(A)

Step Two

$$\frac{818.33(A)}{29{,}401.17\ (TPC\text{-}TIP)} = .027833246$$

Doctor's Account

.027833246 x (33,753.50 - 5550) (PC - PIP) = 785.00(PS of A)

Nurse's Account

.027833246 x 1197.67(PC) = 33.33 (PS of A)

Test One

785.00 + 33.33 = 818.33

This corresponds to appreciation of pension account.

Step Three

Doctor's Account

28203.50(PC-PIP) + 785(PS of A) = 28,988.50(PS of A)

Nurse's Account

1197.67(PC) + 33.33(PS of A) = 1231.00(PS of PA)

Test Two

28988.50 + 1231.00 = 30219.50

This corresponds with value of pension account. Valuations have been made correctly.

PROBLEM FOUR — DEFICIT CONTRIBUTION, NO LIFE INSURANCE

This problem represents a situation where the corporation has failed to contribute the required amount to the pension plan.

Step One

Allocate the amount which was actually contributed to the plan among the participants. This is computed by multiplying the amount which was actually contributed by a fraction, the numerator of which represents the amount which should have been contributed to each participant, and the denominator of which represents the total pension contribution which should have been made for all participants.

$$\frac{PC}{TPC} \times APC = PS\ of\ APC$$

Step Two

Determine the appreciation or losses of the pension account as of the last day of the plan's fiscal year.

$$VPA_c - VPA_p + APC = A$$

Step Three

Determine each participant's share of the appreciation of the pension account as of the last day of the plan's fiscal year.

a. $\dfrac{A}{VPA_p + APC}$ = Percentage Increase

b. Percentage Increase x PS of PA_p + PS of APC = PS of A

Step Four

Determine each participant's share of the entire pension account, including appreciation, for the current year alone.

PS of APC + PS of A = PS of PA

Step Five

Determine each participant's share of the pension account for all years that he has been participating in the plan.

PS of PA_p + PS of PA_c = PS of TPA

Example

Money-purchase Pension Plan

First Year		
Two Participating Employees	*Salary*	*Contribution*
Doctor	$55,953	$12,671.50
Nurse	5,170	840.12
Required Contribution		$13,511.62
Amount Actually Contributed		$10,500.00
Value of Pension Account		$11,125.00

Allocations

Step One

Doctor's Account

$\dfrac{12{,}671.50\ (PC)}{13{,}511.62\ (TPC)}$ x 10,500 (APC) = 9847.14(PS of APC)

Nurse's Account

$\dfrac{840.12\ (PC)}{13{,}511.62\ (TPC)}$ x 10,500 (APC) = 652.86(PS of APC)

Step Two

11,125.00 (VPA_c) - 10,500 (APC) = 625.00 (A)

Step Three

$\dfrac{625}{10{,}500\ (APC)}$ = .059523809 (Percentage Increase)

Doctor's Account

.059523809 x 9847.14 (PS of APC) = 586.14 (PS of A)

Nurse's Account

.059523809 x 652.86 (PS of APC) = 38.86 (PS of A)

Test One

586.14 + 38.86 = 625.00

Allocations are correct since this figure represents appreciation in pension account.

Step Four

Doctor's Account

9847.14 (PS of APC) + 586.14 (PS of A) = 10,433.28 (PS of PA)

Nurse's Account

652.86 (PS of APC) + 38.86 (PS of A) = 691.72 (PS of PA)

Test Two

10,433.28 + 691.72 = 11,125.00

Allocations are correct. This represents value of account.

Example - Deficit Contribution is Made Up

If the deficit is contributed to the pension plan by the corporation in subsequent year(s) in addition to its required contribution, then the amount of the deficit contributed in the subsequent year(s) must be allocated among the participants. The allocation of each participant's share of deficit is then added to his regular allocated contribution for the current year, and the allocation of the appreciation will be made in the same manner as set forth in Problem One.

The allocation of the 3011.62 deficit (previous example) is made as follows:

1. If the entire deficit is contributed in one lump sum, then each participant will receive the portion of the deficit which he would have received had it been made in the year when it was required.

This is computed by subtracting the participant's share of the actual contribution from the required contribution for each participant.

Doctor's account

12,671.50(RPC) - 9847.14(PS of APC) = 2824.36(PS of D)

Nurse's account

840.12(RPC) - 652.86(PS of APC) = 187.26(PS of D)

Thus, the sum of 2824.36 and 187.26 would be added to each participant's respective allocated conribution for the year in which the contribution was made up.

2. If a participant has terminated his employment and has forfeited the contribution made in the year in which the deficit occurred, then the amount to which he would have been entitled will be used to reduce the contribution for that year.

Thus, if the nurse terminated her employment, her share of the deficit, to wit, $187.26, would be used to reduce the contribution for that year.

If the nurse was vested in a portion of her account, then she would be entitled to that portion of the deficit when it is subsequently contributed to the plan.

3. If a portion of the deficit is contributed in subsequent years, each participant will receive a

portion of that deficit which is contributed. The portion each participant will be entitled will be determined by using the following formula:

$$\frac{\text{PC(for year deficit occurred)}}{\text{TPC(for year deficit occurred)}} \times \text{portion of deficit contributed}$$

It is necessary to use the required contribution of the participant in the year the deficit arose. If the contribution for the participant in the year the deficit is made up are used, then there will be an improper allocation of the made up deficit if the required contribution of the participants has changed.

PROBLEM FIVE — DEFICIT CONTRIBUTION, WITH INSURANCE

In this problem, the procedures are essentially the same as set forth in the other problems previously discussed.

Step One

Allocate the amount which was actually contributed to the plan among the participants.

$$\frac{PC}{TPC} \times APC = \text{PS of APC}$$

Step Two

Determine the appreciation or losses of the pension account as of the last day of the plan's fiscal year.

$$VPA_c - VPA_p + (APC - TIP) = A$$

Step Three

Determine each participant's share of the appreciation of the pension account as of the last day of the plan's fiscal year.

a. $$\frac{A}{VPA_p + (APC - TIP)} = \text{Percentage Increase}$$

b. Percentage increase x PS of PA_p + (PS of APC - PIP) = PS of A

Step Four

Determine each participant's share of the entire pension account, including appreciation, for the current year alone.

(PS of APC - PIP) + PS of A = PS of PA

Step Five

Determine each participant's share of the pension account for all years that he has been participating in the plan.

PS of PA_p + PS of PA_c = PS of TPA

PROFIT SHARING PLANS

Contributions in a profit sharing plan are allocated among the participants in proportion to the compensation, which is represented by the following formula:

$$\frac{\text{Participant's Compensation}}{\text{Compensation of all participants}} \times \text{Contribution to Profit Sharing Plan}$$

Thus, if the corporation contributes \$9,750 to its profit sharing plan and the total compensation paid to all participants was \$65,000 and the professional's compensation was \$52,000, then he will be allocated \$7,800.00 of the contribution to the plan.

$$\frac{\text{\$52,000 (Participant's compensation)}}{\text{\$65,000 (compensation of all participants)}} \times \text{\$9,750 (contribution)} = \text{\$7,800 (Participant's allocated share of contribution)}$$

Allocation of appreciation and losses is computed in the same manner as in money-purchase and target or assumed benefit pension plans (See Problems One and Three-Step Two).

a. $\frac{A}{VPA_p + TPC}$ = Percentage Increase

b. Percentage increase x PS of PAp + PC = PS of A

The above formulas assume that the corporation will be making contributions to the plan on a regular basis out of accumulated or current earning and profit of the corporation. As a result, the appreciation is attributable to contributions made during the current year as well as to contributions made in the previous year.

However, in profit sharing plans, it is most common for the corporation to make one contribution to the plan, which is usually at the end of the fiscal year. In such an event, the appreciation would not be attributable to the contribution made for the current year. Formulas which should be used in this instance are as follows:

a. $\frac{A}{VPA_p}$ = Percentage Increase

b. Percentage increase x PS of PAp = PS of A

If a participant has terminated her employment during the current year, that person should still be credited with her share of the appreciation as if she was still a participant, rather than allocating the appreciation among the remaining participants. This should be done, since her contribution was responsible for a portion of the appreciation in the plan.

This will result in a larger participant's account, which will be forfeited. If the plan provides that forfeitures may be reallocated among the remaining participants, then they will receive the appreciation at that time. However, many profit sharing plans require that forfeitures must be used to reduce subsequent years' contributions. If appreciation was not allocated to the terminated participant's account, then the remaining participants would be receiving a larger contribution than what they are entitled.

If forfeitures are permitted to be reallocated among the remaining participants, it is usually allocated in the same manner as contributions are allocated.[9]

$$\frac{\text{Participant's Compenstion}}{\text{Total Participant's Compensation}} \text{ x Forfeiture}$$

Example

Profit Sharing Plan - Contribution equal to 15% of compensation.
Contribution made at end of corporation's fiscal year.

Three Participating Employees	*Salary*
Doctor	$50,000
Nurse	8,500
Secretary	7,200
	65,700

Contribution to Profit Sharing Plan 9,855 (15% of Compensation)

Allocation:
Step One

Allocate contributions among participants.

Doctor

$$\frac{50{,}000 \text{ (Participant's compensation)}}{65{,}700 \text{ (Total compensation)}} \times 9855.00 = \$7500.00$$

(Participant's share of contribution)

Nurse

$$\frac{8500}{65{,}700} \times 9855 = 1275.00$$

Secretary

$$\frac{7200}{65{,}700} \times 9855.00 = 1080.00$$

Second plan year

Secretary terminated her employment during current year and forfeited her entire account. Plan provides that forfeitures are to be reallocated among remaining participants.

Two Participants	*Salary*
Doctor	$50,000
Nurse	8,500
	85,500
Contribution to plan which was made at end of fiscal year (15% of compensation)	$ 8,775
Value of Account, not including current contribution	$10,885

Allocation:
Step One

Determine appreciation of profit sharing account for current year.
10,855 (VPAc) - 9,855 (VPAp) = 1000 (A)

Step Two

Allocate appreciation among all participants, including secretary who has terminated her employment.

a. $$\frac{1000 \text{ (A)}}{9855 \text{ (VPAp)}} = .101471334 \text{ (percentage increase)}$$

Doctor's Account

.101471334 (percentage increase) x 7500 (PS of PAp) = 761.03 (PS of A)

Nurse's Account

.101471334 x 1275.00 (PS of PAp) = 129.38 (PS of A)

Secretary's Account

.101471334 x 1080.00 (PS of PAp) = 109.59 (PS of A)

Test One

7500 + 1275+ 1080 = 9855

Allocation of contributions is correct, since each participant's share equals contribution.

Since contribution was made at end of corporation's fiscal year, there was no appreciation to be allocated among the participants.

Test Two

761.03 + 129.38 + 109.59 = 1000

Allocation of appreciation is correct.

Step Three

Determine each participant's share of profit sharing account, including appreciation, not including contribution or forfeitures for current year.

Doctor's Account

7500 (PS of PAp) + 761.03 (PS of A) = 8261.03 (PS of PA)

Nurse's Account

1275 (PS of PAp) + 129.38 (PS of A) = 1404.38 (PS of PA)

Secretary's Account

1080 (PS of PAp) + 109.59 (PS of A) = 1189.59 (PS of A)

Test Three

8261.03 + 1404.38 + 1189.59 = 10,855.00

Computation was made correctly, since this figure represents value of account.

Step Four

Allocate contribution for current year and forfeiture between remaining participants.

Secretary forfeited - 1189.59

Thus, 8775 (contribution) + 1189.59 (forfeiture) = 9964.59 (Amount to be allocated)

Doctor

$$\frac{\text{50,000 (Participant's compensation)}}{\text{58,500 (Total Compensation}} \times \text{9964.59 (contribution and forfeiture)} = \text{8516.74 (PS of PA)}$$

Nurse

$$\frac{\text{8500 (Participant's compensation}}{\text{58,500 (Total Compensation)}} \times \underset{\text{(contribution and forfeiture)}}{9964.59} = \text{1447.85 (PS of PA)}$$

Test Four

8516.74 + 1447.85 = 9964.59

Computations are correct.

Step Five

Allocate current contribution and forfeitures to each participant's account, including appreciation.

Doctor

8261.03 + 8516.74 = 16,777.77 (PS of TPA)

Nurse

1404.38 + 1447.85 = 2852.23 (PS of TPA)

Total accounts of Doctor and Nurse equal $19630. Allocations are correct, since this corresponds to total contribution for both plan years plus appreciation.

FOOTNOTES

[1]The author acknowledges with appreciation Myron Cooper, C.L.U., Pension Consultant for the Provident Mutual Life Insurance Company, Boston, Massachusetts, for his assistance in writing this chapter.

[2]ERISA§105

[3]All allocations are based upon the dollar method and are not based upon units. In addition, past service is not a factor in making the allocations. Fixed benefit plans are not discussed since the necessary figures will be computed by the actuary.

[4]Valuations may be made at other times during the course of the year. In most cases, however, the trust will be valued and allocations made as of the last day of the plan year.

[5]In allocating each participant's share of the appreciation of the pension account, it is necessary to multiply the percentage increase in appreciation by each participant's account balance for the previous year plus his contribution for the current year to properly reflect the appreciation attributable to his account. That is, the participant's contribution plus appreciation for previous years plus the current year's contribution are responsible for the appreciation for the current year. Otherwise, a participant who enters the plan in the plan's fifth year of operation would receive a greater share of the appreciation if the percentage increase was only multiplied by each participant's allocated contribution for the current year. In other words, the new participant would be sharing in appreciation which, in fact, is attributable to the contributions of the other participants. Furthermore, even if there were no further new participants, this method is necessary to properly reflect the changing contribution of the participants.

[6]Forfeitures: In the event a participant terminates her employment, the portion of her account which is forfeited is used to reduce the subsequent year's contributions that the corporation is required to make to the plan. In determining the value of the forfeiture, the terminated employee's account should be credited with the appreciation of the pension assets for the year in which her employment terminated. If the appreciation was allocated only among the remaining participants, then a "mini" profit sharing plan would be credited which would result in a larger portion of the appreciation being allocated to prohibited group.

[7]Allocation of appreciation in target benefit plans is done in same manner as money-purchase plans.

[8]This example assumes that there is no cash value in the insurance policy. If cash value were present, then the value of the account would be presented as follows:

Value of Pension Account

Insurance policy - cash value	3600.00
Investments	26619.50
Total Value	30,219.50

Only the investment portion would be allocated among the participants. The cash value of each insurance policy will be allocated to the respective owner.

[9]It was customary to allocate forfeitures in proportion to account balances, but the Internal Revenue Service now takes the position that allocations made in this manner may result in discrimination in favor of the prohibited group since they may receive the largest portion of the forfeiture, since they usually remain the longest with the corporation and therefore have the largest account balances.

INDEX